SHAW AND THE PLAY OF IDEAS

SHAW AND THE PLAY OF IDEAS

ROBERT F. WHITMAN

CORNELL UNIVERSITY PRESS
ITHACA AND LONDON

First published 1977 by Cornell University Press.
Published in the United Kingdom by Cornell University Press Ltd., 2–4 Brook Street, London W1Y 1AA.

Passages from *Reason in History* by G. W. F. Hegel, translated by Robert S. Hartman, copyright © 1953 by The Liberal Arts Press, Inc., are reprinted by permission of the Bobbs-Merrill Company, Inc.

International Standard Book Number 0-8014-1072-X
Library of Congress Catalog Card Number 76-29866
Printed in the United States of America by York Composition Co., Inc.
Librarians: Library of Congress cataloging information appears on the last page of the book.

FOR
FANNIE MARIE CROWLEY,
MY MOTHER

Contents

Contents

Preface

The reader should be forewarned that this book has a message. An unashamed attempt to spread the gospel according to George Bernard Shaw, it attempts to proselytize as well as to serve scholarship. Shaw saw himself as prophet and preacher of a "metabiological" religion, which he fondly hoped might become the new faith of the new age. A quarter century after his death that theology has produced no church, few converts, and little if any doctrinal exegesis. But as one of a small band of at least tentative believers (and he asked no more), I feel compelled to continue his mission and to help in disseminating the concepts of Creative Evolution.

My dual role of scholar and propagator of the faith has put me in the position of addressing two different (albeit overlapping) audiences. I hope that the casual reader of Shaw's plays will share my excitement in his ideas and find pleasure in discovering the unity and coherence behind their surface diversity. At the same time the information I bring to light suggesting both a source of that unity, in the philosophy of Hegel, and the means by which it reached Shaw should be a contribution to Shavian scholarship.

There is also an inevitable dichotomy in the organization of the book as a whole. Shaw's ideas, their origins and their evolution in the decade immediately preceding his turn to playwriting, are the subject of the first seven chapters; a discussion of how these ideas emerge in, and help to form, the plays themselves occupies the remaining pages. By looking briefly at ten plays that represent a range of periods, styles, and subject matter, I try to show how the ideas identified in the early chapters "work" dramatically. Specifically, I discuss *Candida, Caesar and Cleopatra,* and *Man and Superman* in Chapter 8; *Major Barbara, The Shewing-up of Blanco Posnet, Androcles and the Lion,* and *Heartbreak House* in Chapter 9; and *Back to Methuselah, Saint Joan,* and *The Simpleton of the Unexpected Isles* in Chapter 10. Although most of my interpretations are not radically new, the argument in the earlier chapters illuminates, and sometimes eliminates, conceptual difficulties that have often plagued critics, and it confirms relationships among plays that have been only surmised before. Most important, perhaps, we can begin to see just how each play stands as a new parable in the evolving gospel of Creative Evolution.

Any serious attempt to write about a major literary figure such as Shaw must owe an incalculable debt to those who have gone before. I am most conscious of my obligations to Archibald Henderson, William Irvine, Eric Bentley, Louis Crompton, and Stanley Weintraub for both information and challenging ideas; but there are many others. J. L. Wisenthal's important book on Shaw's "middle" plays, *The Marriage of Contraries,* appeared only after the manuscript of my own book had already been completed. Approaching from quite different directions, we have come to considerable agreement about thematic and structural elements in the plays, most particularly in *Major Barbara,* and I have found much reassurance in his wisdom.

The success of the kind of literary detective work in which I have been engaged depends heavily on knowledgeable library staffs, and I have been particularly happy in my associations with the Library of Congress, the library at the London School of Economics, the Humanities Research Center at Austin, Texas, and the manuscript room at the British Museum. All students of Shaw are deeply indebted to Dan Laurence for his work in editing the letters, but I owe him special thanks for his encouragement and for steering me to Shaw's diaries, which provided the missing link to support my assumption of Hegelian influences. I have also been especially fortunate in the friendship of The Honorable Rodney Bax, who has helped immeasurably by lending me otherwise unobtainable copies of his grandfather's books.

This study could not have been written without the very generous assistance provided by a Research Fellowship from the National Endowment for the Humanities, as well as a sabbatical leave and travel funds provided by the Faculty of Arts and Sciences of the University of Pittsburgh. And without the kindly guidance and wise suggestions of my late colleague Professor Charles Crow, it might never have progressed beyond its crude and awkward beginnings. I also thank the anonymous readers for the Cornell University Press, whose criticisms and recommendations—whether or not I chose to respond—have helped me to organize and clarify not only my writing, but my thinking, about George Bernard Shaw.

And to my wife, Marina, without whose impatience this volume might never have reached completion, much more than gratitude.

Robert F. Whitman

Pittsburgh, Pennsylvania

Acknowledgments

I wish to express my gratitude to The Bobbs-Merrill Co., Inc., of Indianapolis for permission to quote extensively from Hegel's *Reason in History*, translated by Robert S. Hartman; to the Copp Clark Publishing Co. of Toronto for permission to use material from my article "The Dialectic Structure in Shaw's Plays," which originally appeared in their *Shaw Seminar Papers–65;* to the Humanities Research Center in Austin, Texas, for permission to quote from three unpublished letters in their possession; to the Directors of the British Museum and to The Honorable Rodney Bax for permission to quote from several unpublished letters of Ernest Belfort Bax. All quotation from Shaw's writing, published and unpublished, is by permission of The Society of Authors on behalf of the Bernard Shaw Estate.

Abbreviations

The sources I quote most frequently have been given the following abbreviations and are indicated, with appropriate page references, in the text itself. The same abbreviations replace full citations when used in the footnotes.

Henderson	Archibald Henderson, *George Bernard Shaw: Man of the Century* (New York: Appleton-Century-Crofts, 1956).
IWG	Bernard Shaw, *The Intelligent Woman's Guide to Socialism and Capitalism* (New York: Brentano's, 1928).
Letters, I	Dan Laurence, ed., *Bernard Shaw: Collected Letters 1874–1897* (New York: Dodd, Mead, 1965).
Letters, II	Dan Laurence, ed., *Bernard Shaw: Collected Letters 1898–1910* (New York: Dodd, Mead, 1972).
Plays	Bernard Shaw, *Complete Plays with Prefaces*, 6 vols. (New York: Dodd, Mead, 1962). All citations from the plays are from this edition unless otherwise indicated.
Prose	Diarmuid Russell, ed., *Bernard Shaw: Selected Prose* (New York: Dodd, Mead, 1952).
Q.Ib.	"The Quintessence of Ibsenism," in *Prose,* pp. 534–691.
Reason	G. W. F. Hegel, *Reason in History,* trans. Robert S. Hartman (Indianapolis: Bobbs-Merrill, 1953).
16 S.S.	Bernard Shaw, *Sixteen Self Sketches* (New York: Dodd, Mead, 1949).

SHAW AND THE PLAY OF IDEAS

Introduction: On Taking
Shaw Seriously

It is probably characteristic of any age to preserve its own sense of identity and integrity by rejecting the most conspicuous figures of the age immediately before. Some have already dismissed George Bernard Shaw, on the grounds that his plays are transparent and trivial, his philosophy incoherent, his Fabianism passé, and his Life Force moribund. "G.B.S.," I have been told bluntly, "is a dead duck." Although at one time, during the thirties and forties, it was grumpily suggested that the old man might indeed be immortal, he *is* dead. But he won't stay dead, and there seems to be more interest in his work now than at any time in the past fifty years. Shaw's death in 1950 might seem to make him a member of the "last" generation, but his birth in 1856 would put him among the great-grandfathers and great-great-grandfathers of the present younger generation. As a Victorian he is too far removed to be a threat, or an authority figure against whom there is a compulsion to rebel; at the same time his personality is still too much alive and too vital for him to have become only a historical monument.

Like many Victorians, Shaw was centrally concerned with moral questions; but his moral seriousness does not overwhelm our capacity to respond or to think. He does not come to us as a thinker with significant ideas, but as a writer of comedies; and yet his ideas may be among the most important to survive from the nineteenth century into the twentieth. The ideas have often been criticized as contradictory, ambiguous, and paradoxical, and yet out of those very characteristics there evolved yet another quality, one in which the man himself had a passionate faith: the power of perpetual rebirth and renewal.

Like most figures of any stature in human history, Shaw was at once of his age and apart from it. He possessed a valuable ability to recognize the uses of the past without becoming over-awed by it and at the same time to distrust the past without either arrogance or an indiscriminate admiration for everything new. We are apt, today, to put an emphasis on the uniqueness of the present; but the impulse to turn our backs on the past probably springs less from a faith in the future than from a sense of what we see as failure of traditional values and ways of thinking. Much of Shaw's strength lay in his having found a way of looking at the world that accommodated both past and present and that was at the same time both skeptical and op-timistic.

He was unquestionably a Victorian and an Edwardian, but the closest he ever came to outright contempt was for the stereotypes those labels usually conjure up, of moral rigidity, of domestic tyr-anny, and of self-righteous faith in progress, the scientific method, and the supremacy of Christian duty. He was keenly aware of, and fascinated by, recent advances in science, but he was troubled by its amorality and profoundly resented the cruelties of its ex-periments, the unimaginativeness of its goals, and the mindless-ness of its theories of natural selection. In an age when liberalism seemed to be leading the march of human progress, Shaw saw it as little more than a refuge for a bankrupt individualism, in which progress meant greater protection for the personal rights and private property of those who could afford them. At a time when the vision of human betterment was founded in a faith in the power of the mind, one of the best minds of his day could say that when "you have come to grief as a materialist by rea-soning about something, you are not likely, as a mystic, to im-prove matters by reasoning about nothing."[1]

1. *Q.Ib.*, p. 554, n.

In being suspicious of what was new Shaw did not, however, turn his gaze backward. His complaints against liberalism were not that it was too liberal but too regressive. Science was not too revolutionary but was deficient in vision and daring. His objection to established religion was that it closed its eyes to present realities and refused to take account of science and sex, social injustice and human aspiration. Even Marxism did not go too far, but not far enough. Politicians, scientists, theologians, and thinkers, to say nothing of the great middle classes, were seen by Shaw as the prisoners of formulas, habit, doing things or thinking things because that was the way the world had always been dealt with or conceived of. Tradition and convention, as the first line of defense of the status quo, were to him among the most serious obstacles in the path of human development. And yet it would be a mistake not to recognize the very real values he found in tradition and convention. No matter how unconventional the ultimate formulations, the building blocks for most of Shaw's political, social, biological, and metaphysical theories were hewn from traditional or at least well-established bodies of thought. Indeed, his highly rhetorical style reverberates with echoes of a past that is still very much alive in his present.

Perhaps because of his self-conscious role as middleman between a past that was always dying and a future that was always being born, Shaw was constantly trying to find ways of looking at human problems that would, in their very flexibility, have something more than transient validity. In this he was at least partly successful, and as a result readers coming to Shaw for the first time today may be startled to discover attitudes, perceptions, awareness of problems that they imagined to be the special possession of their own generation. Although Shaw saw the enemies he spent his life fighting as being many and varied, most would be seen today as fitting under the useful umbrella known as The Establishment. The concept is a fiction, to be sure, but it also represents something perfectly real. It stands for inertia and complacency, for resistance to change or to disturbing ideas, for the desire for certainty and security rather than skepticism and experiment. And the sense of the overpowering presence of an establishment, along with a dissatisfaction with what it has wrought, is a substantial bond between Shaw and the reader of today.

Anyone who would be willing to acknowledge the reality of an establishment in any sense would probably associate with it these institutions or characteristics, though not necessarily in the same order: capitalism, militarism, conventional methods of education, social respectability, social inequality, conventional morality, and the unrestricted exploitation of natural resources, justified by the "rights" of private property. These are also just the elements in society that provide the focuses for Shaw's attacks on the status quo.

Shaw's hostility to capitalism, as the source of most of civilized man's economic, social, and moral ills, is both well known and pervasive throughout his writing; and war in general he viewed in Marxist fashion simply as a mechanism whereby capitalists expand markets and consume goods for their own economic advantage. A little less obviously, he found the educational process, at least in England, not only a product of the capitalist system but also a mechanism designed to perpetuate its values. On less polemic grounds Shaw simply considered schools "prisons" in which hapless youths are taught to hate both the subjects and the process of education, and where the inflexibility and lack of imagination of the curriculum stifle whatever natural joy and will to learn the student may have come with. He sounds very contemporary when he complains that "pressing people to learn things they do not want to know is as unwholesome and disastrous as feeding them on sawdust."[2] On the other hand, "when the Pursuit of Learning comes to mean the pursuit of learning by the child instead of the child by Learning . . . the danger will be precocity of the intellect."[3]

The concept and values of social respectability Shaw consid-

2. "Preface" to *Immaturity, Prose*, p. 50.
3. "Parents and Children," prefaced to *Misalliance, Plays*, IV, 72.

ered just another bulwark of the capitalist establishment. At the same time he shows considerable perception into the impulses of the younger generation when he observes that its members often want "to find out a way of getting into trouble that will combine loss of respectability with integrity of self-respect and reasonable consideration for other peoples' feelings . . . on every point except their dread of losing their own respectability."[4]

Conventional religion and its morality Shaw saw as little more than different names for respectability, and like it, props for the status quo. Christianity had become a system that offered a reward of eternal bliss for the benevolence of those who could afford it and eternal damnation for the frustrated violence of those who could not. Indeed, any concern for personal salvation offended Shaw on social as well as moral grounds, for he bitterly resented the energies such notions took away from man's true purpose in the world. The idea of eternal happiness in another world, even in its less naive manifestations, filled him with horror, for he saw it as the ultimate form, not only of boredom, but of onanistic self-indulgence as well. The only meaningful salvation was the salvation of mankind; and that was a salvation of and in *this* world.

Shaw was not in the usual sense a utopian, in that he had no specific program or plan for what he sometimes called "Man Made Perfect," nor was he unqualifiedly optimistic about when or even whether man's potential for perfectibility would ever be realized. But whatever better world might be possible, it could never be achieved until there was an end to exploitation, both of men and of the earth on which they live together. All natural resources, he insisted, were part of the earth and belonged to all its inhabitants, not just to those who wrested it from others; and it belonged to the future as well as to the present. Shaw never used such now-popular terms as environmental pollution and ecological deterioration, but he was explicit in his denunciation

4. "Preface" to *Fanny's First Play*, *Plays*, VI, 87.

of the conspiracy between political leaders and industrialists and landowners to protect their rights to exploit and destroy.

The hard core of Shaw's quarrel with his age, however, lay in the price that was being paid for all the education and religion, the morality and respectability and virtue, namely, the gross social injustice he found in the world around him. One of the central drives of his life was a desire to achieve in the world a condition of absolute equality. Equality was not for him the somewhat facile and popular abstraction on every demagogue's lips, but an elusive concept to be pursued rigorously wherever it fled. His logic ultimately led him to espouse the principle of an equal income for everyone—a degree of egalitarianism even his fellow Marxists found hard to swallow.

A distrust of easy generalizations led Shaw to treat capitalism not as the monolithic villain of Marxist literature but as possessing the virtues of an essential, though outgrown, stage of human social evolution. He was by no means either objective or disinterested; but his refusal to fall back on simplistic bogies, whether called "capitalism" or "the establishment," is a healthy corrective to some of our own destructive tendencies. The ways in which we learn about what is going on in the world, the headline, the news flash, the current affairs magazine that reduces contemporary events to bare essentials, all contribute to our tendency to oversimplify and categorize uncritically elements in our fast-moving age. The world is much simpler to deal with if we can reduce it to black and white, love and hate, good and evil. But as Shaw said, "Good and bad are not enough."

Shaw, of course, could scarcely open his mouth without making a dogmatic, categorical pronouncement. He built his reputation as an impudent upstart, and later as a professional paradoxer, on cocksure generalizations that contradict some apparently self-evident fact. Dogmatic assertions are weapons in his arsenal of shock tactics, and more often than not grow out of his awareness of the very complexity of the issues involved. But when Shaw is not playing games with us—as he very often is—he is much more humble in the face of the world's ambiguities than most of his critics will allow. Indeed, they cry out against his contradictions and inconsistencies as though they had discovered a useful weapon with which to discredit his disturbing insights. Neither he nor I, however, need appeal to Emerson's hobgoblins to justify the inconsistencies. In some ways they are rhetorical devices; but in a larger sense they reflect, and are an attempt to embrace, the more elemental contradictions that he understood and could tolerate in unresolved suspension, while smaller minds fled to the illusory security of simple answers.

Shaw's distrust of oversimplification and his ability to live with ambiguity and uncertainty were not simply a matter of overt statement, but underlay his whole way of seeing the world. For him, affirmations imply their own contradictions, negations must be qualified. His attitude toward religion, with its personal ambivalence and its aversion to dogma, is both characteristic and essentially modern in spirit. He found established creeds universally incredible, yet at the same time he shows none of the easy cynicism that makes contempt for religion so common today. As we shall see, Shaw had fought through the whole question of whether God is dead and come out on the other side with the conclusion that He is indeed alive, and still growing. While he treats traditional religions as inflexible and intellectually dishonest in their inability to take into account the complexity and evolution of reality, he can also say: "We must have a religion if we are to do anything worth doing. If anything is to be done to get our civilization out of the horrible mess in which it now is, it must be done by men who have got a religion."[5]

Cynicism, the escape of the coward, was never a viable alternative for Shaw. Profoundly disillusioned with the established way of doing things, with a government that saw its highest purpose as the protection of private property and the expansion of empire, with religions that had atrophied, with educated classes more

5. "Modern Religion I," in *The Religious Speeches of Bernard Shaw*, ed. Warren S. Smith (University Park, Pa.: The Pennsylvania State University Press, 1963), p. 38.

interested in preserving their own advantages than in social justice, with a world where sentimentality was mistaken for kindness, narrow patriotism for public spirit, and conventionality for
morality, he had sources of despair and spoke a language of dis-
affection in common with many of the questioners, young and
old, in our own day. But at the same time Shaw did not turn in
on himself and reject the conventional world of ordinary people.
If politics and religion and morality and even reason have proved
sterile or corrupt, if they have brought us down the wrong road,
or if they have simply become the tools of selfish men, the solution is not to throw them on the dust heap, but to make them
work for the good of humanity. He speaks to us in tones not of
despair or lamentation, but of anger and renewed vigor. A man
with an idea and a conviction possesses the strength of ten, Shaw
never tires of telling us; and he was not one to be caught short
without an idea.

The road to boredom is paved with good ideas, left there by
sincere men who lacked the power to communicate them. Shaw
had the opposite problem, for he embodied his ideas in such
delightfully witty essays and plays that there has been a very real
danger, then and now, that the wisdom would get lost in the fun.
For a good many years now, Shaw as thinker has, for both critics
and readers, had to play a somewhat sour second fiddle to Shaw
the comic craftsman, Shaw the pre-absurdist, Shaw the post-
Victorian, and of course, Shaw the writer of musical comedy.
The refusal to accept Shaw on his own terms, as philosopher-
playwright, is of course an old story. In the early days many of
his ideas were too unfamiliar and too heretical to be faced with
equanimity, and so the comforting myth of Shaw the Court Jester
was erected as a bulwark against self-criticism. But what was profoundly disturbing to the complacency of the 1890s is apt to be
a commonplace today. The fate of most iconoclasts is that the
broken idols eventually are ground into the dust by the feet of the
multitude, and what was once a new way of looking at things
becomes either a cliché or an anachronism. Shaw has suffered no
less than most; and so Shaw the Marxist, the Fabian, the Vitalist,

the Metabiologist, the Visionary, the preacher of what he boldly proclaimed the "religion of the Twentieth Century" is apt to be treated with the knowing and rather condescending smile of an age that feels sure that it has gone beyond such nonsense.

But while passing over Shaw's essays into metaphysics as rather embarrassing encumbrances on otherwise witty comedies is common, to do so is to be grossly unfair to his achievement as a dramatist and to distort both his intentions and his plays. Certainly he took his role as popular philosopher very seriously. This kind of assertion, it is true, is generally met with a grimace and the observation that Shaw never took anything seriously. Nothing could be further from the truth; and we must take care to avoid the easy assumption that the ability to look at oneself objectively, with humor and irony and a capacity for self-criticism, is the same thing as not taking oneself seriously. He was always aware that it was not The Truth, but the *search* for truth, that he was concerned with, and that the searcher by definition has not what he seeks.

From first to last Shaw was dedicated to the proposal that his plays were important—and indeed any plays were important— only in terms of the ideas they contained. In the preface to one of his earliest collections he observes, as part of a justification of his own dramatic practice: "From the play of ideas—and the drama can never be anything more—[the audience] demands edification."[6] Apparently encouraged by at least the critical furor stirred up by his early work, he could say, in the Preface to *Mrs Warren's Profession*: "So effective do I find the dramatic method that I have no doubt I shall at last persuade even London to take its conscience and its brains with it when it goes to the theatre, instead of leaving them at home with its prayerbook as it does at present" (III, 7). And while the passing decades undoubtedly brought a degree of disillusionment about the power of his plays to mold minds or stimulate thinking, his faith in intellectual content for its own sake never diminished. In one of his

6. "Preface" to *Three Plays for Puritans, Plays,* III, xxxiii.

last public utterances, Shaw reaffirmed the conviction that lies behind most of his work: "Without a stock of ideas, mind cannot operate, and plays cannot exist. The quality of a play is the quality of its ideas."[7]

This faith in the value of the idea pervades all of Shaw's writing, and he was never ashamed to assert the didactic function of his art, or to picture himself as an undisguised preacher. "I write plays," he once wrote Harold Downes,[8] "with the deliberate object of converting the nation to my opinion." But he was under no flattering illusions as to the absolute truth of his ministry or the permanent validity of his message as such. For Shaw ideas, theories, philosophies, whether political or social or metaphysical, are simply stages in the slow and stumbling evolution of the human mind as it pushes itself through gradually ascending levels of self-consciousness. "This body of thought," he reminds us, "is the slowest of growths and the rarest of blossomings, and . . . if there is such a thing on the philosophic plane as a matter of course, it is that no individual can make more than a minute contribution to it."[9] And even those minute contributions are at best tentative. His apparent novelty, he admits, is "simply the novelty of the advanced thought of my day. As such, it will assuredly lose its gloss with the lapse of time."[10] Of even his beloved "Metabiological Pentateuch," *Back to Methuselah*, he could say: "I am not, I hope, under more illusion than is humanly inevitable as to my contribution to the scriptures of Creative Evolution. It is my hope that a hundred parables by younger hands will soon leave mine . . . far behind."[11]

Consequently, what is significant about Shaw's plays is perhaps not so much the specific content of his theories, in terms of par-

7. "The Play of Ideas," in *Shaw on Theatre*, ed. E. J. West (New York: Hill and Wang, 1958), p. 290.

8. Typed note, undated, to Harold Downes, in the collection of Shaw letters at the Humanities Research Center, University of Texas at Austin.

9. "Preface" to *Major Barbara, Plays*, I, 305.

10. "Preface" to *Three Plays for Puritans, Plays*, III, xlix.

11. "Preface" as revised in 1944, to *Back to Methuselah* (New York: Oxford University Press, 1947), p. lxxiv.

ticular political and social and economic programs he espoused, as the fact that the ideas are there, and that there are certain basic philosophical assumptions underlying and tying together the specific articles of his faith. Most importantly, these ideas have an organic relationship to the intellectual structure of the plays. Not only must a play have ideas, but the ideas will inevitably create their own necessary form: "New ideas make their technique as water makes its channel; and the technician without ideas is as useless as the canal constructor without water, though he may do very skillfully what the Mississippi does very rudely."[12]

Looking at his plays to find broad basic patterns of ideas, rather than simply to identify and evaluate specific economic and metabiological doctrines, would not have disturbed Shaw himself, even though he basically distrusted abstraction and generalization. As we have seen, he accepted the fact that particular ideas would, in the slow evolution of human thought, become outmoded and be superseded by new ones. What was important to him was that the act of bringing ideas into the theater—and even more, bringing them into collision with one another, hence making the conflict essential to drama a conflict of *ideas*—was itself contributing to the intellectual, and therefore the spiritual, development of his audience. Although Shaw distrusted rationalists as a species, he had a profound conviction that the future of man rested heavily on his use of his intellectual tools—his self-awareness, his wisdom, above all his drive to know more about himself and his world. By demanding that his audience bring "mind and conscience into the theatre," by stimulating thought and self-criticism, he was furthering that self-knowledge. It is safe to say, I think, that Shaw was more interested in provoking self-analysis and skepticism, in disturbing the complacency of all those who took their values and beliefs for granted, than in promulgating any well-defined philosophical system. At the same time, he did not conceive his function to be primarily negative or

12. "Preface" to *Three Plays for Puritans, Plays,* III, lviii.

destructive, and the essential elements of a positive and creative
system of thought can be found in his writing.

Shaw was in a real sense too tentative in his ideas to be a formal philosopher. He described himself as a "crow who [has] followed many ploughs." "No doubt," he continues, "I seem
prodigiously clever to those who have never hopped, hungry and
curious, across the fields of philosophy, politics, and art."[13] The
eclectic nature of these foragings makes it difficult to identify
Shaw exclusively with any of the major schools or currents of
philosophical thought prevalent during the late nineteenth and
early twentieth centuries. There is a Max Beerbohm cartoon that
represents the critic Georg Brandes as a pawnbroker to whom
Shaw has brought a bundle of clothes. Brandes asks the playwright what he expects for them, to which Shaw replies: "Immortality." Brandes expostulates: "Come, I've handled these
goods before; Coat, Mr. Schopenhauer's, waistcoat, Mr. Ibsen's,
Mr. Nietzsche's trousers. . . ." "Ah," answers Shaw, "but look
at the patches."[14] And indeed, no clown in history has paraded
himself in such magnificent motley.

If the man Shaw immortalized as "The incomparable Max"
had had space, he could have carried the joke farther, down to
Shaw's secondhand handkerchief and shoelaces, with a list that
would have included numerous Marxist and socialist theoreticians
and antisectarian propagandists of the late nineteenth century, as
well as two men he himself acknowledged as major influences,
Samuel Butler and Henri Bergson. But hopping like a crow across
Shaw's work, trying to pick up all the seeds of his thought, is apt to
be a fruitless enterprise, serving to emphasize only their diversity,
and not what is more interesting: the degree to which the disparate elements are molded into an intellectually ordered structure.

Shaw himself never pretended his motley was the elegant robe
of philosophy and was impatient with those who did; but I will

13. Ibid., p. lxi.
14. Cartoon entitled "Life-Force, Woman-Set-Free, Superman, etc.
(1914)," in *Max Beerbohm, A Survey* (London: William Heinemann,
1921), number 44.

defy his disapproval and try, in the following chapters, to identify the most important sources of his ideas and to trace, at least
crudely, their gradual organization into a coherent body of ideas.
The mere identification of sources and influences is always an
uncertain business at best, haunted by disconcerting empty spaces
and huge assumptions. On the other hand, knowing something
about the intellectual or philosophical structures Shaw demon-
strably drew on should help to illuminate the pattern that finally
took shape in his mind. Although no intellectual construction, particularly in a mind as active as Shaw's, remains entirely fixed, by
the time he began writing the plays he had developed an inte-
grated body of ideas that can be called a philosophy and that
dominated his thinking for the rest of his life. What is important,
of course, is not a collection of abstractions, but the way these
ideas impregnate and inform all of Shaw's multifaceted activities.
His economic and political and social and biological theories are
not, as they sometimes seem, fragmented enthusiasms, although
as a man he had quite energy enough to live several complete
and separate lives at the same time. His metaphysics and his
work-a-day ideas are nevertheless all of a piece, growing out of a
few central assumptions about the nature of reality. And the
primary "reality" he sought as a playwright to body forth on the
stage was the reality of his ideas.

1   *Major Motifs: The Foundations of a Philosophy*

Shaw's mind was agile, multifaceted, and elusive; sorting out the themes and ideas in his literary output is not easy. The prefaces loosely attached to the plays are notorious for the abandon with which they range over the whole scope of human society, morals, religion, history, and art.

Beatrice Webb, who probably knew him better than any other of the many women whose lives he touched, called Shaw a "sprite," and the comment was not meant as an unqualified compliment. His thought has a mercurial quality, so that just at the moment when you think you have grasped it, it escapes. This quality can be both enchanting and intensely irritating (as he irritated Mrs. Webb), but it was very much a part of the man. His education was as undisciplined as his thinking, and after he left school at the age of fifteen to help support his family, it was very much at the mercy of his whim and of his rapidly expanding enthusiasms. But neither his whim nor his enthusiasms were frivolous, and he pursued his education with a determination and energy that stand as a rebuke to those of us who take their prescribed education for granted. Shaw often told the story of the incident when, several years after he had followed his mother from Dublin to London, he had occasion to attend a meeting of one of the several Marxist discussion groups then flourishing in the capital. Having spoken out during the question period, he was summarily put down on the grounds that he had scarcely heard of Karl Marx. Embarrassed, he hurried to the British Museum (which he called his "University"), and read the French translation of *Capital,* no English version being then available. At the next meeting of the society he made use of his newfound knowledge and discovered to his amazement that no one there, and few men in England, had read as much of Marx as he. Some years later, puzzled about a certain point in Marxian economics, Shaw engaged in a debate in the columns of a London periodical with the brilliant British economist Philip Wicksteed. Ultimately convinced of his own (and Marx's) error, he joined the Economic Circle, of which Wicksteed was leader, and for several years studied economic theory with one of the best men in the field.

A hunger to know everything he did not know drove him to study and read voraciously. When a new line of thought appeared on his horizon, he did not simply dismiss it; he ran it to the ground, and either absorbed it or buried it. He gobbled up ideas that other people seemed to leave lying around, and the resultant eclecticism, while it gave tremendous range and agility to his thinking, did not lend itself to order and neatness. He reviews his first two decades of playwriting in a list that gives some notion of his encyclopedic interests: "I tried slum-landlordism, doctrinaire Free Love . . . , prostitution, militarism, marriage, history, current politics, natural Christianity, national and individual character, paradoxes of conventional society, husband-hunting, questions of conscience, professional delusions and impostures, all worked into a series of comedies of manners in the classic fashion."[1] Recurring motifs do, however, thread their way through the tangled skein of his enthusiasms, and out of the rich profusion it is possible to discern a pattern, to see a hierarchy of relative importance.

Nothing can be more basic to what a man thinks, or indeed to *how* he thinks, than his image of himself and his sense of the relationship of that self to external reality. At the level of everyday action this kind of question is simple enough to grasp and define; but when we push very far the principle of indeterminateness

1. "Preface" to *Back to Methuselah, Plays,* II, lxxxvii.

seems to take over, and the act of definition in itself distorts the very reality we are trying to grasp. It is something like being confronted with the multiple refractions of the mirror maze, and the self-consciousness of the observer observing himself in the act of observation renders futile the hope of isolating and identifying the true or "real" image.

At least one of the images of himself seen by Shaw, and probably the one most consistently dramatized, was that of the missionary and preacher—not, to be sure, the grimfaced missionary of the Puritan tradition, with the Bible in one hand and a gun in the other, but a unique mutation of the breed, wearing clown's motley, carrying Marx in one hand and a pen in the other. But he was no less passionate a reformer for all the clowning, and he was specifically concerned with the passions—those, as he put it, that "have produced the philosophy, the poetry, the art, and the statecraft of the world, and not merely those which have produced its weddings, coroner's inquests, and executions."[2]

Conviction and passion, wedded to a penchant for preaching, characteristically breed some measure of smugness and self-righteousness, the assumption being that the conviction is based on a uniquely clear perception of the truth. Shaw avoids the implication by neither claiming nor denying his possession of truth. His detractors have not been reluctant to attribute his evasions, his notorious escapes into paradoxes and red herrings, to either cowardice or intellectual dishonesty. A reluctance to make absolute claims about the truth or the nature of reality could also, of course, be a function of humility. Now, humility is not the first characteristic that comes to mind when we think of Shaw, with his bristling, arrogant beard and Mephistophelian eyebrows; but for all his apparent self-assurance, he is a man of profounder paradoxes than are dreamt of by many of his critics. He does not tell us what reality is, because he does not know himself. He only asks that we be realists—and the distinction is important.

2. "Hamlet," in *Dramatic Opinions and Essays* (New York: Brentano's, 1907), II, 314.

The difference, even opposition, between "realism" and the way of looking at things that Shaw characterizes as "idealism" is central not only to his first major philosophical statement, *The Quintessence of Ibsenism* (1891), but also to his thinking throughout his life. In *Quintessence* he goes to considerable lengths to define just what he means by idealism, acknowledging the ambiguity of the term and protesting, even then, against the charge that he is being unnecessarily paradoxical.

If the ideal represents an image of what *ought* to be, and reality is what is, the great danger, as Shaw sees it, is that the "ought" gets confused with the "is," and is mistaken for reality. "We call this sort of fancy picture an Ideal," he explains, "and the policy of forcing individuals to act on the assumption that all ideals are real, and to recognize and accept such actions as standard moral conduct, absolutely valid under all circumstances, contrary conduct or any advocacy of it being discountenanced and punished as immoral, may therefore be described as the policy of Idealism" (*Q.Ib.*, p. 560). Shaw is quite aware of at least one level of confusion that his terminology encourages:

We unfortunately use this word ideal indifferently to denote both the institution which the ideal masks and the mask itself, thereby producing desperate confusion of thought, since the institution may be an effete and poisonous one, whilst the mask may be, and indeed generally is, an image of what we would fain have in its place. If the existing facts, with their masks on, are to be called ideals, and the future possibilities, which the masks depict are also to be called ideals—if again, the man who is defending existing institutions by maintaining their identity with their masks is to be confounded under one name with the man who is striving to realize the future possibilities by tearing the mask and the thing masked asunder, then the position cannot be intelligibly described by mortal pen. [P. 562]

Of the alternatives, Shaw would keep the name "idealist" as a pejorative term, to describe those hypocritical or deluded souls who confuse pretensions to such abstract ideals as virtue, piety, and patriotism with their reality. He clearly identifies himself with those "who [are] striving to realize the future possibilities," and the most passionate desire of his life was to "tear the mask and the thing asunder." He is very much aware that the resistance to such efforts would not come from the Philistine, who would pass him off as a madman, but from the most dedicated and sincere defenders of what Ibsen had called the "claim of the Ideal." "The idealists will be terrified beyond measure . . . at the rending of the beautiful veil they and their poets have woven to hide the unbearable face of the truth. They will . . . brand him as immoral, profligate, . . . and appeal against him to the despised Philistines, specially idealized for the occasion as Society. . . . At his worst, they call him cynic and paradoxer" (p. 561).

The confusion of terminology, however, between idealist as one who seeks to hide reality on the one hand and idealist as one who seeks a better reality on the other is not the only question Shaw's distinction between realist and idealist raises. It is all very well to define reality as "what is," but how can that help us to determine *whether* a thing "is," or to assign comparative degrees of "is-ness"? We need not retreat into Berkeleyan skepticism to wonder whether an idea or a mere hope is less or more real than a physical object, or whether the ultimate realities are adequately characterized as objective or subjective? "The truth" may not be so much unbearable as unrecognizable.

A significant feature of Shaw's image of reality is his willingness to accept its indefiniteness and mutability. And given such uncertainty, no image of a still better reality, no vision of a single way to achieve it, and no moral imperative based on that vision have any permanent or transcendent validity. He believed "that there is no golden rule; that conduct must justify itself by its effect upon life and not by its conformity to any rule or ideal. And . . . life consists in the fulfilment of the will, which is constantly growing, and cannot be fulfilled today under the conditions which secured its fulfilment yesterday" (pp. 663–664). It does not follow, however, that Shaw looked with contempt on hope or aspiration or dreams of a better future, for his own inclinations in that direction ran strong. It was simply that he saw much of the evil in the world being committed in pursuit of a better world, in the name of justice, virtue, purity, and godliness. Whether used to rationalize self-interest and laziness or elevated to the status of an eternal law, no ideal for Shaw has any absolute authority: and the illusion that it has absoluteness makes even sincere ideals and honest idealists potentially dangerous. It is not that such concepts as goodness and honor and beauty cannot be given a meaning, but that they can be given too many too easily, and so twisted to serve any man's will.

The antithesis between idealism and realism is the source of the dynamics in most of Shaw's writing, and because it provides the basis for conflict, it is most conspicuous in the plays. This particular polarity, which seems to underlie his sense of drama, is perhaps illustrated most explicitly in the third act, the dream sequence, of *Man and Superman*. The central action and controlling symbolism of the "Don Juan in Hell" episode are based on the opposition between the angelic and the diabolic temperaments, which is at the same time "only the difference between two ways of looking at things." The distance between heaven and hell is essentially the distance between idealism and realism. Juan confuses Ana with a typical Shavian paradox, assuring her on one hand that "heaven is the home of the masters of reality," and on the other that "hell is the home of honor, duty, justice, and the rest of the seven deadly virtues." When Ana protests, "I am going to heaven for happiness. I have had quite enough of reality on earth," he replies, "Then you must stay here; for hell is the home of the unreal and of the seekers for happiness." The Statue confirms Juan by describing hell as "a place where you have nothing to do but amuse yourself."

One might suppose, on the basis of assertions such as these, that Shaw is simply expressing a puritan contempt for pleasure; it is not the self-indulgence Shaw despises and fears, however, but the self-delusion. He felt it was suicidal for man to indulge his proclivity for making a virtue of his weaknesses, for glamorizing his instincts, for flattering his laziness and idealizing what is comfortable. In hell no reality exists to limit this tendency; and here, Juan tells the idealist, "you call your appearance beauty, your emotions love, your sentiments heroism, your aspirations virtue, just as you did on earth; but here there are no hard facts to contradict you."

Ideals, duties, conventions, virtues, all are words, "words which I or anyone else can turn inside out like a glove," Juan complains; but the reality of heaven allows no place for glib abstractions. There you "live and work instead of playing and pretending. You face things as they are; you escape nothing but glamor; and your steadfastness and your peril are your glory." "Thither," says Juan, "I shall go presently, because there I hope to escape at last from lies and from the tedious, vulgar pursuit of happiness."

A strong underlying strain of snobbishness in Shaw erupts in this characteristic sneer at the vulgarity of happiness. It reveals an elitism more than a little suggestive of Calvinist election, but justification is by will and work, not by faith and divine grace. And since salvation to Shaw is not merely a private matter, but the future of mankind, he measures the scale from damnation to blessedness in terms of commitment *to* the self and commitment *of* the self to the purposes of the universe. A scorn for the pursuit of personal happiness, as something unworthy of man's highest aspirations and efforts, runs all through Shaw's writing. In a relatively early bit of music criticism, Corno di Bassetto observes: "I am unfortunately so constituted that if I were actually in heaven itself I should have to earn my enjoyment of it by turning out and doing a stroke of work of some sort, at any rate of at least a fortnight's hard labor for one celestial evening hour. There is nothing so insufferable as happiness, except perhaps unhappiness."[3] Many years later he affirmed that "the secret of being miserable is to have leisure to bother about whether you are happy or not . . . . A perpetual holiday is a good working definition of hell."[4] There is in this something of the so-called "work ethic," the *laborare est orare* of the more earnest Victorians; but Shaw did not really worship work for its own sake, or trust its

3. Quoted by Hesketh Pearson, *George Bernard Shaw: His Life and Personality* (New York: Atheneum, 1963), p. 130.
4. "Parents and Children," *Plays*, IV, 34–35.

idealization any more than any other. On the other hand, he did worship creativity, and happiness was to him self-centered, transient, sterile, and uncreative. With Captain Shotover, he feared "the accursed happiness . . . of yielding and dreaming instead of resisting and doing, the sweetness of the fruit that is going rotten."[5]

For Shaw the rejection of happiness in favor of a commitment to work for something outside the self was what he called a moral passion, which had all the characteristics of genuine religious fervor. Quite late in his career his spokesman, the Little Black Girl, announced: "I do not seek happiness: I seek God."[6] Much earlier he had written to the actress Janet Achurch in his elitist vein: "Happiness is insufferably tedious to those who have once gained the heights." Later, discussing a passage in *Candida,* in which the actress played the title role, he told her: "Now you know . . . what Eugene means when he says: 'I no longer desire happiness: life is nobler than that.' That is the language of the man recreated by a flash of religion" (*Letters,* I, 472, 506). It was poignantly appropriate that these admonitions against the seductions of happiness should be addressed to Janet Achurch, since at just that time Shaw was fighting desperately for her soul against the devil of drug addiction. In his long life Shaw fought many battles and lost most of them; but none was as tragic as this hopeless struggle to save his friend, ostensibly for the theater, but essentially for herself and for the world. And the contest was as much a question of principle as a personal matter. He looked on the use of drugs, at least while choice was still possible, as a vicious consequence of making happiness the primary personal value. And by the same token the search for happiness was, like the taking of drugs, a futile and self-defeating effort to escape reality. At about the same time he was writing to Janet Achurch, Shaw warned another actress against all those "who prefer liberty, happiness and irresponsibility to care, suffering and life;

5. *Heartbreak House, Plays,* I, 568.
6. *The Adventures of the Black Girl in Her Search for God* (1933; rpt. New York: Capricorn, 1959), p. 58.

who live for and in themselves instead of for and in the world"
(*Letters,* I, 679). At the opposite end of Shaw's moral scheme
of things from the search for personal happiness is "the true joy
in life, the being used for a purpose recognized by yourself as a
mighty one; the being thoroughly worn out before you are thrown
on the scrap heap; the being a force of Nature instead of a fever-
ish selfish little clod of ailments and grievances complaining that
the world will not devote itself to making you happy."[7] Such
pronouncements were for public consumption, to be sure; but
his more private communications reveal the same theme. "It is
good for me to be worked to the last inch," he wrote Ellen Terry;
and in another letter: "I want to be *used,* since use is life." On
still another occasion he wrote: "It is only when I am being used
that I can feel my own existence, enjoy my own life. . . . Everything real in life is based on need" (*Letters,* I, 676, 723, 770).

"Use is life." We will hear the phrase again, for if any single
maxim can define a man's life and thought, this one does so for
Shaw. The sense of his own reality he found in the conviction
that he was being used for what he believed to be a mighty purpose. Shaw's lifelong war against idealism, then, was founded on
the presumption that behind that way of seeing the world lies a
denial of all that gives life meaning. In the pursuit of either personal happiness or personal virtue he could find no "mighty purposes"; and in being more concerned with conventionality than
with new ideas, with abstractions than with facts, and with social
proprieties than with social change, in looking backward rather
than forward, and in these ways denying him a goal worthy of his
use, idealism seemed the impulse of death, not of life. He saw
himself as a "realist [who] at last loses patience with ideals alto-
gether, and sees in them only something to blind us, something to
numb us, something to murder self in us, something whereby
instead of resisting death, we can disarm it by committing
suicide" (*Q.Ib.,* p. 564).

The most sinister feature of idealism for Shaw was that its appeal is not to the vicious but to the virtuous. Writing of Ibsen's

---

7. "Epistle Dedicatory" to *Man and Superman, Plays,* III, 510–511.

plays, he says: "Since it is on the weaknesses of the higher type of character that idealism seizes, his most tragic examples of vanity, selfishness, folly, and failure are not vulgar villains, but men who in an ordinary novel or melodrama would be heroes" (*Q.Ib.*, p. 656). And elsewhere he speaks of "the terrible mischief and misery made every day, not by scoundrels, but by moral people and idealists in their inexorable devotion to what they call their 'duty' " (*Letters*, I, 277).

It should be evident that the flaw in idealism is not, as some critics have claimed, that "it set unrealizable norms of conduct,"[8] but that its norms are based on an irrelevant system of values. Shaw wrote in a letter to William Archer concerning *Arms and the Man:* "I do not accept the conventional ideals. To them I oppose in the play the practical life & morals of the efficient, realistic man, unaffectedly ready to face what . . . must be faced. . . . My whole secret is that I have got clean through the old categories of good & evil, and no longer use them even for dramatic effect. Sergius is ridiculous through the breakdown of his ideals, not odious from his falling short of them. . . . They don't work; but . . . there is something else that does work" (*Letters*, I, 427).

The "something else" is clearly realism. A character in one of Shaw's playlets says: "When I believe in everything that is real . . . then I shall be a man at last."[9] Shaw himself says elsewhere that man "raises himself from mere consciousness to knowledge by daring more and more to face facts and tell himself the truth" (*Q.Ib.*, p. 558). His concept of his role in furthering the process for others may have been only slightly overstated in a comment to the friend and neighbor of his later years, Stephen Winsten: "The world will never be the same again because I have educated four generations to see things as they are, and not what they imagine them to be or want them to be."[10]

8. Louis Crompton, *Shaw the Dramatist* (Lincoln: University of Nebraska Press, 1969), p. 14.

9. "The Glimpse of Reality" (1909), *Plays,* IV, 743.

10. S. Winsten, *Days with Bernard Shaw* (London: Hutchinson, n.d.), p. 88.

Shaw wanted to discredit idealism because it makes men insensitive to the problems and functioning of human nature in the real world. But it is almost always easier to define what it is we do not believe than what it is we do; and while the idealistic abstractions he so distrusts are not hard to identify, the many implications of realism are not quite so obvious. At one level, he uses the word in the most literal sense of the ability to see things as they actually are, the ugly "facts of life" of poverty, greed, social injustice. Realism represents the capacity to recognize human selfishness behind its disguises of poetry and romance and, at the other extreme, to respond to flights of the human spirit without cant and self-congratulation. "Reality," however, was something much more basic to Shaw than the unvarnished truths of man's nature.

Talking about any reality beyond the immediately evident and sensuous world carries with it the inherent difficulty of finding a language sufficient to the perception. The immense possibilities that the mind can only guess at are difficult to articulate except through symbols, parables, crude approximations, and generalizations. There is in Shaw an element of mysticism: he wants to come to grips intellectually and morally with larger realities he dimly perceives behind the veil of appearances. At the same time he tries to avoid the language of abstraction he renounced so vehemently in his wide-ranging attacks on idealism.

When Shaw speaks passionately about finding his sense of life in "use," in feeling himself used by an unspecified force for mighty purposes, it is clear that both the force and the purpose lie at the heart of his "reality." Traditionally, such feelings have been associated with reverence for some form of deity; but for Shaw the conventional worship of the Christian God was simply another mask of idealism. In a letter to William Archer describing the lecture that eventually grew into *The Quintessense of Ibsenism*, he says: "Above all, we are fairly free from that arch-ideal called God, which concentrates into a single concept all the essential evil and incidental good of idealism" (*Letters*, I, 258). The sense in which this was true for him is illuminated in a speech by Don Juan in *Man and Superman:* "Religion [had been reduced] for me to a mere excuse for laziness, since it had set up a God who looked at the world and saw that it was good, against the instinct in me that looked through my eyes at the world and saw that it could be improved" (*Plays,* III, 641–642).

For all this, Shaw was intensely and genuinely religious; but he self-consciously avoided, or tried to revitalize with new meaning, what he considered the sterile and stultified terminology of conventional Christianity. Sometimes his pronouncements on religion can be misleading, as in the following passage, where only the parenthesis reveals the tongue well lodged in the cheek: "My own faith is clear: I am a resolute Protestant; I believe in the Holy Catholic Church; in the Holy Trinity of Father, Son (or Mother, Daughter) and Spirit; in the Communion of Saints, the Life to Come, the Immaculate Conception, and the everyday reality of Godhead and the Kingdom of Heaven."[11] The tongue may have been in the cheek; but Shaw was being in no way cynical. He meant what he said; but his meaning was quite different from that of the orthodox Christian using the same words. He was a Protestant in the original sense of a protester against authority; he believed in the true catholicism of the universal and primitive church, before it was organized and debased into the worship of martyrdom, what he contemptuously calls "crosstianity;" he took Christ at his word, and believed all men the sons, and women the daughters (Shaw was very modern in his sexual egalitarianism), of God, and God the son of Man, and both partaking of the universal spirit; he believed in the Communion of Saints as long as he was included, and that all conceptions were immaculate. He believed in a life to come, not as "an eternity spent . . . in a sort of bliss which would bore any active person to a second death," but as "a better life to come for the whole world," *in* this world:[12] "As the kingdom of heaven is

11. "On Going to Church," in *Shaw on Religion,* ed. Warren S. Smith (New York: Dodd, Mead, 1967), p. 23. The essay originally appeared in the first issue of *The Savoy,* Jan. 1896.
12. "Preface" to *Major Barbara, Plays,* I, 320–321.

within us we need not go about looking for it and crying Lo here!
and Lo there!"[13] And the "everyday reality of Godhead" was to
be taken very literally. "He who can see that not on Olympus,
not nailed to the cross, but in himself is God: he is the man to
build [a] bridge between the flesh and the spirit."[14]

Such turning of language to his own ends was obviously and
intentionally subversive; but Shaw had no desire to overthrow
religion as such. He wrote his friend Frederick Evans, London
bookseller and amateur photographer, in 1895: "I want to write
a big book of devotion for modern people, bringing all the truths
latent in the old religious dogmas into contact with real life—a
gospel of Shawianity, in fact" (*Letters*, I, 551). And it is not
stretching the point to say that this is precisely what he spent
most of his career doing. In his old age he told his friend Winsten: "I have never wanted to preach the worship of a great man
as Carlyle did; nor achieve greatness at the expense of others, but
I always did want, and still want, to put ideas into people's
heads, so that they can conceive of something better than themselves and strive to bring it into existence. . . . I have been described as a man laughing in the wilderness. That is correct
enough, if you accept me as preparing the way for better things."[15]

As this passage suggests, there was a conceptual element and a
willful element in Shaw's religion: he would create both *awareness* of "something better," and the *will* to "bring it into existence." "What I want to do is to make people more and more
conscious of their souls and of the purpose which has evolved the
soul as its special organ."[16] Awareness, then, is not simply a
function of the intellect, but of the soul; and the will to create
something better presupposes an awareness of purpose, the purpose for which the individual soul and will were created. Shaw's
religion was fully developed long before he found, in the writings

13. "Preface" to *Androcles and the Lion, Plays*, V, 382.
14. *Q.Ib.*, p. 589. Shaw is here describing Maximus's "Third Empire."
15. Winsten, *Days with Shaw*, pp. 195–196.
16. *The Religious Speeches of Bernard Shaw*, ed. Warren S. Smith
(University Park, Pa.: The Pennsylvania State University Press, 1963),
p. 48.

of Henri Bergson, a name for it; but in writing the Preface to
Back to Methuselah (1920) he says retrospectively: "I had always known that civilization needs a religion as a matter of life or
death; and as the conception of Creative Evolution developed I
saw that we were at last within reach of a faith which complied
with the first condition of all religions that have ever taken hold
of humanity: namely, that it must be, first, and fundamentally,
a science of metabiology" (*Plays*, II, lxxxvii–lxxxviii). Although
he has been accused of both puckish eccentricity and fatuous
pretentiousness, it was just this quasi-scientific religion that gave
Shaw a purpose in life, a sense of being an integral and creative
part of the order of things: "I believe myself to be the servant
and instrument of creative evolution. . . . That is to say, a person to whom eating, drinking and reproduction are irksome
necessities in comparison with the urge to wider and deeper
knowledge, better understanding, and greater power over ourselves and our circumstances."[17]

When Shaw speaks of himself as the "servant and instrument"
of this creative will, he means it not in the traditional and figurative Biblical sense of the "servant of God," but in a very literal
and biological way: "God . . . is will. But will is useless without hands and brain. . . . That evolutionary process to me is
God: this wonderful will of the universe, struggling and struggling, and bit by bit making hands and brains for himself, feeling
that, having this will, he must also have material organs with
which to grapple with material things. And that is the reason we
have come into existence. If you don't do his work it won't be
done."[18]

There is a paradox in Shaw's references to God that is in fact
no more of a contradiction than the orthodox concept of the
Trinity. Often, as in the passage just cited, God is treated as will
or impulse, the desire to be something better, what in the Preface
to *Saint Joan* is called the "evolutionary appetite." But He is not

17. *Everybody's Political What's What?* (London: Constable, 1944), p.
327.
18. *Religious Speeches*, p. 6.

only the will to struggle higher, He is also the act, the evolutionary process itself, the hands and the mind that "grapple with
material things"; and at the same time He is the end result of
that process, the goal of what Shaw calls "the aspiring will of
humanity towards divinity." "We are," he says, "all experiments
in the direction of making God. What God is doing is making
himself. . . . We are not very successful attempts at God so
far."[19] God, in other words, is not complete; but Shaw would say
with Lavinia in *Androcles and the Lion:* "I'll strive for the coming of the God who is not yet." The deity Shaw envisioned is in
Yeats's phrase both the dancer and the dance, as well as the
Aristotelian "final cause," that final perfection toward which the
dancer aspires. He is Creator, the Created, as it is and as it will
be, and the Will to Create—or, as Shaw says, Father, Son, and
Holy Spirit.

Most of the passages cited to describe Shaw's religion of Creative Evolution have been taken from relatively early work. One
final quotation may be legitimate, however, both because it
neatly summarizes the main points and because it is taken from
one of his last major efforts, *Everybody's Political What's What?*
(1944), and consequently serves to illustrate the comparative
stability of the central ideas in his "metabiological religion." In
the passage he is discussing the qualities of the ideal statesman,
who

must be religious; but he must discard every element in his religion
that is not universal. . . . If he personifies the creative factor in
biology as God he must not nationalize it as Jehovah or Allah,
Buddha, or Brahma. Above all he must not look to God to do his
work for him. He must regard himself as the fallible servant of a
fallible God, acting for God and thinking for God because God,
being unable to effect His purposes without hands or brains, has
made us evolve our hands and brains to act and think for Him: in
short, we are not in the hands of God; but God is in our hands. A
ruler must not say helplessly "Thy Will be done": he must divine it,
find out how to do it, and have it done. His God must not be an
existing Omnipotent Omniscient Perfection, but as yet only an ideal

19. Ibid., p. 35.

towards which creative evolution is striving, with mankind merely its best attempt so far, and a very unsatisfactory one at that, liable to be replaced at any moment if creative evolution gives it up as hopeless. He must face the evil in the world, which apparently reduces the goodness of God to absurdity, as but the survival of errors originally well intended. He must treat life as everlasting, but treat his contemporaries as ephemeral mortals having no life beyond the grave to compensate them for any injustices they may suffer here and now. [P. 329]

The views here stated are often taken as a materialistic rationalization of the deity, and it is easy to fall into the trap of assuming that because Shaw used quasi-scientific terminology and spoke of his religion as the "science of metabiology" he was therefore in any important sense a rationalist in his thinking. This he repeatedly denied. In a public address made in 1911, he said: "As for my own position, I am, and always have been, a mystic. I believe that the universe is being driven by a force that we might call the life-force. I see it as performing the miracle of creation, that it has got into the minds of men as what they call their will. Thus we see people who clearly are carrying out a will not exclusively their own."[20] In an undated letter to Charles Morgan, he is even more explicit: "Creative Evolution . . . is both mystical and matter of fact, inasmuch as though it occurs visibly and instantly it is utterly inexplicable and unaccountable and fits into no theory. It defies deduction and is an ultimate phenomenon."[21] He was quite aware that his own emphasis on the importance of the mind could be misleading, and when G. K. Chesterton went wrong in his commentary, Shaw wrote: "Nothing is more natural than that you should reconstruct me as the last of the Rationalists . . . ; and nothing could be more erroneous. It would be much nearer the truth to call me, in that world, the first of the mystics" (*Letters,* II, 762).

It is doubtful that Shaw was a mystic in any technical sense, and he would surely not have settled comfortably into one of

20. Ibid., p. 33.

21. Shorthand draft, undated, of letter to Charles Morgan, in the collection of Shaw letters at the Humanities Research Center, University of Texas at Austin.

William James's categories. At the same time, the vision by which
he lived and wrote was not seen by the clear light of reason, and
it seems to lie largely outside the rationalist scheme of things.
This is not to say that Shaw scorned reason, for again and again
he called on man to respect and develop the powers of his mind.
The modesty of his lines to Ellen Terry may have been only
whimsical: "Curious, how little use mere brains are: I have a
very fine set; and yet I learn't more from the first stupid woman
who fell in love with me than ever they taught me" (*Letters,* I,
672); but the point he was making, that experience precedes
reason, and that reason must have something solid on which to
operate, was very serious. In a letter to William Archer, Shaw
put his finger on a crucial distinction: "The real and of course
eternally indispensable function of Reason is to devise the means
for the satisfaction of the will, whereas the essence of Rationalism
is to set it up as being the prime motor of human action—the
steam instead of the engine" (*Letters,* I, 316).

The will that reason serves is not to be identified with impulse,
assertion of the ego, or any similarly personal or self-centered
drives. "Good conduct," he says elsewhere, "is not dictated by
reason but by a divine instinct that is beyond reason. Reason only
discovers the shortest way: it does not discover the destination."[22]
This universal dimension of the will, elsewhere identified with the
Life Force, as distinct from the individual dimension, needs to be
kept in mind when, as in the *Quintessence of Ibsenism,* he says:
"Ability to reason accurately is as desirable as ever; for by accurate reasoning only can we calculate our actions so as to do what
we intend to do: that is, to fulfill our will" (p. 554).

In other words Shaw, in a typical paradox, was an antiration-
alist with a profound respect for the powers and uses of the human
mind. Reason as a logical process seemed to him cold and mechanical—the engine, as he put it, rather than the steam. Thought,
however, as imagination, as comprehension, as the ability to understand ourselves, the world, and our purposes in it, was a creative and ultimately mystical function, the highest activity of
which the human animal is capable. The Life Force had two

22. Quoted by Hesketh Pearson, p. 348.

components or vectors, and without the physical and procreative element the species would die; still, it is quite obvious that for Shaw it is man's mind that must find the way to something better, and lift the man to the superman.

One of the paradoxes inherent in Shaw's concept of the mind emerges even more strikingly in a suggestion to St. John Ervine that the passion for thought might be the strongest of all the passions: "Intellect is a passion; that is, an activity of life, far more indispensable than physical ecstasy or reproduction"; and went on to explain that the Ancients in *Back to Methuselah* live in a "permanent ecstasy of that sort of enjoyment raised to powers of which we have no experience."[23] Years later, writing about his friends, Beatrice and Sidney Webb, Shaw made even more explicit the synthesis of the physical and intellectual: "[I] was confirmed in my peculiar doctrine that a point will be reached in human mental development when the pleasure taken in brain work by St. Thomas Aquinas and the Webbs (and saints and philosophers generally) will intensify to a chronic ecstasy surpassing that now induced momentarily by the sexual orgasm and produce a normal enjoyment of life such as I have only experienced a very few times."[24]

The urge to find identity and purpose in service, to gain a sense of importance by becoming necessary to others, is a fairly common and not always healthy human characteristic. Shaw shared the impulse; but he lacked the resources to be financially indispensable to anyone, he despised emotional dependency, on or by others, and he was notoriously incapable of fixing anything. Further, there seems to have been little predilection for self-denial in his nature. The self he would put to the service of the Life Force's mighty purposes was his unique gift, his mind. In its use he found the satisfactions of creation, and the works of his mind were his children. Whether he would have grandchildren had to be a matter of faith.

23. St. John Ervine, *Bernard Shaw: His Life, Work and Friends* (New York: William Morrow, 1956), p. 491.

24. "The Webbs and Social Evolution," *New York Times Book Review*, Nov. 18, 1945, p. 1. The *Times* was not at this point up to "orgasm," and printed it "organism."

2 *Major Motifs:*
Socialism

Shaw considered himself a mystic, but only so far as mysticism would be consistent with thorough-going realism. He dreamed of the superman, but experience told him that if salvation was to be in this world and not the next, it would have to be for everyone, not just a few, and that human progress toward that salvation came in infinitesimal increments. In a way, the relationship between reason, or logic, and the highest functions of the human mind was for Shaw not unlike the relationship between the political philosophy called socialism and the metaphysical vision he labeled Creative Evolution. It is true that Shaw, as a pragmatic and intensely energetic human animal, probably spent more of his time and passion and energy in the service of socialism than on any other facet of his many-faceted life; but it was always a means to an end.

The importance it had for him personally, the quality of the passion he put into it, and the sheer volume of the writing it produced make Shaw's socialism too large a topic to be dealt with adequately in anything less than a book devoted to it alone. It was, after all, an activity that held the focus of his attention for the twenty-five or thirty years of his creative prime. And it is scarcely coincidental that his political and dramatic productivity went hand in hand. The publication of *Fabian Essays* (1889) antedates the first performance of *Widowers' Houses* by three years. *Saint Joan,* which can reasonably be called the finest flowering of his dramatic genius, appeared five years before the fulfillment, and most explicit statement, of his economic and political thinking in the long, dense, yet lucid and closely reasoned *Intelligent Woman's Guide to Socialism and Capitalism* (1928). Late in his life he complained to one of the myriad of would-be biographers whose efforts, in sheer self-defense, he conscientiously read: "Here you shew . . . that you think of me only as a playwright. Yet for every play I have written I have made hundreds of speeches and published big books on Fabian Socialism. There is behind my plays a thought-out sociology which makes them fundamentally unlike those by authors to whom knowledge of society means that peas should not be eaten with a knife."[1]

For my purposes, it seems advisable to concentrate here on those distinctive features of Shaw's socialism that serve to define it, or that are in some way significantly related to other, non-political, aspects of his thinking. There is, to begin with, the question of the relationship between Shaw's brand of socialism and that of Karl Marx and communism in general. Throughout his life, even at times when it obviously did harm to his public image, Shaw was not only frank but even insistent about the extent of his admiration for Marx personally, and of his debt to him for the substance and form of his own ideas. "I was a coward until Marx made a Communist of me and gave me a faith," he announced; "Marx made a man of me."[2] Elsewhere he claims, somewhat more ambiguously: "Marx made me a Socialist and saved me from becoming a literary man"—although there is perhaps more irony here than ambiguity (*16 S.S.*, p. 84).

The admiration for Marx was not limitless, however, and nothing irritated Shaw more than the doctrinaire Marxist's claims for the master's infallibility. It was the violent diatribes against the moral horrors of bourgeois capitalism in *Capital* that first evoked

1. "Biographers' Blunders Corrected," *16 S.S.*, pp. 159–160. For an exhaustive description of Fabian Socialism, see A. M. McBriar, *Fabian Socialism and English Politics: 1884–1918* (Cambridge: Cambridge University Press, 1962), a volume to which this chapter is much indebted.
2. Quoted by R. F. Rattray in *Bernard Shaw: A Chronicle* (Luton, Eng.: The Leagrave Press, 1951), p. 44.

Shaw's sympathetic response, and even the abstract social theories seemed written in words of fire. In time, however, Shaw discovered that Marx's "lack of administrative experience and of personal contact with English society, both proletarian and capitalistic, disable him dangerously as a practical politician in spite of his world-shaking exposure of the villainies of Capitalism, and his grasp of its destiny in the Communist Manifesto" (*16 S.S.,* p. 132). Whether the criticism reflects realism or merely provincialism, the comment on Marx's lack of familiarity with the English tradition provides a clue to a major difference between Shaw's program for socialism and Marx's.

Although he was aggressively and at times flamboyantly an Irishman, and amused himself by attributing English constitutionalism to sheer fecklessness, if not to a positive preference for servitude, Shaw nevertheless shared the English respect for stability and aversion to political violence and upheaval. Social rigidity might make the process of change infuriatingly slow, but because of the tradition of constitutional flexibility it tended to be bloodless because it was continuous rather than discontinuous and violent. Shaw was, by personality as well as principle, a gradualist, an evolutionist, and he profoundly distrusted instant solutions as the oversimplifications of idealists. For him the class war and worldwide proletarian revolutions preached by Marx were an ongoing and comparatively orderly phenomenon rather than a cataclysm bringing overnight utopia. Although as time went on he became increasingly disillusioned with the capacity of Parliament to accommodate new ideas, Shaw continued to see the gore on the blood-red flag as symbolic of the suffering of oppressed humanity rather than as flowing from the throats of slaughtered capitalists.

Shaw's divergence from traditional Marxist views arose from a recognition that the conflicts, whether of interest or of ideology, did not follow strict class lines, and that even utopia cannot be created by force. "The war would not be as the Marxist doctrinaires of the Class War seem to imagine," he observed, because "the line that separates those . . . interested in the maintenance of Capitalism from those interested in its replacement by Socialism, is a line drawn not between rich and poor, capitalist and proletarian, but right down through the middle of the proletariat to the bottom of the very poorest section" (*IWG*, p. 373). Furthermore, although "the ocean of Socialism cannot be poured into the pint pot of a nineteenth century parliament," the solution is not to smash the pot, which would quench no one's thirst, but to build a bigger one (Henderson, p. 285). The operative concept here is "to build," for Shaw realized that socialism was as much a state of mind as a political program, and that its acceptance required something more than the dissolution of capitalism, whether violent or peaceful: "Though a political revolution may be necessary to break the power of the opponents of Socialism if they refuse to accept it as a Parliamentary reform, and resist it violently either by organizing what is now called Fascism or a *coup d'état* to establish a Dictatorship of the Capitalists, yet neither a violent revolution nor a peacefully accepted series of parliamentary reforms can by themselves create Socialism" (*IWG,* p. 376).

Although by instinct a pacifist, Shaw was not doctrinaire even on that point, and was willing to acknowledge that "great social changes, if conscious and intentional, are not made until their advocates are sufficiently in earnest to be prepared to kill those who obstruct them"—a sentiment repeated later, but mistakenly often discounted by critics, in *Major Barbara* (Henderson, p. 277). The opposition to violence, in other words, is not so much on moral as on practical grounds. "If the change could be made catastrophically," he acknowledges, "it would be well worth making"; but the fact is it cannot. "At the end of the fighting we shall be the poorer, none the wiser, and some of us the deader. If the Socialists win, the road to Socialism may be cleared; but the pavement will be torn up and the goal as far off as ever."[3] Although it was Shaw's lifelong friend and fellow Fabian, Sidney

3. "Transition," in *Fabian Essays in Socialism,* ed. G. Bernard Shaw (London: 1889; rpt. New York: Doubleday, n.d.), p. 224; see also *IWG,* p. 377.

Webb, who much later made famous the notion of "the inevitability of gradualness" as applied to the movement toward socialism, the idea had already been propounded by Shaw: "On the ground of abstract justice, Socialism is not only unobjectionable, but sacredly imperative. I am afraid that in the ordinary middle-class opinion Socialism is flagrantly dishonest, but could be established off-hand to-morrow with the help of the guillotine, if there were no police, and the people were wicked enough. In truth, it is as honest as it is inevitable; but all the mobs and guillotines in the world can no more establish it than police coercion can avert it."[4] However staunchly Shaw disavowed the catastrophic view of world communism, he found small satisfaction in the pragmatically necessary principle of gradualism, as he makes clear in one of the many eloquent passages the cause of socialism drew from his pen:

Let me . . . disavow all admiration for this inevitable, but sordid, slow, reluctant, cowardly path to justice. I venture to claim your respect for those enthusiasts who still refuse to believe that millions of their fellow creatures must be left to sweat and suffer in hopeless toil and degradation, whilst parliaments and vestries grudgingly muddle and grope towards paltry instalments of betterment. The right is so clear, the wrong so intolerable, the gospel so convincing, that it seems to them that it *must* be possible to enlist the whole body of workers . . . under the banner of brotherhood and equality; and at one great stroke to set Justice on her rightful throne. Unfortunately, such an army of light is no more to be gathered from the human product of nineteenth century civilization than grapes are to be gathered from thistles. But if we feel glad of that impossibility; if we feel relieved that the change is to be slow enough to avert personal risk to ourselves; if we feel anything less than acute disappointment and bitter humiliation at the discovery that there is yet between us and the promised land a wilderness in which many must perish miserably of want and despair: then I submit to you that our institutions have corrupted us to the most dastardly degree of selfishness.[5]

4. *Fabian Essays*, p. 221.
5. Ibid., pp. 245–246.

After such ardor, it is not particularly surprising that Shaw should have developed serious doubts about the ponderously slow evolution, often looking like paralysis, of constitutional political forms. After his visit to the Soviet Union in 1931 he and the Webbs reluctantly abandoned the principle of "the inevitability of gradualness," and acknowledged that violent revolution might under certain circumstances be better than no revolution at all, and that it was becoming increasingly evident that the available options were shrinking rather than expanding.[6]

Shaw's repudiation of the Marxist ideal of anarchy, however, was absolutely unqualified, as a violation of *both* theory and experience, to say nothing of British common sense. "Anarchism, as a panacea, is just as hopeless as any other panacea, and will still be so even if we breed a race of perfectly benevolent men. . . . Applied to the industrial or political machinery of modern society, anarchy must always reduce itself speedily to absurdity."[7] At the heart of Shaw's socialism lies the conviction that the health of the community is tied directly to the equitableness with which it distributes its wealth and the force of its laws. "Distribution must be made according to some law or other. Anarchy (absence of law) will not work. We must go on with our search for a righteous and practicable law" (*IWG*, p. 30). The "righteous law" will not be provided by capitalism, for, according to Shaw, it breeds its own form of anarchy even more destructive than that of communism, and justifies itself on the appeal to natural law. "They loved to believe that a right and just social order was not an artificial and painfully maintained legal edifice, but a spontaneous outcome of the free play of the forces of Nature," namely competition. Following this self-serving ideal, capitalist "political economy [has] declared for industrial anarchy; for private property; for industrial recklessness of everything except individual accumulation of riches."[8]

6. See Henderson, pp. 310 ff., for a more detailed analysis of the Russian expedition.

7. *The Perfect Wagnerite: A Commentary on the Niblung's Ring* (New York: Brentano's, 1909), p. 79.

8. *Fabian Essays,* p. 217.

Capitalism has, of course, its altruistic side, in its appeal to the ideal of personal freedom. But, says Shaw, "even the modified form of anarchy on which modern civilization is based: that is, the abandonment of industry, in the name of individual liberty, to the upshot of competition for personal gain between private capitalists, is a disastrous failure, and is, by the mere necessities of the case, giving way to ordered Socialism." Shaw had his own version of natural law, but it is a far cry from the law of competition: "Liberty is an excellent thing; but it cannot begin until society has paid its daily debt to Nature by first earning its living. There is no liberty before that except the liberty to live at somebody else's expense, a liberty much sought after nowadays, since it is the criterion of gentility, but not wholesome from the point of view of the common weal."[9] And the primary claim of the common weal in its most literal sense is perhaps the central concept of Shaw's political and social thought.

It is precisely this intense concern for the community at large that caused Shaw to respond as sympathetically as he did to Marx's denunciations of the destructive exploitation of both people and resources—that is, what is common wealth—by the capitalist bourgeoisie. "Karl Marx . . . seized on the blue books which contained the true history of the leaps and bounds of England's prosperity, and convicted private property of wholesale spoliation, murder and compulsory prostitution; of plague, pestilence, and famine; battle . . . and sudden death. This was hardly what had been expected from an institution so highly spoken of."[10] These are hard words, but their logic lies in the built-in need of the capitalist economy for constantly expanding markets, and hence Shaw's "exasperated sense of the mischief done by our system of private Capitalism in setting up huge vested interests in destruction, waste, and disease."[11] Of course, if the destruction and disease were distributed equitably amongst

9. *The Perfect Wagnerite*, pp. 79–80; see also "The Impossibilities of Anarchism," published as Fabian Tract No. 45 (see n. 18).

10. *Fabian Essays*, p. 220.

11. "Preface" to *The Applecart*, *Plays*, IV, 227.

the population, then at least it could be argued that there was common woe, if not common weal; but this is scarcely the case: "The tendency of private enterprise, with . . . its natural desire to make the rate of profit as high as possible, is . . . clearly an anti-social one. Through its operation the various inventions which are the sole real assets of modern civilization, instead of raising the standard of life of the whole population, may remain for a long time the toys of the rich, who themselves cannot escape from an overwhelming environment of primitive poverty, to which more civilization means only less air, less house room, less decency, less health, and less freedom."[12]

Just as the object of Shaw's concern is the common weal, so the cure for the common illness is a common rather than an individual responsibility: "It is not our disorder but our order that is horrible, it is not our criminals but our magnates that are robbing and murdering us. . . . The condition of the civilized world is deplorable, and the remedy is far beyond the means of individual righteousness. . . . Until Society is reformed, no man can reform himself except in the most insignificantly small ways. He may cease picking your pockets of half crowns; but he cannot cease taking a quarter of a million a year from the community for nothing at one end of the scale, or living under conditions in which health, decency and gentleness are impossible at the other."[13]

Shaw recognized that Marx was not only cut off from English tradition but from the whole proletarian world he imagined he was addressing, and consequently had misjudged his audience badly. It was not the oppressed worker but the middle-class intellectual who had the education and the energy and the will to respond actively to the outraged appeal to humanity's conscience. Shaw explained: "I read Marx. Now the real secret of Marx's fascination was his appeal to an unnamed, unrecognized passion:

12. "The Common Sense of Municipal Trading," *Prose*, p. 764; this originally appeared as a Fabian Essay in 1908.
13. Shaw's Introduction to Charles Dickens, *Hard Times* (London: Waverley, 1912), reprinted in *Hard Times: An Authoritative Text*, ed. George Ford and Sylvere Monod (New York: Norton, 1966), p. 334.

the hatred in the more generous souls among the respectable and educated sections for the middle-class institutions that had starved, thwarted, misled, and corrupted them spiritually from their cradles. Marx's *Capital* is not a treatise on Socialism: it is a jeremiad against the bourgeoisie, supported by a mass of official evidence. . . . It was addressed to the working classes; but the working man respects the bourgeoisie, and wants to be bourgeois. It was the revolting sons of the bourgeoisie itself . . . like myself, . . . who painted the flag red" (*16 S.S.,* p. 83). Shaw was somewhat more realistic than Marx, not only in the question of who would provide the leadership of the communist cause, but in recognizing also who would be the backbone and the muscle. He understood, as Marx did not, the extent to which the worker might be tied, both economically and in his values, to capitalism, and hence reluctant to bite the hand that fed him, no matter how meanly or insolently.

It is evident that Shaw had no special reverence for what he called the "Dogma of Finality and Infallibility" with which some of his fellow socialists surrounded the sacred words of Karl Marx. Uncritical acceptance and mindless worship were not Shaw's style. And his differences with the author of *Capital* were not simply on practical matters of the validity of violence or the reality of the class war, but also on theoretical questions.

When Shaw first read *Capital* in 1882 he had absorbed and accepted as part of the formulae of communism Marx's interpretation of what is known as "value theory." Marx, following the lead of the early-nineteenth-century English economist Ricardo, expounded a theory according to which the value of an object or commodity is determined by the labor involved in producing it. The difference between the cost of materials, including such things as transportation, and the exchange value, whether measured in terms of equivalence in another commodity or of market price, is attributable to the labor put into the object; and hence the key Marxian precept that since it was the worker who, through his labor, gave the object value, that portion of the "surplus value" which the capitalist calls profit or return on investment should go to the worker rather than be siphoned off by the employer by virtue of his private monopoly of the means of production.

Speculating on the proposition that if all the workers in the world devoted themselves to making millions of tea tables, the exchange value of tea tables would be virtually zero, regardless of how much time and labor went into the making of them, Shaw found the Marxian labor theory of value unconvincing. He turned instead to the economic principles of another English economist, W. S. Jevons, where utility, rather than labor, was the measure of value. Utility is not quite the same thing as usefulness, since it includes the dimension of demand. As the supply of a commodity increases, both the exchange value and the "utility" tend to decrease, because, as Shaw puts it, "when people have had some of a commodity, they are partly satisfied, and do not value the rest so much. The usefulness of a pound of bread to a man depends on whether he has already eaten some. Every man wants a certain number of pounds of bread per week: no man wants much more; and if more is offered he will not give much for it—perhaps not anything. One umbrella is very useful: a second umbrella is a luxury: a third is mere lumber. . . . Now the exchange value is fixed by the utility, not of the most useful, but of the least useful part of the stock. . . . And since the least useful unit of the supply is generally that which is last produced, its utility is called the final [or "marginal"] utility of the commodity."[14] Given the fact that the capitalist system depends for its existence on the maximization of profits, it behooves the producers to make sure that prices are not forced down through careless overproduction, and that wages are kept as low as possible. Shaw argued that minimizing wages presented little difficulty, since labor too was a commodity, subject to the marketplace laws of marginal utility as much as umbrellas or tea tables. In an uncontrolled market, then, with an increasing population, the marginal utility of unskilled labor would in principle approach zero, although in fact it must be sufficient to keep a worker alive

14. "The Basis of Socialism," *Fabian Essays,* pp. 27–28.

and capable of doing his job. But the cost may be more than society can afford: "Their poverty breeds filth, ugliness, dishonesty, disease. . . . It is sometimes said that during this grotesquely hideous march of civilization from bad to worse, wealth is increasing side by side with misery. Such a thing is eternally impossible: wealth is steadily decreasing with the spread of poverty. But riches are increasing, which is quite another thing."[15] Shaw's whole concept of the virtues of socialism and the viciousness of private property really hinges on this distinction between individual riches and common wealth. Salvation, as we have seen, is not a private, but a public thing; and the claim that the affluence and luxury of the few are essential to the welfare of the whole seemed to him the most evil of rationalizations.

It is the economic phenomenon known variously as unearned increment or rent or profit or return on investment that distressed Shaw—not on grounds of abstract justice so much as because its existence meant that while individual riches increased, the wealth of the community as a whole was being lessened by the spread of poverty and its attendant social costs. He agreed with Marx as to the moral intolerability of capitalism, but he differed substantially in his solutions. He acknowledged that the application of the principle of marginal utility in the area of labor kept wages at a minimum and hence the disparity between labor cost and exchange value at a maximum. But he did not accept Marx's labor theory of value, and consequently did not suggest that the difference be simply returned to the worker. What Marx had called "surplus value" Shaw recognized as the function of complex social and economic laws, and properly "belonging" not to either capitalist or worker, but to society as a whole.

By the same token, he saw land and its resources as part of the heritage of the community, not of individuals, and hence the rent derived from it as belonging to the community: "Economic rent, arising as it does from variations of fertility or advantages

15. Ibid., pp. 36–37.

of situation, must always be held as a common or social wealth."[16] "What the achievement of Socialism involves economically," he says elsewhere, "is the transfer of rent from the class which now appropriates it to the whole people. Rent being that part of the produce which is individually unearned, this is the only equitable method of disposing of it."[17] Shaw was quite aware that the appropriation of rent by the whole community removes the whole basis of private ownership, and that the "socialization of rent would mean the socialization of the sources of production by the expropriation of the present private proprietors, and the transfer of their property to the entire nation."

The purpose behind the appropriation of rent and behind the limitations on private property was not, of course, simply to frustrate and get revenge on the bourgeoisie, as so often seems the case with Marx, nor was the accommodation of private industry inconsistent, for the ultimate purpose of both was a higher level of communism than mere community ownership of resources. "There are doctrinaire Socialists," explained Shaw, "who will be shocked at the suggestion that a Socialist Government should not only tolerate private enterprise, but actually finance it. But the business of Socialist rulers is not to suppress private enterprise as such, but to attain and maintain equality of income. The substitution of public for private enterprise is only one of several means to that end; and if in any particular instance the end can be best served for the moment by private enterprise, a Socialist Government will tolerate private enterprise, subsidize private enterprise, or even initiate private enterprise" (*IWG*, pp. 338–339). The principle of equal income, probably the most radical and least likely to be realized feature of Shaw's socialism, did not crystallize in his writing until well after his Marxist and early Fabian periods; but by the time he wrote *The Intelligent Woman's Guide* he was totally committed to a policy of "dividing-up the income of the country equally between everybody, making no distinctions." There are, he acknowledged, "a great many people who call themselves

16. Ibid., p. 42.
17. "Transition," *Fabian Essays*, p. 220.

Socialists . . . who would be shocked and horrified. . . . They
would assure you . . . that no Socialist believes in such crazy
nonsense. What they want, they will tell you, is equality of opportunity, by which I suppose they mean that Capitalism will not
matter if everyone has an equal opportunity of becoming a Capitalist, though how that equality of opportunity can be established
without equality of income they cannot explain. . . . Socialism
means equality of income and nothing else" (pp. 93–94).

Any proposal to equalize income will of necessity arouse the
bitter antagonism of a substantial number of people—in fact most
of those who imagine their incomes to be at or above the proposed new norm. Shaw was made well aware of this, and it took
considerable courage to stick to his guns in the face of the outraged cries of his detractors and the embarrassed silence of his
friends. Even the Fabians, at least officially, pretended they
hadn't heard, and never included equal income as part of their
program. But while he was often accused of making outrageous
pronouncements for the sake of self-dramatization and publicity,
Shaw does not in this case seem to have been trying either to out-
flank the radical left or to play to the gallery and curry favor
with the proletariat. In reply to the criticism that his principles
gave recognition only to the lowest common denominator, and
thereby glorified mediocrity, Shaw insisted that his primary purpose was to escape from the confusion of income and social status
with merit that is most likely to frustrate genuine worth: "Only
where there is pecuniary equality can the distinction of merit
stand out. Titles, dignities, reputations do more harm than good
if they can be bought with money. . . . Between persons of un-
equal income all other distinctions are thrown in the background.
. . . Between persons of equal income there is no social distinction except the distinction of merit" (*IWG,* p. 71).

It is evident that Shaw would have liked to make sure that
genuine worth was adequately recognized and valued, as a matter
of simple equity; and yet his primary concern was not with such
abstractions as justice. The division of society into the "haves" and
"have nots" was not merely unjust, but inefficient and potentially
self-destructive as well—a situation in which both poverty and

wealth, being parts of the same body, were being paralyzed by the same poison. And the evil of capitalism lay as much in its moral as in its economic impact, for Shaw considered it based on a system of values that encouraged the philosophy of getting as much as possible for doing as little work as possible: "There is no sincere public opinion that a man should work for his daily bread if he can get it for nothing. Indeed, it is just the other way: public opinion has been educated to regard the performance of daily manual labour as the lot of despised classes. The common aspiration is to acquire property and leave off working."[18] The most vicious aspect of this situation is the disparity it creates between actual and professed values, for "the association of prosperity with idleness, and praise with industry, practically destroys morality by setting up that incompatibility between conduct and principle which is the secret of the ingrained cynicism of our own time."[19] A system in which the achievement of an unearned income is not only tolerated but made the object of admiration, and hence a reward for idleness and a justification for producing nothing, was not for Shaw simply inequitable, it was insane.

The root of the evil is of course to be traced back to private property: "The income of a private proprietor can be distinguished by the fact that he obtains it unconditionally and gratuitously by private right against the public weal, which is incompatible with the existence of consumers who do not produce."[20] Shaw even complained once that "the Labor Party is anti-social in that it supports the producer against the consumer and the worker against the employer instead of supporting the workers against the idlers";[21] and one of the most consistent goals of his life was what he described as the "Disestablishment and Disendowment of Idleness."

With a passion that may well have owed something to his early reading of Carlyle, Shaw considered idleness the first of the

18. *The Impossibilities of Anarchism,* Fabian Tract No. 45 (London: The Fabian Society, 1893), p. 14.
19. *Fabian Essays,* p. 20.
20. Ibid., p. 42.
21. Letter to Augustine Hamon, quoted in Rattray, *Chronicle,* p. 188.

deadly sins because it is counterproductive, a dead weight holding back social progress. "When every possible qualification of
the words Idle Rich has been made, and it is fully understood
that idle does not mean doing nothing (which is impossible), but
doing nothing useful, and continually consuming without producing, the term applies to the class, numbering at the extreme
outside one-tenth of the population, to maintain whom in their
idleness the other nine-tenths are kept in a condition of slavery so
complete that their slavery is not even legalized as such" (*IWG*,
p. 62). And the rationalization that the rich, even if they contributed less to the public welfare than they consumed, at least
stimulated the economy with their demand for luxuries Shaw
treated with contempt, on the ground that "luxuries are not
social wealth: the machinery for producing them is not social
wealth: labor skilled only to manufacture them is not socially
useful labor."[22]

Shaw's hatred—and hatred is probably not too strong a term
—of the rich, on the grounds that they represent useless and unproductive parasites on the community as a whole, was no
greater than his hatred of the poor, for what were essentially the
same reasons: they were a burden that depressed the common
welfare. "Class hatred," he asserted, "is not a mere matter of
envy on the part of the poor and contempt and dread on the part
of the rich. Both rich and poor are really hateful in themselves.
For my part I hate the poor and look forward eagerly to their
extermination. I pity the rich a little, but am equally bent on
their extermination. . . . And yet I am not in the least a mis-
anthrope" (*IWG*, p. 456).

The "extermination," to be sure, is not to be understood literally, but in the sense of rendering the condition impossible. The
existence of socially unproductive affluence, on the one hand, and
on the other a poverty that for very different reasons consumed
more than it produced seemed to Shaw a criminal waste of scarce
human resources, a burden that in the long struggle between the
forces of life and the forces of death might well tip the balance
against life.

22. *Fabian Essays*, p. 38.

The distance between rich and poor represented an intolerable antithesis, and yet disparity, like a differential in voltage, is a source of energy. A society torn apart by the violent antagonism of idle rich and overworked laborer may be headed for suicide, but a society in which all differentiae whatever have been eliminated may be headed for paralysis and entropy. Shaw did not seek to obliterate all distinctions between human beings, only those based on money and class. The energy that moves society need not come from such essentially destructive sources as the lust for power and indolence at one extreme and the raw competition for survival at the other. What he sought was a structure within which the real and natural differences, conflicts, and antitheses of human nature might be harnessed to work for the *common* wealth and welfare.

For such reasons as these Shaw was especially outraged by all efforts, whether of public legislation or private charity, to sweeten the consequences of extreme economic inequalities while ignoring the causes. The abolition of poverty is not to be achieved by giving handouts as conscience money, as he made clear in *Major Barbara,* and he had no patience with those who viewed "Socialism as a charitable enterprise for the benefit of the poor. Nothing could be further from the truth. Socialism abhors poverty, and would abolish the poor. . . . Socialism loathes almsgiving, not only sentimentally because it fills the paupers with humiliation, the patrons with evil pride, and both with hatred, but because in a country justly and providently managed there could be neither excuse for it on the pauper's part not occasion for it on the patron's" (*IWG,* pp. 95–96). Elsewhere he warns: "Do not let your mind be disabled by excessive sympathy. What the true Socialist revolts against is not the suffering that is not cumulative, but the waste that is" (*IWG,* p. 455).

Shaw was perfectly well aware that in espousing gradualism rather than revolution, in discounting the importance of the class war, in repudiating Marx's theory of value and holding out for a universal equality of income, and especially in shifting the focus of attack from capitalism per se to nonproductivity of either the rich or the poor he had strayed far from the ways of the gospel. The influence of such latitudinarian thought—which the orthodox called "revisionism"—has led such historians of Marxism as George Lichtheim to bemoan the fact that the period from the 1880s to the 1930s "represents almost a complete blank so far as England is concerned" because "British Socialism was at the critical moment captured by the Fabians."[23] Shaw never claimed to be a purist; but by insisting on his admiration for Marx, and by clinging to the label of communist, he earned the scorn of the faithful, and the accusation that what he called Marxism was only another of his paradoxical poses.

During most of his public life Shaw had to defend himself against those, friends as well as foes, who were outraged by his failure to fit their stereotypes. His socialist colleagues were horrified when, at the time of the Boer War, he openly supported imperialist Britain against the outnumbered but fanatical army of Paul Kruger. During the First World War he was denounced as a traitor because he publicly criticized the frenzy of jingoistic chauvinism that carried away most of his countrymen, and then as a hypocrite for the playlets, public appearances, and speeches with which he tried to contribute to the war effort. His own explanation was straightforward: "I have no ethical respect for modern Capitalist society, and therefore contemplated the British, German, and French sections of it with impartial disapproval. I felt as if I were witnessing an engagement between two pirate fleets, with, however, the very important qualification that as I and my family and friends were on board British ships I did not intend the British section to be defeated if I could help it. All the ensigns were Jolly Rogers; but mine was clearly the one with the Union Jack in the corner."[24] Characteristically, his frankness was viewed as merely another instance of perverse Shavian paradox by his piratical shipmates.

Somewhat more convincing charges of muddleheadedness were

23. George Lichtheim, *Marxism: An Historical and Critical Study* (New York: Praeger, 1961), p. 225.
24. *What I Really Wrote about the War* (London: Constable, 1931), p. 2.

leveled against Shaw for his rather uncritical whitewash of Stalinist Russia after his visit in 1931, and later for his qualified praise of the early efforts by Mussolini and Hitler to create order out of chaos. His speeches on Russia in the mid 1930s and the Preface to *On the Rocks* (1933) do suggest a naiveté that may be only partly explained by the urgency of his desire to find a socialist experiment that worked. Having spent fifty years preaching the theory of socialism, his image of his life's work depended heavily on its practical validity. But wishful thinking did not overwhelm Shaw's moral sense; and in fact he did not try to defend totalitarian governments in moral terms. He did, however, claim that they were, as institutions, acting on realistic rather than idealistic grounds, as pragmatists rather than moralists, justifying actions only by the good accruing to the state as a whole. He was not insensitive to the harshness and repression fundamental to the police state, but found that less offensive—at least for rhetorical purposes—than the occasion it gave for a sense of moral superiority and a complacent blindness to comparable evils on the part of his countrymen.

In a letter to fellow socialist H. M. Hyndman, Shaw explained his seemingly paradoxical views on the Boer War on the basis that Paul Kruger had converted a war of self-interest into a moral crusade of Good against Evil, of Jehovah against Mammon: "And as Mammon can be developed into a Socialist power in proportion as men become Socialistically minded, whereas Jehovah makes any such change of mind impossible, and stands for false categories of moral good and evil in nature, and consequently for implacable war, punishment, enmity, aggression & repression between men, my sympathies are with Mammon" (*Letters*, II, 162). But, he complained, "the moralist side being the . . . one which I attack, I have the air of attacking everything for the sake of singularity."

In the Preface to *On the Rocks* Shaw defends Stalinist Russia on much the same grounds. He observes that virtually every government or ruling class from the times of Socrates and Christ on have engaged in the literal or figurative extermination of those considered threats to their power. At worst this is done by torture and murder, at best by physical isolation, as in reservations or ghettos, or through economic isolation as "inferior peoples." Shaw does not make a moral judgment of this behavior, but simply describes it as a fact of political life. What does outrage him is that in virtually every case the pretended justification is the moral superiority of victor to victim, of exterminator to exterminated. What Shaw found unique in the Soviet Union, and the source of a faith in its future beyond the violence of its birth pangs, were its efforts to base policies and programs, to make decisions about whom to suppress and whom to encourage, not on grounds of moral superiority or inferiority but on the basis of *usefulness* to society as a whole.

Shaw's enthusiasm for the Russian experiment in state socialism did not, however, blind him to the fact that a revolutionary movement runs the danger of becoming even more dogmatic and self-righteous than the entrenched establishment it seeks to overthrow. "In Russia the State will sooner or later have to break the temporal power of the Marxist Church and take politics out of its hands, exactly as the British and other Protestant States have broken the temporal power of the Roman Church. . . . But until then the Church of Marx, the Third International, will give as much trouble as the Popes did formerly." "Still," he goes on, "our Protestant repudiation of the authority of the new Marxist Church should not make us forget that if the Marxist Bible cannot be taken as a guide to parliamentary tactics, the same may be said of those very revolutionary documents the Gospels. We do not on that account burn the Gospels and conclude that the preacher of the Sermon on the Mount has nothing to teach us; and neither should we burn Das Kapital and ban Marx as a worthless author whom nobody ought to read. Marx did not get his great reputation for nothing; he was a very great teacher," especially for those "who have really learnt from him instead of blindly worshipping him as an infallible prophet" (*IWG*, pp. 442–443).

Although Shaw may have been overly optimistic in his hope that Marxism might not become as narrowly moralistic and as blinded by "ideals" as any more traditional creed, he was clearly aware of the dangers of elevating a social and economic theory to the level of a religion. And yet socialism was for him something more than a logically structured political program for the betterment of human conditions. It was a faith and a passion that had become deeply rooted in his whole emotional and intellectual nature, and he could be no more coldly objective about it—nor did he ever claim to be—than any deeply involved partisan. The diaries Shaw kept from 1885 to 1897 reveal a man who devoted incredible amounts of time and energy to socialist activities. Scarcely a day passed when he did not attend several meetings of socialist clubs, debating societies, discussion groups of diverse sorts, workingmen's associations, street corner gatherings, committees of the Fabians or, later, of the St. Pancras Vestry (later Borough Council), where he served conscientiously and by all reports effectively on the public health, electricity, parliamentary, housing, and drainage committees—at most of which affairs he delivered a prepared or unprepared address. He carried this burden of activity lightly enough, and there were many who, like Ernest Rhys, were surprised to discover that when Shaw set aside the facade of wit and irreverence "he talked seriously, even emotionally, about the Socialist campaign and the work to be done in London and the country at large."[25] The secret of Marx's fascination for him, he had said, was "his appeal to an unnamed, unrecognized passion," a passion that seems to have provided the source of, rather than a drain on, inexhaustible energies, a passion that transfigured his life. "Here am I," he said, "by class a respectable man, . . . yet I am, and have always been, and shall now always be, a revolutionary writer."[26] It was a passion dedicated to the proposition that the purpose of life is to improve the quality of life for the whole community; and while it may begin in individualism, it must pass beyond: "When a man is at last brought face to face with himself by a brave Individualism, he finds himself face to face, not with an individual, but with a

25. Ernest Rhys, *Wales England Wed* (London: J. M. Dent, 1940), p. 85.
26. "Preface" to *Major Barbara, Plays,* I, 336.

species, and he knows that to save himself, he must save the race. He can have no life except a share in the life of the community; and if that life is unhappy and squalid, nothing that he can do to paint and paper and upholster and shut off his little corner of it can really rescue him from it" (*Q.Ib.*, p. 640).

The breadth of its object gives Shaw's passion much of its depth and substance. But the community of man exists in two dimensions: that of his immediate social and economic condition, for the amelioration of which socialism seemed to Shaw to offer the most promising program, and that of his ultimate condition or purpose or role in the universe—or at least in our tiny corner of it. The world of Now is a very small though possibly decisive instant in the total evolution of man from an obscure insensate past to some unimaginable future; and it is this infinitely broader dimension that Shaw tried to cope with in the constellation of theories surrounding the principle of the Life Force. Socialism and Creative Evolution, as well as most of the other ideas that provided the center of Shaw's thought, are simply different ways of thinking about, or coming to terms with, some central questions about the nature of man. They form a reasonably consistent and coherently structured body of thought; and once Shaw had worked them out to his own tentative satisfaction they did not undergo any major transformations. But how the pieces fell together during a critical decade in his life, and where a young man whose formal education ended at the age of fifteen found the pieces in the first place, are problems of intellectual history that are interesting in their own right, and the answers to which throw valuable light on both the substance of those ideas and the ways in which they became incarnate in the dramatic and intellectual structures of the plays. And if it seems paradoxical to speak of ideas achieving material and mortal substance in an intellectual structure, the implied contradiction between mind and matter suggests the dialectic tension that exists, at once stable and unresolved, at the heart of Shaw's thinking.

3   *Consolidation and Synthesis*

The critical, and in a sense climactic, decade in Shaw's intellectual and philosophical development lies somewhat tentatively between 1883 and 1893. In 1883 he had ended his literary apprenticeship and completed the last of his five unsuccessful novels; the *terminus ad quem* represents a point at which his philosophy seems to be fairly well thought through and developed—as evidenced in *The Quintessence of Ibsenism*—and he was embarked on his career as a playwright. Of course, Shaw was seriously involved in working out his ideas before 1883; and it would be absurd to suppose that his thinking stopped developing and petrified, like Roebuck Ramsden's, at the age of thirty-seven. Nevertheless, nowhere in Shaw's career was there such rapid and obvious development as in this decade. His mind seems to have been at white heat, operating with that incredible energy that characterized the man, putting together pieces and fragments, and emerging with a philosophic structure that was admittedly eclectic, but surprisingly sophisticated and complete for a young man who had done no formal study, and very little reading, in the systems of the professional philosophers.

Not long after Shaw arrived in London from Dublin in 1876, following his mother, who had come some years earlier, he settled on—or perhaps "drifted into" is a more accurate description —writing as a profession. "I was driven to write," he says, "because I could do nothing else. . . . It's not what a man would like to do, but what he can do, that he must work at in this world. I wanted to be another Michael Angelo, but found that I could not draw. I wanted to be a musician, but found I could not play—to be a dramatic singer, but had no voice. I did not want to write: that came as a matter of course without any wanting."[1] The reminiscences of the novel-writing days reveal a great deal about Shaw's character—the energy, as well as a kind of dogged aggressiveness that sometimes would allow quantity to substitute for quality:

In 1879 . . . I had done what every literary adventurer did in those days, and many do still. I had written a novel. My office training [in Dublin] had left me with a habit of doing something regularly every day as a fundamental condition of industry as distinguished from idleness. I knew I was making no headway unless I was doing this, and that I should never produce a book in any other fashion. I bought supplies of white paper, demy size, by sixpennorths at a time; folded it in quarto; and condemned myself to fill five pages of it a day, rain or shine, dull or inspired. . . . On this plan I produced five novels in five years. It was my professional apprenticeship, doggedly suffered with all the diffidence and dissatisfaction of a learner with a very critical master, myself to wit, whom there was no pleasing and no evading, and persevered in to save my self-respect.[2]

Self-discipline and valuable experience were the only rewards novel-writing brought at the time. Of the five, four did not appear in book form until after Shaw had acquired notoriety as a playwright—the exception being *Cashel Byron's Profession,* which was published in stereotype in 1886, and in hard cover in 1889. All except the first, *Immaturity,* appeared in the mid-1880s only as serials in relatively obscure socialist journals. Although prevented at the time by his own inexperience from understanding what was wrong, Shaw later identified some of his

1. *Nine Answers,* an 1896 interview recast into a pamphlet privately published for Jerome Kern in 1923, quoted by Stanley Weintraub in *Shaw: An Autobiography 1856–1898* (New York: Weybright and Talley, 1969), p. 77.

2. "Preface" to *Immaturity, Prose,* pp. 58–59.

limitations, both general and specific: "When I had to come out of the realm of imagination into that of actuality I was still uncomfortable. I was outside society, ouside politics, outside sport, outside the Church. If the term had been invented then I should have been called The Complete Outsider. But . . . I had the intellectual habit; and my natural combination of critical faculty with literary resource needed only a clear comprehension of life in the light of an intelligible theory: in short, a religion, to set it in triumphant operation. It was the lack of this last qualification that lamed me in those early days in Victoria Grove."[3] Of course, this observation was made with the clarity of perception characteristic of hindsight, and Shaw knew perfectly well what religion it was that he then lacked and was soon to be opened up to him. The early novels, however, were written in complete ignorance of Marx and, while that does not make all the difference, it does make some.

The first four novels are admirable in their energy, their unconventional but provocative ideas, and an essential high seriousness behind the emergent wit; but one senses that taken as a group they lack the organizing force, the unifying purpose and direction of the plays. Before he wrote the fifth and last novel Shaw had, as he later termed it, "found a religion"; and the consequences are dramatically and at times outrageously evident in *An Unsocial Socialist*. Undoubtedly the liveliest of the novels, it also puts the greatest strain on the reader's patience. Shaw seems to have swallowed Marx hook, line, and sinker, and returns them here with slight evidence that his digestive juices have had any chance to operate. The hero, Sidney Trefusis, is in violent reaction against a successful capitalist father who is clearly a precursor of Andrew Undershaft: "My father had to choose between being a slave and enslaving others."[4] Trefusis's socialism is irrepressible, and at the slightest provocation he delivers disquisitions on the difference between value of use and value of exchange, on nineteenth-century economic history, on capitalist exploitation,

3. Ibid., p. 66.
4. *An Unsocial Socialist* (New York: Brentano's, 1930), p. 292.

ad infinitum. Minor characters of rural origin and no education reveal an astounding awareness of the economic implications of population growth and the marginal utility of labor; and even the author cannot refrain from inserting a three-page discussion of the difficulties involved in determining the true value of a tombstone. The most outrageous affront to the reader is the scene in which Trefusis, pursued by the angry headmistress of Alton College, two parsons, and a posse of police, stops to lecture his wife on Marx's theory of surplus value for some fifteen pages. But it is all in good fun; and Shaw is learning early that outright impudence can make palatable opinions that in solemn pronouncement would be insufferable.

Sidney Trefusis possesses what one of his uncomfortable aristocratic victims calls a "Portfolio of Paradoxes," and indeed *The Unsocial Socialist,* filled as it is with observations on marriage, happiness, evolution, revolution, husband-hunting, and a dozen other typical Shavian concerns, is a gold mine for anyone looking for early expressions of characteristic ideas. But rich as the novel is in this one sense, in another it is surprisingly thin: the assertions tend to be dogmatic, theoretic, and abstract, with little to hold them together or give them focus beyond the broadly iconoclastic socialism of the hero. *The Unsocial Socialist* was, Shaw tells us, merely a fragment, the beginning of "a novel which should be a gigantic grapple with the whole social problem. But, alas! at twenty-seven one does not know everything. When I had finished two chapters of this enterprise—chapters of colossal length, but containing the merest preliminary matter—I broke down in sheer ignorance and incapacity."[5] "A last," he says elsewhere, "I grew out of novel-writing, and set to work to find out what the world was really like."[6]

It was not in the pliant world of fiction but in the tough world

5. "Bernard Shaw's Works of Fiction: Reviewed by Himself," *The Novel Review* ("with which is incorporated Tinsley's Magazine"), No. 33, n.s. (Feb. 1892), p. 240.

6. "Preface" to 1901 ed. of *Cashel Byron's Profession;* quoted by Weintraub in *Autobiography 1856–1898,* p. 99.

of political struggle and economic realities that Shaw's new "religion" of socialism was tested, strengthened, and ultimately hammered into a full-fledged philosophy that owed only an incidental debt to Marx. But important as Marx was in providing both a rationale and a nucleus around which Shaw's scattered thoughts could crystallize, the very rapidity with which he recognized a spiritual home in *Capital* is indicative of the bias his thinking already had in that direction. Shaw himself traces the source of this bias back to his earliest memories—although it is worth noting that the poverty he remembers is obviously not, as is sometimes supposed, his own: "My ordinary exercise whilst I was still too young to be allowed out by myself was to be taken out by a servant, who was supposed to air me on the banks of the canal or around the fashionable squares where the atmosphere was esteemed salubrious and the surroundings gentlemanly. Actually she took me into the slums to visit her private friends, who dwelt in squalid tenements. . . . Thus were laid the foundations of my lifelong hatred of poverty, and the devotion of all my public life to the task of exterminating the poor and rendering their resurrection for ever impossible." Speaking of these childhood experiences elsewhere he talks of his "esthetic hatred of poverty and squalor. . . . My artist nature, to which beauty and refinement were necessities, would not accept poor people as fellowcreatures, nor slum tenements as fit for human habitation. To me they were places where I could not possibly live" (*16 S.S.*, p. 45–46). Depending on one's view this can be seen as revulsion at the prospect of human suffering or merely squeamishness in the presence of grime and garbage, and probably there is something of both.

Certainly the intense class consciousness of the Protestant Irish middle-class community of Dublin from which Shaw sprang contributed an element of snobbery. In *Sixteen Self Sketches*, published when Shaw was in his nineties, he "confesses" that at thirteen he had spent six months at a school which, "with its hosts of lower middle class Catholic children, sons of petty shop-

7. "Preface" to *London Music in 1888–89, Prose*, p. 76.

keepers and tradesmen, was inconceivable from the Shaw point of view." In spite of the objection of relatives, he was "sent to Marlborough Street, and at once lost caste outside it and became a boy with whom no Protestant young gentleman would speak or play" (pp. 42–43). For eighty years he kept this shameful secret from the world, his wife, and his biographer; but it is not entirely clear whether his sense of guilt arose from the experience itself or his reaction to it.

During this period of his youth Shaw's reading was undergoing a drastic expansion of horizons. Although he claimed he was "saturated" with the Bible, Bunyan, and Shakespeare before he was ten, his removal from the socially exacerbating Catholic school on Marlborough Street to a less academically demanding Protestant school left him with a surplus of time to indulge his favorite pastimes: visiting the National Gallery, where he daydreamed of becoming a latter-day Michelangelo, and reading. He was soon saturated with Dumas and Scott, whose romantic idealism he always distrusted, and Dickens, whom he admired throughout his life above all other novelists. Of the poets, he seems to have enjoyed Byron, although he could never take him quite seriously, and Blake, whose inversions of the conventional hierarchy left a much deeper mark.[8] But his tastes ran more to prose writers. Even as a schoolboy he seems to have read Darwin, Tyndall, Herbert Spencer, although his rebellious impulses were most attracted by "Paine . . . Voltaire and Rousseau [who], I was taught, were blasphemers whose deathbeds were made frightful by their certainty of going to hell. It was then part of the education of a gentleman to convince him that the three most religious men in Europe had been impious villains. . . . Shelley cured me of all that. I read him, prose and verse, from beginning to end. This took place at the end of my teens" (*16 S.S.*, pp. 169–170).

Shaw affirmed that he was "an out-and-out Shelleyan," and there is no question but what the poet exercised a tremendous

8. See Irving Fiske, "Bernard Shaw's Debt to William Blake," *The Shavian*, Tract no. 2 (1951), reprinted in *G. B. Shaw: A Collection of Critical Essays*, ed. R. J. Kaufmann (Englewood Cliffs, N.J.: Prentice-Hall, 1965), pp. 170–178.

influence on Shaw. In 1911 he identified Shelley as one of the early prophets who had tried to provide materials for a Bible of the religion of Creative Evolution, to which effort his own *Man and Superman* was a contribution.[9] But that was later; and Shelley's early appeal was doubtless as a rebel against all varieties of moral, intellectual, religious, and political tyranny, a rebel who took a positively Shavian delight in shocking respectability by both action and word. Shaw described Shelley, in terms highly congenial to his own thinking, as a "Republican, a Leveller, a Radical of the most extreme type. He was even an anarchist . . . up to the point which he perceived Anarchism to be impracticable." In fact, his writings "leave no reasonable doubt that if he had been born half a century later he would have been advocating Social-Democracy with a view to its development into the most democratic form of Communism practically attainable and maintainable."[10]

In 1886 Shaw joined the Shelley Society, which had just been started by Dr. F. J. Furnivall. Furnivall was a great founder of literary societies, and Shaw was almost as enthusiastic as a joiner, partly, no doubt, out of love for literature, but also for the opportunity it gave him to acquire poise and self-confidence by appearing and debating in public. In 1883 he had joined both the Browning and the Shakespeare societies, and their minutes provide a lively record of his iconoclastic critical pronouncements, as well as his respectable scholarly papers. According to his own report of the first meeting of the Shelley Society: "I . . . announced that as a good Shelleyan I was a Socialist, an Atheist, and a vegetarian, [and] two of them resigned on the spot."[11] Shaw affirmed it was Shelley's example that converted him to vegetarianism, a regimen that, after the establishment of vegetarian restaurants

9. "Foreword" to 1911 ed. of *Man and Superman*, quoted in R. F. Rattray, *Bernard Shaw: A Chronicle* (Luton, Eng.: The Leagrave Press, 1951), p. 177.

10. "Shaming the Devil about Shelley," *The Albermarle*, 2, no. 3 (Sept. 1892), p. 91.

11. "Notes by George Bernard Shaw," Appendix I to *Thomas J. Wise in the Original Cloth*, by Wilfred Partington (London: Robert Hale, 1946), p. 316.

in 1880 made it practical, he followed strictly, even in the face of death. During an illness in 1898 both friends and doctors assured him that his refusal to touch meat was destroying him, and he responded with this delightful proof that a vein of real whimsy underlay his more characteristically sardonic tone: "My situation is a solemn one. Life is offered to me on condition of eating beef-steaks. My weeping family crowd about me with Bovril and Brand's [Beef] Essence. But death is better than cannibalism. My will contains directions for my funeral, which will be followed not by mourning coaches, but by herds of oxen, sheep, swine, flocks of poultry, and a small travelling aquarium of live fish, all wearing white scarves in honor of the man who perished rather than eat his fellow-creatures. It will be, with the single exception of the procession into Noah's Ark, the most remarkable thing of the kind ever seen."[12]

Although the seriousness with which Shaw took his vegetarian-ism may be some measure of Shelley's influence, the poet's major contribution was to introduce Shaw to some of the main elements of socialism before he ever left Dublin, and so to lay the founda-tion for the enthusiasm with which he embraced the socialist cause as soon as it entered his ken. And it was appropriate that the seeds of his socialism should have been sown by Shelley, for whom it represented revulsion against tyranny, visionary social justice, the triumph of Love, in other words was idealistic in the best—that is, not the Shavian—sense. Shaw became deeply in-volved in unromantic problems of making socialism work in the everyday world and often found that when confronted with reality Shelley's naiveté was simply inadequate; and yet for all his pose of hardheaded common sense, Shaw's socialism never entirely lost its deeply idealistic and humanitarian dimension.

Soon after he arrived in London, Shaw was introduced by a friend to the Zetetical Society, an offshoot of the older Dialecti-cal Society, founded, Shaw says, "to discuss John Stuart Mill's Essay on Liberty when that was new." The orientation of the

12. "Wagner and Vegetables," letter by Shaw in "The Contributors' Playground," *The Academy*, 55 (15 Oct. 1898), p. 79.

Zetetical Society was "strongly individualistic, atheistic, Malthusian, . . . Darwinian, and Herbert Spencerian," in other words reflecting the liberal impulses of Mill's early work more than the essentially socialistic direction of his later writing. Shaw found the views of the society congenial, but its most important contribution to his development, apart from introducing him to his lifelong friend, Sidney Webb, was to begin the breakdown of his defensive cocoon of shyness.

To readers familiar only with the public image of the later Shaw, dogmatic, self-assured to the point of arrogance, seeking every and any opportunity to dramatize and publicize himself, the suggestion that he was essentially a shy person may seem ludicrously inept. Yet there is every reason to take quite literally his account of his early terrors and of the self-discipline with which he fought against them: "I haunted all the meetings in London where debates followed lectures. I spoke in the streets, in the parks, at demonstrations, anywhere and everywhere possible. In short, I infested public meetings like an officer afflicted with cowardice, who takes every opportunity of going under fire to get over it and learn his business" (*16 S.S.*, pp. 95–96). It was this almost obsessive pursuit of experience in confronting his own cowardice at public meetings that on September 5, 1882, brought Shaw into the Nonconformist Memorial Hall in Farringdon Street to hear a speech that he later claimed "changed the whole current of [his] life." "The speaker of the evening . . . was Henry George, American apostle of Land Nationalization and Single Tax. He struck me dumb and shunted me from barren agnostic controversy to economics" (*16 S.S.*, p. 96). George's plan for a unified tax did not long hold Shaw's imagination, but his allusions to Marx were the first tremors of an earthquake, the half-grasped promise of a new world.

The name of Karl Marx is now so ubiquitous, and his influence, for good or ill, so pervasive, that it is very easy to forget how comparatively recently he has become a real force in the economic and political life of the English-speaking world. Although the *Communist Manifesto* was already notorious on the Continent, Marx was living unknown and ignored in London in 1880. At the same time a wealthy and somewhat eccentric political dilettante, Henry Mayers Hyndman, had read and been tremendously impressed by the French translation of Volume One of *Capital,* and had sought Marx out in his humble Haverstock Hill quarters. Hyndman spent many hours at Marx's feet, absorbing his theories and spinning fantasies of personally leading the English workingman into a brave new Utopia. He already had a plan to rally the "advanced" men and women to his leadership in an attack on "liberal" Gladstonian imperialism, but Marx provided him with a newer and more far-reaching cause. In spite of a warning from the aging Disraeli that "England was a very difficult country to move," Hyndman went ahead and formed the Democratic Federation, the first socialist political organization in Great Britain.[13]

Shaw, already overflowing with socialist impulses and more specifically excited by his recent exposure to Henry George, gravitated naturally to the Democratic Federation as an appropriate forum for his new enthusiasms. It was here, at his first meeting, that he was told no one was qualified to discuss economics without having read Marx and then discovered, having tracked down a French edition of *Capital* at the British Museum, that only he and Hyndman had read a word of it. "That was the turning point in my career. Marx was a revelation. His abstract economics, I discovered later, were wrong, but he rent the veil. He opened my eyes to the facts of history and civilization, gave me an entirely fresh conception of the universe, provided me with a purpose and a mission in life."[14] As he says elsewhere, "From that hour I was a speaker with a gospel, no longer only an apprentice trying to master the art of public speaking" (*16 S.S.,* p. 97).

In spite of some doubts as to the seriousness of their socialism, Shaw applied for membership in the Democratic Federation and

13. See Henry Mayers Hyndman, *The Record of an Adventurous Life* (New York: Macmillan, 1911).

14. Quoted by Hesketh Pearson, *George Bernard Shaw: His Life and Personality* (New York: Atheneum, 1963), p. 68.

would have joined had he not discovered first an even more congenial socialist organization. In 1881 an American transcendentalist of Scottish background, Thomas Davidson, had come to London with the idea of founding a society based on the principles "of living a simple, strenuous, intellectual life, so far as possible communistically, and on a basis of natural religion."[15] Early companions in this project, Havelock Ellis, William Clarke, and Henry Hyde Champion, all went on to become much more widely known than the founding father; but in the early days the magnetic personality and intellectual brilliance of Davidson dominated and provided the driving spark for a small group that in 1883 organized itself as The Fellowship of the New Life. Very early in its career, however, the new organization developed a split between the ethicalists, for whom "the cultivation of a perfect character in each and all" was the first and essential step toward a better world, and those who felt moral perfection was possible only where physical needs had been satisfied. In November 1883 H. H. Champion introduced a resolution affirming: "The members of the Society assert that the Competitive system assures the happiness and comfort of the few at the expense of the suffering of the many and that Society must be reconstituted in such a manner as to secure the general welfare and happiness."[16] The priorities proved too incompatible for compromise, and the two groups agreed to disagree in a friendly separation. On January 6, 1884, the split became official, and the Fabian Society, the organization that had more to do than any other in bringing Great Britain down the road to socialism, was born. On the title page of its first publication appeared a passage, of uncertain origin, that doubtless caught Shaw's eye: "Wherefore it may not be gainsaid that the fruit of this man's long taking of counsel— and (by the many so deemed) untimeous delays—was the safe-holding for all men, his fellow citizens, of the Common Weal."

Shaw turned his back on the Democratic Federation: "On dis-

15. See Henderson, p. 208.
16. This and the following quotation are given by Henderson, pp. 209–210.

covering the newly founded Fabian Society, in which I recognized a more appropriate *milieu* as a body of educated middle-class intelligentsia: my own class in fact. Hyndman's congregation of manual-working pseudo-Marxists could for me be only hindrances" (*16 S.S.,* p. 97). Shaw was never particularly reticent about the reasons that led him to turn to the Fabians; and he describes the process in a little more detail in his contribution to the biography of an associate in the Society, Mrs. Hubert Bland: "At that time I had read Marx and become a strong Socialist, but I was in doubt about throwing in my lot with the Social Democratic Federation—not because of snobbery, but because I wanted to work with men of my own mental training. The Fabian Society's [first] tract, *Why are the Many Poor?,* fell into my hands. The moment I saw the words 'Fabian Society' on it, I realized that here was a good title which immediately suggested an educated body, so I found out the Society's address from the tract and turned up . . . for the next meeting."[17]

That was on May 16, 1884. On September 5 of that year Shaw was elected a member of the Fabian Society; on September 19 Tract No. 2 of the Society, a "Manifesto" for Fabians, was read at their meeting, and it was written by Shaw. So was Tract No. 3. On January 2, 1885, Shaw was elected to the Executive of the Society, to which he was re-elected every year until his voluntary retirement from the position in 1911.

The history of the Fabian Society and of Shaw's relationship to it has been told elsewhere in much greater detail than is appropriate here.[18] There is no question but that both the organization and the man gained immeasurably from the association. The Society could not help but have both its tone and its thinking conditioned in part by the personality of its most colorful and flamboyant member, as is evident from Shaw's description of the ambience of Fabian discussions: "We contracted the invaluable

17. Note by Shaw in *E. Nesbit: A Biography,* by Doris Langley Moore, rev. ed. (Philadelphia: Chilton, 1966), pp. 83–84, note 6.
18. See Edward Reynolds Pease, *The History of the Fabian Society* (New York: Barnes and Noble, 1963).

habit of freely laughing at ourselves which has always distinguished us, and which has saved us from becoming hampered by
the gushing enthusiasts who mistake their own emotions for public movements. From the first, such people fled after one glance
at us, declaring that we were not serious. Our preference for
practical suggestions and criticisms, and our impatience of all
general expressions of sympathy with working-class aspirations,
not to mention our way of chaffing our opponents in preference
to denouncing them as enemies of the human race, repelled from
us some warm-hearted and eloquent Socialists. . . . If our debates are to be kept wholesome, they cannot be too irreverent or
too critical. And the irreverence, which has become traditional
with us, comes down from those early days."[19] Shaw's efforts at
playing the obstreperous *enfant terrible* were sometimes strained,
but they served the practical purpose of helping to hold the
Society together: "In the Fabian Cabinet . . . there was considerable strife of temperaments; and in the other Socialist societies splits and schisms were frequent. . . . I believe that some of
my own usefulness lay in smoothing out these frictions by an
Irish sort of tact which in England seemed the most outrageous
want of it. Whenever there was a quarrel I betrayed everybody's
confidence by analyzing it and stating it lucidly in the most exaggerated terms. Result: both sides agreed that it was all my
fault. I was denounced on all hands as a reckless mischiefmaker,
but forgiven as a privileged Irish lunatic" (*16 S.S.*, p. 112).

Clearly, however, Shaw's contribution to the Fabians was not
simply that of professional skeptic, court jester, and literary hack
whose skill with words was useful on the public platform and in
spelling out for the lay audience ideas generated by academically
trained experts. The bump of irreverence and the insistent questioning of authorities were not merely negative qualities by which
Shaw steered the Fabians from the pitfalls of infallibility or the
snares of mawkish clichés; they also led directly to some substantial contributions to socialist thinking and policy. It was

19. "The Fabian Society: What it has Done; & How it has Done it,"
Fabian Tract No. 41 (August, 1892), pp. 4–5.

Shaw, for example, after he had affirmed that Marx had made a man of him and given him a faith, who also wooed the Fabians away from Marxism.

The defection began with the March 1884 number of the newly founded socialist journal *Justice,* to which Shaw later became a frequent contributor, but which on this occasion published a letter from one G. B. S. Larking, entitled "Who is the Thief?" In it Mr. Larking whimsically suggested a possible flaw in the logic of Marx's economics by which, if followed to its conclusion, not only the capitalist but every consumer as well shared in the guilt of exploiting the proletariat. As Shaw explained it, he simply "could not make the two ends of Marx's economic argument meet exactly," and characteristically couched his exposition of the problem in humorous terms as a kind of defense against the anticipated scorn of a thoroughgoing Marxist reply. But the reply never came; and his faith was shaken.

At about the same time another enthusiastic amateur was also having doubts about the soundness of Marx's economic theories. The Reverend Philip H. Wicksteed, a Unitarian minister, had a year or so earlier been preaching what was then called The Higher Criticism through the English countryside when a colleague persuaded him to read Henry George's *Progress and Poverty.* As in Shaw's case, it changed his life, and, inspired by George's vision of the world capitalism was creating, he devoted his career to the study of economics. Early in that study he read Marx's *Capital* and, again like Shaw, was not satisfied with the explanation he found there of the sources of economic value. But being already much more widely read and hence more sophisticated in his grasp of the subject than Shaw, he recognized the source of the problem and found a more viable value theory in the writings of Stanley Jevons.

Wicksteed quickly acquired a reputation as a critic of Marx; and in 1884 was challenged by the broad-minded Fabian editors of another socialist journal, *To-Day,* to explain his position in their pages. He accepted, and in the October issue his *"Das Kapital:* a Criticism" appeared, to the scandal of all good Marxists. H. M. Hyndman, as leader of what by that time was known as the Social Democratic Federation, was invited to reply, but refused on the grounds that this defiance of Marxian omniscience was beneath his contempt. Fortunately, the editors were not satisfied with this, and asked Shaw, already notorious as a debater, who also refused, but on the grounds of incompetence. When one of the editors, R. P. B. Frost, offered to take on the job, however, Shaw hastily changed his mind, but stipulated that Wicksteed must be guaranteed space for a response. His article, "The Jevonian Criticism of Marx," appeared in the January, 1885, issue of *To-Day* and offered the unusual spectacle of a Shaw who was thoroughly unsure of himself. After acknowledging Wicksteed's ability, and assuring himself that some more competent economist would dispose of his arguments, Shaw turned to what was little more than humorous irrelevance and question-begging, such as the rationalization that since someone once pulled on him the old schoolboy trick of "proving" one is equal to zero, all efforts to express economic relationship in algebraic terms must be suspect. There is much wit but little logic in the article, and Shaw knew he was building on shifting sands. Wicksteed's rebuttal appeared in the April issue, disposing easily of the red herrings Shaw had introduced, clarifying his own argument, and taking a wry dig at an adversary who "renounced mathematical reasoning in favour of the literary method which enables a clever man to follow equally fallacious arguments to equally absurd conclusions without seeing that they are absurd."[20]

Wicksteed obviously respected his opponent's intelligence and was gentle with his ignorance. Shaw, for his part, recognized his master and went out of his way to meet Wicksteed and gain his friendship. This strategy gained him access to an informal group known as the Economic Circle, made up primarily of professional economists and members of the faculty of London University,

---

20. "The Jevonian Criticism of Marx: A Rejoinder," reprinted along with the other documents in this controversy, in *Bernard Shaw and Karl Marx: A Symposium, 1884–1889,* ed. Richard W. Ellis (New York: Random House, 1930), pp. 96–97.

and ultimately expanded into the Royal Economic Society, which met biweekly to discuss Jevonian economics under Wicksteed's leadership. It was the closest Shaw had ever come to university education, and indeed the level at which it was conducted was that of the faculty colloquium; but Shaw was neither contemptuous nor overwhelmed. He very soon, and very characteristically, shared the leadership of the group with Wicksteed at the same time that he was exploiting the situation as an intensive course of formal economic study. During just this period, that is from 1885 to 1889, the leadership of the Fabian Society formed a study group called the Hampstead Historical Society, initially to teach themselves economic history from a Marxian perspective. Fortunately for Shaw the two associations met on alternate weeks and he could, like the proverbial busy bee, absorb the doctrines of Jevons, as developed by Wicksteed, F. Y. Edgeworth, and Alfred Marshall at the economic study group, and then disseminate the results of his listening and reading and thinking later to the receptive Fabians at the Hampstead Society. Graham Wallas, from the beginning one of the Fabian leaders, later reported that "after we had finished *Das Kapital,* we continued the Hampstead Circle for three years more and both there and in the preparation of Fabian and other lectures, worked at the history of social thought. Our interest in history and the constant stimulus of Shaw's insight and genius made us reject the Marxist economic interpretation."[21]

Since the Fabians, both directly and through their policy of "permeating" other organizations and institutions, came to be the most powerful single force in English socialism, Shaw's influence in turning them away from Marxian economics had farreaching and permanent consequences. But the real point of this episode in Shaw's crowded career is not his importance to British history, but its revelation of something important about his personality and the nature of his mind. What is significant is not so much the substance of the particular ideas he rejected or of those

21. Graham Wallas, *Men and Ideas* (London: George Allen and Unwin, 1940), p. 105.

he ultimately espoused as the restless curiosity, the eagerness to learn, the willingness to give up one enthusiasm when it was found wanting and to work long and hard to hammer out a superior faith. As Undershaft was to say some years later: "If your old religion broke down yesterday, get a newer and better one for tomorrow."

What offended Shaw in Marx was not only the dogmatism, but the simplistic black and white view of the world. Marx's solution to social injustice was to take surplus value away from a villainous, exploitative bourgeoisie and give it to a virtuous, downtrodden proletariat. Such doctrine might well appeal, both in its simplicity and in its economic implications, to the laboring class, and hence have practical political value. But Shaw could not accept the simple social polarization propounded by Marx.

Shaw did not scorn the laboring man as an individual, and he often addressed meetings of various workingmen's associations with considerable success; but he felt strongly that political power lay not in sheer numbers, but in education, in economic power, and in access to parliamentary processes. Marx, of course, was not wholly unaware of this possibility; but his contempt for the middle-class intellectual persuaded him to put his faith in the economic clout of the huge mass of workers who, he said, created value. Hyndman's Social Democratic Federation followed the party line and conscientiously tried to woo the laboring man to the communist cause, though with little success. It was Shaw's faith in ideas and their ultimate political efficacy that almost surely was responsible in large part for the Fabian policy of education and permeation in preference to following the more direct path of party politics and social action.

It is true that eventually Shaw's faith in ideas alone became somewhat modified, and so too Fabian policy in practice shifted so as to include active involvement with the Independent Labour Party. But that was later; and in the formative years—formative for both the Fabians and for Shaw—his commitment to the power of ideas had far-reaching consequences. He in effect rejected a theory of value that had been subordinated to, and made to justify, the class struggle, even though it was easily intelligible to the economically untrained, and turned to one that affirmed that socially created values, instead of belonging to a single limited class, accrue to the community as a whole. The more sophisticated and broadly based concepts derived by Shaw through Wicksteed from Jevons, although lacking in popular appeal, appeared to him both closer to the social realities and healthier in their political implications. Marx, for all his Hegelian discussion of a classless society as the synthesis of the historical dialectic of class conflict, in fact talks as though the proletariat simply triumphed over and eliminated the capitalist bourgeoisie. In the shift away from the Marxist emphasis on production to an emphasis on equitable distribution to the whole community, Shaw and the Fabians steered a course that both in practical effects and in its intellectual configuration seems much closer to a true synthesis.

The significance of Shaw's contributions to the Fabian Society must always be balanced with the efforts of his coworkers. His own tributes to them are neither exaggerated nor clouded by false modesty: "As my colleagues were men of exceptional character and attainments, . . . the reputedly brilliant extraordinary Shaw was in fact brilliant and extraordinary because he had in the Fabian Politbureau an incomparable critical threshing machine for his ideas. . . . My colleagues knocked much nonsense, ignorance and vulgar provinciality out of me; for we were on quite ruthless critical terms with one another" (*16 S.S.*, p. 111). What he calls the Politbureau consisted of Sydney Olivier (1859–1943), later Lord Olivier, and Governor of Jamaica (1907–1913); Graham Wallas (1858–1932), sociologist, author, and later Professor of Political Science at London University; Hubert Bland (1856–1914), described by Shaw as a "Tory Democrat," also a well-known socialist writer and one of the founders of the Fabian Society; Shaw; and, most important from his point of view, Sidney Webb (1859–1947).

Shaw's relationship with Webb was extraordinarily long, strong, and fruitful. Many years later he said: "Quite the wisest thing I ever did was to force my friendship on him and to keep it; for from that time I was not merely a futile Shaw but a committee of Webb and Shaw" (*16 S.S.*, pp. 107–108). And he wrote to Archibald Henderson: "Webb is one of the most extraordinary and capable men alive; and the difference between Shaw with Webb's brains and knowledge at his disposal, and Shaw by himself, is enormous. Nobody has yet gauged it, because as I am an incorrigible mountebank, and Webb is one of the simplest of geniuses, I have always been in the centre of the stage whilst Webb has been prompting me, invisible, from the side. I am an expert picker of other men's brains; and I have been exceptionally fortunate in my friends" (Henderson, p. 222).

Shaw was indeed fortunate in his friends, for they included some of the finest minds of the late nineteenth and early twentieth centuries; but there was certainly very little luck in the matter. Doubtless he did at first have to force himself on Webb, who was extremely shy, and for whom Shaw was virtually the sole lifelong friend. They made an odd pair, the witty, ebullient, impudent Irishman and the hard-working, retiring, somewhat formal and pedantic man with the encyclopedic memory, who had risen through the British Civil Service by virtue of consistently astounding scores on every examination he took. Although it seems probable—if such equations have any validity at all—that Webb possessed as able a mind as Shaw's, they were in almost every respect complementary personalities. Not wholly lacking in imagination, Webb was nevertheless careful in his logicality, exhaustive in his research, almost obsessed with the importance of facts. He was not unkindly, or lacking in humor, although his somewhat wry wit was more obvious in his private correspondence than in his public utterances. Shaw was very much aware that Webb shone in the possession of qualities that he himself lacked; and while that fact did not by itself make them virtues, he admired them sincerely, and even extravagantly, determining to put this complementary brilliance to work in the service of the cause that was to consume a large part of their joint energies for many years. It took great pressure on Shaw's part to persuade Webb to join the Fabian Society, for in that first year the group's orientation was ill-defined, and it included anarchists and wild-

eyed revolutionaries as well as "Tory Democrats" like Hubert
Bland, and seekers after the New Life. Apparently Shaw convinced him that the Fabian Society would provide the best possible forum and vehicle for their political convictions and that
between them they could shape its future. Webb joined, and
shortly, in sharp contrast to the witty, striking, but essentially
rather incoherent pronouncements of Fabian Tracts Two and
Three, by Shaw, there appeared No. Five, "Facts for Socialists,"
by Sidney Webb. Once the facts were straight, the Fabians pulled
themselves out of their slough of uncertainty and set themselves
on the path that they were to follow successfully for several
decades.

Webb's enthusiasm for amassing, documenting, and arranging
facts has in fact made him vulnerable to his detractors, but it is
a quality too easy to sneer at and too rarely found. Facts were not
ends, valuable in themselves, but ammunition in the war against
social injustice that consumed the life of both Sidney Webb and
his equally dedicated, equally intense, wife, Beatrice. In a sense
they were continuing the work of Marx: documenting in great
detail the evidence for the charge against capitalism—but they
did their job more thoroughly, with less vehemence, and, in
England at least, with more success. Shaw stood in profound awe
of such conscientiousness, but needless to say did not therefore
alter his own ways: "As both Sidney and Beatrice conscientiously
refrained from forming their conclusions until they had with inexhaustible industry investigated all the available evidence, they
had furious disputes with me at almost every step. . . . I never
collect authorities nor investigate conditions. I just deduce what
happened and why it happened from my flair for human nature,
knowing that if necessary I can find plenty of documents and
witnesses to bear me out in any possible conclusion. This is a
shorter method than that of the Webbs."[22]

Shorter, perhaps, but not necessarily sounder. This is the artist,
the imaginative re-creator of human nature, confronting the hard-
shelled realist, the self-confessed Philistine. Webb doubtless found

22. "The Webbs and Social Evolution," *The New York Times Book
Review,* Nov. 18, 1945, p. 19.

Shaw infuriating at times, for he was intolerant of intelligent people who refused to deal with facts. He was indulgent of Shaw's fondness for buffoonery and self-dramatization; the plays he found trivial and irrelevant; and the habit of apparent self-assurance on the basis of very insecure facts he considered at best irresponsible. But in spite of all Webb's disapprovals, the two men acted together as an effective and influential team, virtually dominating the councils and policies of the Fabian Society for more than twenty-five years. It does not appear that Sidney was ever very much influenced in an intellectual way by Shaw. Beatrice viewed his Irish gallantry and mercurial nature with a somewhat priggish disapproval, not untouched, perhaps, with a private disappointment. And yet both Webbs acknowledged their tremendous debt to and dependence on Shaw, not only as the witty and colorful writer and platform speaker who contributed incalculably to the appeal of Fabian socialism, but also as a theoretician and generator of ideas. He both edited and organized their mountains of facts for them, and with the suspect qualities of an artist's imagination and intuition transformed dull data into essays and books, appearing over both his name and theirs, that certainly constitute the most important socialist literature of their time.

But while without Shaw the Webbs might very well have gone down in history as very minor amassers of social data, and without the Webbs Shaw, at least as music critic, and playwright, probably would have developed much as he did, the fact remains that Sidney, as his closest and most respected friend, could not help but have had some effect on Shaw's thinking. At the most obvious level, he certainly had a generally restraining influence, keeping Shaw's feet at least within several yards of the ground. But while Webb treated this mad Irish genius with a patience bordering on saintliness, the two frequently locked horns in what Shaw described as a vital dialectic relationship. Years later he claimed: "The importance of the fact that Webb was intensely English and I ineradicably Irish, so that our views often clashed at first impact and our fierce arguments worked out to a unique conclusion of which we would have been separately incapable, has never been grasped" (Henderson, p. 349). Since during these years when he was shaping his philosophy, at least until his marriage in 1898, Shaw spent a large amount of time with the Webbs, usually arguing furiously, it was almost inevitable that this continuing dialectic with Sidney should have contributed something to the forging of his ideas into a coherent structure.

Sidney Webb was not, for all his brilliance, a particularly original thinker, so that his contribution to the formulation of Shaw's philosophy was largely in his role of foil. To the degree that he was a man of ideas, however, much of his thinking derived from a source he shared with his friend. George Lichtheim, in his history of Marxism, identifies as a key figure in the evolution toward collectivism in nineteenth-century England "John Stuart Mill— Marx's contemporary and in a sense his only serious rival, insofar as he is one of the ancestors of Fabianism and welfare socialism generally."[23]

Webb and Shaw vehemently distrusted and disavowed the "genteel Liberals" who in their day claimed Mill as their own, but it is not difficult to discern the heritage of his social and economic principles in both men's work. Although rarely made explicit, the doctrine of the greatest good for the greatest number lies behind many of their most basic assumptions. Pragmatic in approach and empirical in method, they shared with Mill a view of man that was evolutionary and optimistic and a vision of social justice that was ultimately egalitarian. Like him they had a faith in the orderly development of human organization, and preferred to work within existing parliamentary and democratic structures, while recognizing the need for change. And all three men believed that the leadership for such evolutionary change would come from the much despised and often ignored but dynamic and increasingly powerful middle class.

Both Webb and Shaw had digested the meat of Mill's social philosophy before they became a Fabian team, and each had come to the philosopher of utilitarianism in his own way and for

23. George Lichtheim, *Marxism, An Historical and Critical Study* (New York: Praeger, 1961), p. 26.

his own reasons. At the heart of much of Mill's work lay the conviction that "the establishment of a science of society [was] an essential step toward implementing rational policies of social change."[24] Webb found in Mill's systematic approach the outlines of a program that satisfied his zeal for organizing the data of man's social experience, and hence made possible a "science" of sociology—a science dedicated not only to the description but to the improvement of the human condition. Webb was attracted to a vision of social evolution that was both ordered and humanitarian, and he was the epitome of the reasonable and well-educated social scientist Mill envisaged as guiding that evolution.

Although Shaw also wanted to find a system, a controlling purpose, a basis for a faith in a better future, in man's social development, he had considerably less confidence than his friend in the power of reason alone. In appealing to a "Life Force," he was in fact much closer to being an "intuitionist" than Mill would have accepted or than Webb *did* accept. On the other hand, insofar as Mill distrusted appeals to intuition because they often became unarguable defenses for prejudice and tradition and the status quo, he was making a judgment comparable to Shaw's distinction between idealists and realists.[25] Mill was one of Shaw's realists; and he was supremely the man of ideas. He may indeed have been a model for Shavian eclecticism, someone who was willing to take ideas from diverse and often incongruous sources, a pragmatist who judged them on the basis of whether they "worked." Undershaft's admonition regarding a morality that does not fit the facts, "Scrap it and get one that does fit," was basic to Mill's ethics.[26]

Mill and Shaw shared a distrust for passion, except when it was what the latter called the "moral passion," a passion for ideas and the power they have in the development of human affairs. Mill too saw "ideas [as] the most significant sources of social

24. Alan Ryan, *John Stuart Mill* (New York: Random House, 1970), p. 104.
25. Ibid., p. xiv.
26. Ibid., pp. xix and 187–211.

change," and Shaw certainly considered himself, like Mill, "an intellectual participant in a transitional period, with the role . . . of encouraging mental regeneration."[27] But along with the commitment to ideas per se, Shaw would have been attracted, and probably influenced, by Mill's essential sanity, his cautious distrust of ultimates, and his conviction that the closest we come to truth is when ideas are allowed to exist in conflict and even contradiction.[28] In knowledge, as in ethics, absolutes were for both men unattainable, and any system or religion or political party that claimed a monopoly on truth was by its nature inimicable to, and even destructive of, human moral and social progress.

It was probably in their passionate and lifelong commitment to the progressive evolution of human institutions toward a goal of equity and ultimately equality that the two men were closest. Such a faith included for Mill as for Shaw an intense hatred of poverty as both an economic and a human fact, a belief in the equality between women and men, a repudiation of unearned property, and a recognition that while no individual is exempt, except by incapacity, from sharing in the work required by the good of the community, all equally require the leisure necessary to escape the brutalization which is the concomitant of unremitting labor.[29]

It is difficult, then, not to see Mill as a spiritual and intellectual "father" to the socialism of both Webb and Shaw. It is true that Mill in his early writing tended to distrust socialism as the institutionalization of the tyranny of the majority; and yet toward the end of his life he evidently accepted the possibility that it might in fact offer freedom from even more oppressive tyrannies. Indeed, it is hard to read some of the later passages in his *Auto-*

27. Graeme Duncan, *Marx and Mill* (Cambridge: Cambridge University Press, 1973), pp. 215–217.

28. See *Marx and Mill*, pp. 16 and 214–215; also John M. Robson, *The Improvement of Mankind: The Social and Political Thought of John Stuart Mill* (Toronto: University of Toronto Press, 1968), pp. 185, 191, 197–198; and Mill's *On Liberty*, Chap. 2.

29. See Pedro Schwartz, *The New Political Economy of J. S. Mill* (London: Weidenfeld and Nicolson, 1972), pp. 197–198, 213–217; also *Marx and Mill*, p. 226.

biography without wondering from which of Shaw's Fabian tracts it might have been taken:

We . . . looked forward to a time when society will no longer be divided into the idle and the industrious; when the rule that they who do not work shall not eat, will be applied not to paupers only, but impartially to all; when the division of the produce of labor, instead of depending, as in so great a degree it now does, on the accident of birth, will be made by concert, on an acknowledged principle of justice; and when it will no longer either be, or be thought to be, impossible for human beings to exert themselves strenuously in procuring benefits which are not to be exclusively their own, but to be shared with the society they belong to. The social problem of the future, we considered to be, how to unite the greatest individual liberty of action, with a common ownership in the raw material of the globe, and an equal participation of all in the benefits of combined labor.[30]

In the last of his exhaustive and invaluable biographies of Shaw, Archibald Henderson spends a good deal of time refuting the widely held view that Sidney Webb had "invented" the notion of "the inevitability of gradualness," which became closely identified with the evolutionary socialism of the Fabian Society. He argues on the grounds that, although Webb first used the phrase in an address as President of the Labour Party in 1922, Shaw had enunciated the principle at least as early as 1889. But the concept can not legitimately be credited to either man, since years earlier Mill had talked about the moral and institutional evolution of man toward what can only be described as a socialistic future.

Webb and Shaw each owed much to Mill. Webb found the outline and method for a "science of sociology"; and he dedicated his life and talents to making Mill's vision a reality. Shaw too—or part of him, the Fabian socialist Shaw—found a sense of commitment and "use" in giving his energies to a rationally based program of human progress. But a science of man could not in the end wholly satisfy a mind that passionately desired a religion of man as well.

30. *Autobiography* (New York: Liberal Arts Press, 1957), p. 148.

4   *Beyond Fabianism: The*
Search for a Religion

Just as, in its early days, Shaw played a major role in shaping the Fabian Society's formulation of socialist doctrine, that activity played a significant and reciprocal role in shaping the personality, the style, and the thinking of G.B.S. Socialism was always a means to an end for Shaw, personally as well as politically. His initial involvement with the movement, as we have seen, sprang as much from a need for self-confidence as a need for a philosophical home. His shyness was genuine, and the triumph over it was complete. It could only have been achieved at a price, however—not only the price of exposing one's sensitive nature to the painful abrasions of ridicule, but also that of developing a slightly calloused pose to cover the naked soul. With typical perceptiveness Shaw described the process: "Therefore I had to become an actor, and create for myself a fantastic personality fit and apt for dealing with men, and adaptable to the various parts I had to play. . . . In this I succeeded later on only too well. In my boyhood I saw Charles Mathews act in a farce called Cool as a Cucumber. The hero was a young man just returned from a tour of the world, upon which he had been sent to cure him of an apparently hopeless bashfulness; and the fun lay in the cure having overshot the mark and transformed him into a monster of outrageous impudence. I am not sure that something of the kind did not happen to me."[1]

1. "Preface" to *Immaturity, Prose,* p. 65.

Shaw never tired of affirming, in a variety of ways that "G.B.S. . . . [is] one of the most successful of my fictions. . . . G.B.S. is a humbug" (*16 S.S.,* p. 89). It is quite possible that most of Shaw's more flamboyant and, to many of his admirers, less attractive traits—his arrogance, his self-publicizing antics, his obstreperous rudeness and pretensions to omniscience—are only part of an elaborate role played both to protect the private man and call attention to his ideas. His "official" biographer, Archibald Henderson, asserts that Shaw "was never a participant in English society; and really made a place for himself in its literary life largely by creating an artificial personality, quite unlike his own, which amused the English people" (p. 133). From a source even closer to the "real" Shaw we have the corroborative evidence of Beatrice Webb, who says in her diary for 1893, the year of her marriage to Sidney: "Now I am not so sure that the vanity itself is not part of the *mise en scène,* whether, in fact, it is not part of the character he imagines himself to be playing in the world's comedy" (Henderson, p. 329).

It is quite possible that the mask worn so assiduously in later life had its beginnings when the young immigrant, painfully shy, and sensitive about his uncitified clothes, his Irish accent, his unfamiliarity with London ways, first raised his voice in a gathering of what seemed to him unapproachably educated and sophisticated young radicals. But masks have a nasty way of becoming so firmly attached that it is often very difficult to discriminate between the mask and the face behind it. A pose is no less real for being self-conscious, and in time may replace the *other* reality it was intended to hide. And the fact that someone points publicly to the mask and says "that is not the real me" may make the Pirandellian paradox more complex, but does not make the mask less "real" than any other aspect of the personality. Standing between two facing mirrors we can, if we wish, point to one reflection and say that *it* is the true one; but in fact there is no hierarchy of realities among the infinitely regressing images. Shaw took on a public role, but both the fact that he did so and the form that it took are part of what he was, and it is too easy to dismiss one personality as irrelevant while accepting the other as real. Both must be taken account of and fitted into the composite picture of the man and his ideas; to try to discriminate precisely at every point between "mask" ideas and "real" ideas would mean getting hopelessly sidetracked in a mirror maze largely of our own construction.

Shaw acquired both the mask of self-confidence and effectiveness as a public speaker stumping for socialism, on street corners, at dockyards, in large assemblies, in the hothouse atmosphere of Marxist discussion groups. His socialism was not one whit less genuine for all that; but it did give a particular cast to his political style. His is a kind of forensic socialism, a debater's socialism, one that becomes a reality neither on the barricades nor in the voting box, but in the mind. It is lucid and articulate, reasonable without being rationalistic, dialectic in its development, and espoused with a moral passion. Shaw very consciously developed a language for his socialism, for his public speaking, and in the end for his writing. It is flexible, rich, balanced, both in its rhythms and in its presentation of pros and cons; it is given to periodic climaxes of logic and rhythm, and can legitimately be termed poetic, although the poetry is more of sound than of imagery. Indeed, it is rhetorical in the fullest and best sense of the word. Of course, many of Shaw's essays began as platform speeches; but even those that did not, such as the prefaces to the plays, reveal the background of platform polemics. The form is characteristically argumentative and combative; building up the opposition's case in such a way that it can be demolished with a quip, reducing to absurdity what he pretends are its most basic assumptions, piling up arguments in a rhetorical rush of words that simply overwhelms disagreement.

When Shaw came to write plays, it was almost inevitable that the voice that had held audiences spellbound in the hallowed halls of the Browning Society, in William Morris's home in Hammersmith, in Fabian and other meeting rooms the length and breadth of England, and that is evident not merely in political writing, but in the art and music and drama criticism as well, should burst forth again in the mouths of his dramatic characters. William Irvine has said that "Shavian drama invented itself when Shaw walked into a debating society,"[2] and this is true both of plays as a whole and of the handling of particular scenes. The broader question of how the conflict of ideologies was introduced and developed in the structure of the plays will be discussed later, but even a casual look at a few of Shaw's striking debates will reveal how much the verbal fencing of the plays owes to his Zetetical and Dialectical and Fabian experiences: between Juan and the Devil in *Man and Superman;* Dick Dudgeon and General Burgoyne in *The Devil's Disciple;* Undershaft, Cusins, and Barbara in *Major Barbara;* Joan at her trial; or the subtle orchestration of innumerable debates into the dramatic whole called *Heartbreak House.*

Argument and dialectic, the language of debate and the rhetoric of persuation—these were not just techniques adopted for the political or dramatic moment. After the early 1880s propagandizing became a way of life for Shaw; and virtually everything he undertook from that time on was tainted—or inspired—by the image of himself as preacher, missionary, promulgator of a new gospel. But while Shaw may have cut his intellectual teeth on Fabian socialism, that cause also seems too restricted to the pragmatic problems of everyday political maneuvering and propagandizing to have engaged his highest imaginative powers, or to have placed an essentially shy man on the public platform literally hundreds of times a year.

The difference between the novels and the plays was not simply the Marxism that had "made a man" of him before he wrote *An Unsocial Socialist.* He had dropped the larger opus of which that last novel was to have been only the beginning, not only because he felt unprepared and ignorant, but because he lacked the broader philosophical basis, the larger scheme of things, in terms of which socialism itself might take on meaning and importance. He had said at the end of the Preface to *Immaturity*

2. William Irvine, *The Universe of G.B.S.* (New York: McGraw-Hill, 1949), p. 155.

that what was lacking, to give direction and purpose to his intellectual and literary resources, was "only a clear comprehension of life in the light of an intelligible theory: in short, a religion." In spite of the pyrotechnic glare with which Marx had burst onto his spiritual landscape, he did not really provide a religion. He identified and defined evil: capitalism and poverty; and he provided both facts and invective for ammunition. Mill's ameliorative view of social evolution provided a model. But as Shaw never tired of saying, reason can tell you the best means of getting to any particular objective, but it cannot tell you why you should want to go there. Socialism, then, was only a rational means of reaching an objective that may not itself have been rationally definable.

In looking further, Shaw was in no sense denigrating socialism; indeed, for him a solid grasp of its principles and the energy and wisdom to realize them in practice was the highest life man could achieve in the existing world. But the fact remains that "Political Science means nothing else than the devizing of the best ways of fulfilling the will of the world."[3] The political science of socialism, then, represented for Shaw the intellect in the service of some superpersonal will. The object of this will, the ultimate goal of life, will not be subject to individual reason; and while it may express itself *through* the private will, its origins lie in sources beyond and more universal than the individual. There is a tendency among readers to assume that because strong individuals emerge in many of Shaw's plays—Lady Cicely Waynflete, Undershaft, Caesar, Saint Joan come first to mind—that he was essentially an individualist in his attitudes. But, as we shall see, the superiority of these figures derives precisely from their identification with some essential vitality and will outside themselves.

The need to "give" of himself was unquestionably an essential part of Shaw's nature. As we have seen, he told Ellen Terry in 1896: "It is only when I am being used that I can feel my own existence, enjoy my own life" (*Letters*, I, 676), and in the Preface to *Man and Superman* he affirmed that the true joy of life was

3. "Preface" to *Getting Married, Plays*, IV, 339.

"being used for a purpose recognized by yourself as a mighty one." Later, in an address, "Modern Religion" (1912), he defined the religious person as "one who conceives himself or herself to be the instrument of some purpose in the universe which is a high purpose. . . . Any person who realizes that there is such a power, and that his business and joy in life is to do its work, and his pride and point of honor to identify himself with it, is religious."[4] Giving oneself to socialism may in this sense be a religious act, if socialism is *itself* an instrument of a higher purpose in the universe. But it is still only a method of social and economic organization, and while it may perhaps be "the best way of fulfilling the will of the world," it does not create or define that will. In these terms neither Marxism nor Fabian socialism could of itself have provided Shaw with a religion. What he obviously sought was a philosophy in which the giving of oneself constituted the central act of faith, not as an act of self-abnegation or self-sacrifice, but as a creative act.

In a different age, or a different man, "giving oneself to God" in the traditional Christian sense might have sufficed; but for a variety of reasons that road was closed to Shaw. For one thing, the central symbol of Christianity, the cross, did not represent for him either the reality of Grace or the significance of incarnation, both of which he could have accepted but chose to ignore, so much as an emphasis on guilt, repentance, and the fact that Christ's blood had relieved man of the burden of sin. Shaw had a very keen sense of sin: "My conscience is the genuine pulpit article: it annoys me to see people comfortable when they ought to be uncomfortable; and I insist on making them think in order to bring them to a conviction of sin."[5] The creative response to an awareness of sin did not for Shaw lie in repentance or in accepting vicarious atonement, but in doing one's best to undo the consequences and prevent its continuance. It is perfectly true that

---

4. *The Religious Speeches of Bernard Shaw,* ed. Warren S. Smith (University Park, Pa.: The Pennsylvania State University Press, 1963), p. 38.
5. "Epistle Dedicatory" to *Man and Superman, Plays,* III, 486.

Shaw was reacting against a particular brand of Nonconformist
Protestantism, a kind of genteel Calvinism that in Ireland "was
not then a religion: it was a side in political faction, a class
prejudice, a conviction that Roman Catholics are socially inferior
persons, who will go to Hell when they die, and leave Heaven in
the exclusive possession of ladies and gentlemen" (*16 S.S.*, pp.
75–76). His revulsion and flight from the established church of
his boyhood were further encouraged by a large streak of irreverence growing out of the personalities and circumstances of his
home environment.

The more colorful of Shaw's tales of his boyhood have been
told often enough, by himself as well as others; yet a few are
worth repeating for the light they throw on some of the most
characteristic features of his personality and view of the world.
According to him, his first experience in loss of faith was the
traumatic discovery of his father's alcoholism. Although it would
be, he says, "a rhetorical exaggeration to say that I have never
since believed in anything or anybody," he affirms that "then
the scoffer began."[6] A sensitive boy who has "seen 'the governor,'
with an imperfectly wrapped-up goose under one arm and a ham
in the same condition under the other (both purchased under
heaven knows what delusion of festivity), butting at the garden
wall in the belief that he was pushing open the gate, and trans-
forming his tall hat to a concertina in the process," is not very
likely to harbor much in the way of deeply rooted respect for
authority, parental or otherwise. But Shaw's father, sober as well
as drunk, contributed more than a little to his son's skepticism
toward the conventional pieties: "He was in the grip of a humorous sense of anticlimax which I inherited from him and used
with much effect. . . . The more sacred an idea or a situation
was by convention, the more irresistable was it to him as the
jumping-off place for a plunge into laughter."[7]

It would be very wrong to suppose that Shaw's youth was
characterized by family jollity stimulated by his father's droll

6. Letter to Ellen Terry, *Letters*, I, 773, and *16 S.S.*, pp. 27–28.
7. "Preface" to *Immaturity, Prose*, pp. 45 and 41.

debunking of sacred cows. Indeed, his father was as often as not lost in "joyless drunkenness," and his mother, in bitter disillusionment, withdrew into herself and her music, leaving her son to grow up as best he might in what he described to Ellen Terry as "a devil of a childhood, Ellen, rich only in dreams, frightful & loveless in realities" (*Letters*, I, 773). And yet, as he said in a lighter mood, "What sort of gravity could a boy maintain with a family history of this kind? . . . The immediate result of my family training . . . was that I presented myself to the unprepared stranger as a most irreverent young man."[8]

Compounded as he was of conflicting elements—disregard, amounting to outright contempt, for authority; little respect for the traditional objects of reverence, familial, social, or institutional; almost total skepticism in religious matters; all these combined with a strong urge to give himself to some power outside himself—Shaw in his late twenties was still going through that stage traditionally known as "finding himself." Another man might have found in love the fulfillment of giving up the self to another; but the curious *ménage à trois* in which Shaw grew up, consisting of his parents and the brilliant and eccentric singing teacher, conductor, entrepreneur, and charlatan, George Vandeleur Lee, although extraordinarily rich musically, was emotionally sterile. Although the psychological impact on the young Shaw can never be accurately determined, his early environment certainly provided a weak foundation for satisfying emotional relationships in later life. As an adult he seems to have had his share of sexual liaisons, the most durable being those with the ladies not very circumspectly indicated in his diaries as J. P. (Jenny Patterson) and F. E. (Florence Farr Emery).[9] But physical attraction by no means had the highest priority among his desiderata for female friends, and his most intense relationships

8. Ibid., pp. 46–47.
9. Shaw's diaries, kept between 1885 and 1897, along with a longhand transcription from the original shorthand by his secretary, Blanche Patch, are in the British Library of Political and Economic Science at the London School of Economics, and I wish to express my gratitude for their kindness in making that material available to me.

seem to have been more intellectual than emotional. He tried very sincerely to forge strong and intimate ties with many women, notably Janet Achurch (Charrington), Ellen Terry, and Mrs. Pat Campbell, and at least in the first two cases gave freely and unselfishly of his attention and energy and wisdom. But the emotional limitations could not be overcome, and his passion is both literate and literary, and a little abstract, not so much bookish as a delightful fiction. He was, as always, well aware of his inadequacy, and wrote to Ellen Terry: "It is not the small things that women miss in me, but the big things. My pockets are always full of the small change of lovemaking; but it is magic money, not real money." And then he adds, a little defensively: "I am fond of women (or one in a thousand, say) but I am in earnest about quite other things" (*Letters,* I, 801). What the "other things" are is more explicit in another letter: "I cannot manage *people.* I can only manage schemes and ideas and arrange the drama of the thing" (*Letters,* I, 606). Shaw's emotions, it would seem, became fully involved not with individuals so much as with ideas and with causes.

If in his floundering after a faith Shaw clung to Marx, and somewhat later gave himself to Fabian socialism, it should not be supposed that he was grasping after straws. The groundwork had been laid, as we have seen, by Shelley and John Stuart Mill. Karl Marx, by giving his somewhat vague utopian dreams of human justice an economic basis and a political formula, had provided Shaw with a cause, a cause that had the double appeal of exciting genuine emotional commitment and appearing to have a sound scientific foundation. By insisting that social and economic changes were manifestations, not of chance, but of a universal principle, Marx had suggested an area where fact and faith might meet.

The evolutionary principle that was central to Fabian socialism may have been directly or indirectly forced on the Society's attention by Shaw, but he certainly did not invent it. The concept of slowly evolving organic forms goes back far beyond Darwin, although he did much to popularize the idea in the area of biology, and by the later years of the nineteenth century thinkers were boldly applying it in many other areas of natural and human activity. Mill had, especially in his later writing, applied the principle to social forms and institutions, seeing man as evolving systematically toward the socialist structure of society.

The first major document produced by the Fabians, the *Fabian Essays in Socialism* (1889), reveals the heritage of Mill's ideas on ameliorative social evolution very clearly. Sidney Webb characteristically stated the argument in terms of Darwinian selection and man's increased capacity to grasp social facts:

We know now that in natural selection at the stage of development where the existence of civilized mankind is at stake, the units selected from are not individuals, but societies. . . . If we desire to hand on to the afterworld our direct influence, and not merely the memory of our excellence, we must take even more care to improve the social organism of which we form part, than to perfect our own individual developments. . . . Accordingly, conscious "direct adaptation" steadily supplants the unconscious and wasteful "indirect adaptation" of the earlier form of the struggle for existence; and with every advance in sociological knowledge Man is seen to assume more and more, not only the mastery of "things," but also a conscious control over social destiny itself.[10]

Shaw, just as characteristically, rejected the Darwinism and placed even more emphasis on man's highest impulses. Also taking a historical perspective, he observed that with the advent of science and secularism, and the discrediting of supernaturalism, "we relapsed into a gross form of devil worship, and conceived Nature as a remorselessly malignant power," which manifested itself in "the struggle for existence—the remorseless extirpation of the weak—the survival of the fittest—in short, natural selection at work." The error was possible only because men failed to realize "that Nature was unmoral and indifferent, . . . and that there is no cruelty and selfishness outside Man himself; and that his own active benevolence can combat and vanquish both.

10. *Fabian Essays in Socialism,* ed. G. B. Shaw (London: 1889; rpt. New York: Doubleday, n.d.), pp. 78–80.

. . . It is to economic science—once the Dismal, now the Hopeful—that we are indebted for the discovery that though the evil is enormously worse than we knew, yet it is not eternal—not even very long lived, if we only bestir ourselves to make an end of it."[11]

The *Essays,* with Shaw's in the lead, were a challenge to men to use the powers of their minds to control their economic and social destinies. It is significant, however, that Shaw should have so explicitly renounced the Darwinian principle of natural selection. He had written the essay just quoted, "The Basis of Socialism," for presentation to the Society on October 5, 1888. Slightly more than a year before he had read, for review in the *Pall Mall Gazette,* Samuel Butler's *Luck or Cunning?* a book that, although it did not exactly set all London on its ears, opened up a whole new dimension of philosophical possibilities to Shaw. Butler had been temporarily attracted to Darwin for essentially the same reasons as had Shaw: not because he had "invented" the principle of evolution, but because he had apparently taken the supernaturalism and superstition out of the explanations of human development and put evolution on a sound scientific basis of organic biology. As Shaw put it: "At that time it was generally assumed that Darwin invented Evolution. He had done just the opposite. He had shewn that many of the evolutionary developments ascribed to a divine creator could have been produced accidentally without purpose or even consciousness. This process he called Natural Selection" (*16 S.S.*, p. 122). As a consequence, "all we clever people who called ourselves Secularists, Freethinkers, Agnostics, Atheists, Positivists, Rationalists, or what not, . . . were all anti-Clericals snatching at any stick big enough to whack the parsons with; and the biggest stick was the Natural Selection of Darwin. . . . We all, Butler included, grabbed it joyously."[12] But while Shaw was happy enough to get rid of the parsons and their omniscient, omnipotent, and intrusively paternalistic deity,

11. Ibid., pp. 44–45.
12. "Butler When I Was a Nobody," *Saturday Review of Literature,* 29 April 1950, p. 10.

he was instinctively repelled by the mechanistic implications of natural selection, where blind chance, and the responses of the brute instinct for survival, rule an aimless universe. Butler, being something of a scientist, expressed his misgivings explicitly, and went right to the heart of Shaw's problem: "The farseeing Samuel Butler, after being carried away by the reaction for six weeks, suddenly realized that by banishing purpose from natural history Darwin had, as Butler put it, banished mind from the universe" (*16 S.S.*, p. 123).

The extent to which Shaw was impressed by Butler's arguments is evident in the large number of characteristically Shavian ideas that appear to have their origin in *Luck or Cunning?* That book was very specifically an angry and detailed attack on all "those who had been foremost in preaching mindless designless luck as the main means of organic modification." Of course, the villain is Darwin, representing the principal proponent of "an essentially mechanical mindless conception of the universe."[13] What galled Butler most was Darwin's refusal to acknowledge design, which was really what he means by "mind": "The accumulation of accidental variations which owed nothing to mind either in their inception, or their accumulation, the pitchforking, in fact, of mind out of the universe, or at any rate its exclusion from all share worth talking about in the process of organic development, this was the pill Mr. Darwin had given us to swallow; but so thickly had he gilded it with descent with modification, that we did as we were told, swallowed it without a murmur, . . . and, for some twenty years, . . . ordered design peremptorily out of court."[14]

Rejecting all such efforts to "get rid of feeling, consciousness, and mind generally, from active participation in the evolution of the universe," Butler turned for an alternative to the earlier evolutionary theories of Jean Lamarck, who, although acknowledging the influence of external changes, such as climate, fluctu-

13. *Luck or Cunning?*, vol. 8 of *The Works of Samuel Butler*, ed. Henry F. Jones and A. T. Bartholomew (London: Jonathan Cape, 1924), p. 118.
14. Ibid., p. 6.

ations in food supply, geological upheavals, and the like, on the
development of living organisms, had in effect argued that such
organisms changed because they "wanted" to, as an effort of
will. For Butler this brought the essential element back into the
picture: "His system was in reality teleological, inasmuch as
. . . it makes the organism design itself. . . . He in effect
makes effort, intention, will, all of which involve design . . .
underlie progress in organic development."[15] Carrying this line
of thinking further, Butler argues that "divergent form is the
embodiment and organic expression of divergent opinion. *Form
is mind made manifest in flesh through action.*"[16] And at the
farthest limits of evolutionary development, mind creates itself:
"The more a thing knows its own mind the more living it becomes, for life viewed in both the individual and in the general
as the outcome of accumulated developments, is one long process
of specializing consciousness, . . . that is to say, of getting to
know one's own mind more and more fully upon a greater
and greater variety of subjects."[17] Summing up his argument,
Butler concludes:

**We must have evolution. . . . We must also have mind and design.
. . . What, then, remains but . . . the supposition that the mind
or cunning of which we see such abundant evidence all around us
is, like the kingdom of heaven, within us, and within all things at all
times everywhere? There is design, or cunning, but it is . . . not
despotically fashioning us from without as a potter fashions his clay,
but inhering democratically within the body which is its highest outcome, as life inheres within an animal or plant. . . . The view that
God is in all His creatures, He in them and they in Him, is only
expressed in other words by declaring that the main means of organic modification is, not luck, but cunning.[18]**

Shaw rewarded Butler's return of mind to the universe with
lifelong admiration, even though the concept of mind involved

15. Ibid., p. 7.
16. Ibid., p. 224.
17. Ibid., p. 125.
18. Ibid., pp. 234–235.

did not entirely satisfy him. Although Butler identified mind with design, the association is misleading, for he seems by the term to have meant "intention," that which "wants" something better which it does not have, whether it is the means to reach inaccessible food or the capacity to see or the ability to control the environment. There is room, in this concept, for a billion organisms following a billion different wants in a billion different directions. And even if, as Lamarck had suggested, the sheer weight of generations of "wanting" somehow produced the biological change, there was in the theory no framework of a common purpose or a common will in which the individual participates that might have linked cause and effect. Butler's view may have been basically teleological, but in a sense only one step at a time, limited strictly by the range of the creature's immediate needs and powers of imagination. His "mind" seems more physiological than intellectual, more concerned with perfecting the organs "within the body, which is its highest outcome," than with perfecting man as a social or moral entity. The orientation here is too individual and its designs too haphazard to have offered Shaw a coherent philosophy for the whole man. So while Butler freed Shaw from the aimlessness, the mindless struggle for survival, of Darwin, he did not really provide him with a purpose.

Schopenhauer, however, makes a significant distinction between intellect and will, and between individual and universal will, which would seem to take care of any inadequacies Shaw found in Butler's response to Darwin. There can be no question but that Shaw knew something of Schopenhauer's ideas by the 1880s. He may possibly have discussed them with his university-educated friends, such as Olivier and Webb, at the Fabian Society. At the very least he had, during much of 1887, been reading Ernest Belfort Bax's *Handbook of the History of Philosophy,* a work to which Shaw, as we shall see, was much indebted, and which contained a detailed and fairly technical exposition of Schopenhauer's thinking. Of course, Butler's "mind" or "design" probably owed a direct debt to Schopenhauer's "will," which "guides the growth of the animal and directs all its activities. . . . The will creates for itself an organism suitable to its needs; function precedes organization: the desire to butt is the cause of the appearance of the horns." But Schopenhauer's will is both more basic and more sophisticated than Butler's. According to Bax's analysis, "Will, in Schopenhauer's sense, is to be understood as all impulse whatsoever, mechanical, physical, chemical, no less than organic and psychic." It is, he says, a universal "force" in which lies "the infinite potentiality of the world"; and "the body is the immediate objectification of the will."[19] Indeed, Bax continues, the whole phenomenal world is only a manifestation of this primal will. It is evident that Schopenhauer's "will" bears more than a little resemblance to Shaw's later characterizations of the Life Force, as is suggested by this summary of the will's operation: "In man, it becomes conscious of itself. . . . It creates intelligence as its organ or instrument; intelligence is the lamp that illuminates the will's way through the world. The will makes for itself a brain; the brain is the seat of the intelligence; intelligence and consciousness are functions of the brain. . . . On the lower stages of existence, the will is blind craving, it works *blindly*, without consciousness; in man it becomes conscious; intelligence is grafted on the will and becomes the greatest of all instruments of self-preservation. But it always remains in the service of the will; will is the master, intellect the servant."[20]

Although the force of the will leads to the creation of new organs and new self-consciousness, the object of this "voluntarism," as it is called, is simply self-preservation. Schopenhauer's system does not have any sense of ameliorative evolution, or belief that there is satisfaction or joy in becoming something better than what was. On the contrary, greater self-consciousness only brings a greater awareness of frustration, suffering, and despair. The individualized manifestations of the will eventually come

19. Ernest Belfort Bax, *A Handbook of the History of Philosophy*, 3d ed., revised (London: George Bell, 1904), pp. 293–294.
20. Frank Thilly, *A History of Philosophy* (New York: Henry Holt, 1914; rpt. 1945), p. 487.

in conflict with either the universal will or other equally selfish and struggling individual wills. "The progress of knowledge and civilization does not mend matters; it simply brings with it new needs and, with them, new sufferings and new forms of selfishness."[21] Since the will is only a source of pain for Schopenhauer, the best way of finding peace in this world is through the negation, mortification, and death of the individual will in the ascetic, or will-less, life. This was a degree of pessimism that was totally foreign to both Shaw's personality and his ideas.

Shaw's formulation of the religion of the Life Force had distant roots and covered many years; the first document in which its foundations are clearly visible, however, is *The Quintessence of Ibsenism,* begun in 1890 and published in 1891. It is not certain just when or how Shaw became familiar with Ibsen's work. William Archer, with whom he began a lifelong friendship in 1884, was one of a small group of Englishmen—he estimated no more than a half dozen—who had heard of Ibsen as early as 1880. In that year Archer, who knew Norwegian, translated *Pillars of Society,* although it was not printed until 1888; and in 1881 he got to know Ibsen personally in Rome. Although unqualifiedly enthusiastic about the new playwright, Archer was experienced enough as a London drama critic to have serious doubts about the flexibility and tolerance of English tastes; and after witnessing a continental production of *Ghosts* in 1883 announced that "the play could not possibly be produced on the English stage."[22] Thanks largely to his and Shaw's efforts, however, he was proven wrong within seven years—although the violence of the critical reaction to that British performance of *Ghosts* was one of the stimuli for *The Quintessence of Ibsenism.* The first truly successful production of Ibsen in England was of Archer's translation of *A Doll's House,* offered in 1889 by Shaw's friends, Charles Charrington and Janet Achurch (Mrs. Charrington), and reviewed by him for the *Manchester Guardian.*

Archer's enthusiasm seems to have communicated itself

21. Ibid., p. 489.
22. Quoted by Henderson, p. 403.

quickly, for by March of 1885 Shaw was sufficiently familiar
with the Norwegian playwright's work to write Archer, regarding a play sent for his criticism: "I . . . think it good so far.
It smells of Ibsen" (*Letters*, I, 75). Later that year Shaw's
Ibsenism was reinforced through his friendship with Philip
Wicksteed, who, in addition to being an influential economist
and noted Biblical scholar, was also an early Ibsen enthusiast.
Hostility to Ibsen, however, was so strong in England that
Wicksteed was on several occasions denied permission to give
lectures on the playwright—in one instance by London Univer-
sity. The talks were finally given in 1888 in the Chelsea Town
Hall and were published in 1891, the year of Shaw's *Quintes-
sence*.

In a variety of ways, then, Shaw was thoroughly familiar with
Ibsen and his works for at least five years before he wrote his
book. The sources of the Norwegian's appeal are not hard to
imagine: his skeptical attitude toward conventionally received
ways of seeing things, his contempt for the complacency and
hypocrisy of moral people, and perhaps most specifically, what
Shaw called his "forensic technique of recrimination, disillusion,
and penetration through ideals to the truth, with a free use of
all the rhetorical and lyrical arts of the orator, the preacher, the
pleader, and the rhapsodist" (*Q.Ib.*, p. 687). This sounds very
much like a Shavian self-portrait; and indeed, critics ever since
1891 have congratulated themselves on discovering Shaw's
secret: that his little book on Ibsen is in fact about himself. But
as usual Shaw got there first, and as early as August of that
year wrote a friend that he had "written a book called The
Quintessence of Ibsenism which is really the Quintessence of
Shawism."[23]

In his preface Shaw defended himself against the charge of
"finding more than was there" in Ibsen's plays by arguing "that
the existence of a discoverable and perfectly definite thesis in a
poet's work by no means depends on the completeness of his

23. Typed letter, dated Aug. 21, 1891, to Lady Bayles; in the collection of Shaw letters at the Humanities Research Center, University of
Texas at Austin.

own intellectual consciousness of it" (p. 544). The criticism that Shaw was simply projecting his own ideas has some justification, and yet a great deal that is legitimately Ibsen does come through. One thing is clear, however: in writing his first extended analysis of another creative artist, Shaw was forced to pull together a number of ideas that had been floating around, in suspension, as it were, in the back of his head. In the process of thinking through Ibsen's ideas he had to think through his own; and the two are sometimes difficult to distinguish.

The most obtrusive, and probably illegitimate, imposition of Shavian ideas lay in his efforts to attribute his own socialism to Ibsen. Shaw found, for instance, that in *Little Eyolf* "Ibsen . . . explicitly insists for the first time that 'we are members one of another.' . . . Thus we see that in Ibsen's mind, as in the actual history of the nineteenth century, the way to Communism lies through the most resolute and uncompromising Individualism" (p. 639). Ibsen may possibly have been heading in that direction, but he protested vehemently—in response to such assertions—that he had not yet gotten there.

Shaw's compulsion to see almost everyone he admired as either an active or a latent socialist is usually easy to spot, and hence to discount. It is, on the other hand, much more difficult to sort out the subjective and objective realities in his treatment of Ibsen's handling of other bodies of ideas, such as Schopenhauer's ideas about the world will, and the central distinction between will and intellect. It appears certain that Ibsen was reasonably familiar with the work of most of the German Romantic philosophers. But Shaw, too, had already been introduced to Schopenhauer's thought, and since the process of assimilation had clearly begun, it is difficult to make accurate distinctions. What Shaw, for instance, represents as Ibsen's differentiation between idealist and realist lies at the heart of the discussion of the plays in *The Quintessence*. Idealist and realist, as there described, had already been associated more or less explicitly by Schopenhauer with the realms of intellect and will respectively; but Shaw, without contradicting that association, puts those concepts to work for his own quite different purposes. What is finally significant, perhaps, is the consistency with which Shaw, in his reading of Ibsen, is drawn to ideas that appear to have had their origin in Schopenhauer and, as we shall see, in Hegel.

To Shaw, Ibsen's Peer Gynt is little more than a representation of Schopenhauer's individual will ensnared and deluded by idealism, "setting up as his ideal the realization of himself through the utter satisfaction of his own will." But still "the world-will is outside Peer Gynt as well as inside him," and by blinding himself to the disparity, by thinking he could affirm his own will in defiance of the world will, he is left with nothing but emptiness, frustration, and despair (pp. 578–582). In Shaw's reading of Ibsen, "life consists in the fulfillment of the will" only when the individual will, seeing things realistically, is in accord with the world will. Shaw even sees the playwright's artistic development in terms of Schopenhauer's distinction between will and intellect. "Ibsen, by merely giving the rein to the creative impulse, had produced Brand and Peer Gynt. . . . His will, in setting his imagination to work, had produced a tough puzzle for his intellect. In no case does the difference between the will and the intellect come out more clearly than in that of the poet" (p. 583).

Earlier in the essay Shaw had been even more explicit:

Since all valid human institutions are constructed to fulfil man's will, and his will is to live even when his reason teaches him to die, logical necessity . . . is, in short, not necessity at all. . . . In our own century the recognition of the will as distinct from the reasoning machinery began to spread. Schopenhauer was the first among the moderns to appreciate the enormous practical importance of the distinction, and to make it clear to amateur metaphysicians by concrete instances. . . . Now to a generation which has ceased to believe in heaven . . . the fact that life is not rationally worth living is obvious. . . . Plainly then, the reasonable thing for the rationalists to do is to refuse to live. But as none of them will commit suicide in obedience to this demonstration of 'the necessity' for it, there is an end of the notion that we live for reasons instead of in fulfilment of our will to live. [Pp. 552–553]

Shaw felt it necessary in a footnote to call attention to the pessimistic implications of Schopenhauer's line of thinking and to "warn those who fancy that Schopenhauerism is one and indivisible, that acceptance of its metaphysics by no means involves endorsement of its philosophy." In an annoyed letter to William Archer, who subbornly refused to understand the essay, Shaw repeated the warning against confusing Schopenhauer's metaphysics with his philosophy; and while he made the extent of his use of Schopenhauer's ideas even clearer than in the essay itself, he also emphasized his selectivity, and rebuked Archer: "You have done just what you think I did: you have fished one notion out of Schopenhauer, or rather out of his reputation, and you call that Schopenhauerism" (*Letters,* I, 316–317).

After having created "two great dramatic poems" through the power of poetic impulse, or will, Ibsen, according to Shaw, entered "on a struggle to become intellectually conscious of what he had done," in his next play, *Emperor and Galilean.* Shaw obviously found this somewhat obscure play of particular importance, and spent more time discussing it than any of Ibsen's other works. The particular feature of this "struggle" of Ibsen's intellect to understand his will that seemed to fascinate Shaw was its emphasis on "the growth of the spirit of man." In *Emperor and Galilean* the "growth of the spirit" is in fact the growth of the soul, subsuming as Schopenhauer says, both will and intellect. In the play Shaw found several parallel antitheses established, perhaps the most basic being that between flesh and spirit, although it could also be described in terms of body and soul, matter and mind, or will and intellect.[24]

The commentary begins with the observation that in periods of cultural transition, when the infallibility of one moral system has been shattered and has not yet been replaced by another commonly accepted faith, "men's uncertainty as to the rightness and wrongness of their actions keeps them in a continual perplexity" (p. 588 ff.). Julian is a victim of such perplexity, caught in the

24. See also J. L. Wisenthal, *The Marriage of Contraries* (Cambridge, Mass.: Harvard University Press, 1974), pp. 1–3.

dilemma "as to whether he will dare to choose between Christ and the imperial purple of Rome." Julian's mentor and spiritual advisor is the mystic sage, Maximus, who sees the true conflict as one not merely between Julian's professed creed and his ambition for empire, but "between Christ and Julian himself." Maximus's vision is based on the central antithesis between what he characterizes as "the first empire" of pagan sensuality and self-indulgence and freedom and "the second empire" of Christian self-denial, asceticism, and "self-abnegatory idealism." There is no going back to the first, he realizes, and the second is unnatural and "already rotten at heart." The synthesis to which he looks forward is "the third empire: . . . the empire of Man asserting the eternal validity of his own will. He who can see that not on Olympus, not nailed to the cross, but in himself is God: he is the man to build [the] bridge between the flesh and the spirit, establishing this third empire in which the spirit shall not be unknown, nor the flesh starved, nor the will tortured and baffled." The metaphor Maximus uses in the play is that it "shall be founded on the tree of knowledge and the tree of the cross together, because it hates and loves them both."

At the beginning there is much of Peer Gynt in Julian, an idealist who would assert the absolute authority of his self-centered will, but would cloak himself in gratifyingly high-sounding ideals. Of Maximus's assurance that "in himself is God," he understands only that part which flatters him, and comes to the conviction that he is indeed God on earth, and sees Christ "not as the prototype of himself, as Maximus would have him feel, but as a rival god over whom he must prevail at all costs." "Tell me who shall conquer, the emperor or the Galilean," he asks of Maximus, whose reply Shaw quotes at length:

"Both the emperor and the Galilean shall succumb. . . . Whether in our time or in hundreds of years I know not; but so it shall be when the right man comes." "Who is the right man?" says Julian. "He who shall swallow up both emperor and Galilean. . . . Both shall succumb; but you shall not therefore perish. Does not the child succumb in the youth and the youth in the man: yet neither child nor youth perishes. . . . You have tried to make the youth a child again. The empire of the flesh is fallen prey to the empire of the spirit. But the empire of the spirit is not final, any more than the youth is. You have tried to hinder the youth from growing: from becoming a man. Oh fool, who have drawn your sword against that which is to be: against the third empire, in which the twin natured shall reign." [P. 590]

Trying to make clearer what he means by "twin-natured," Maximus calls him: "The God-Emperor. . . . Logos in Pan, Pan in Logos. . . . He is self-begotten in the man who wills." "But," Shaw goes on in his own words, "it is of no use. Maximus's idea is a synthesis of relations in which not only is Christ God in exactly the same sense as that in which Julian is God, but Julian is Christ as well." Julian can go as far as to say: "The spirit has become flesh and the flesh spirit"; but he spoils it all by continuing: "All creation lies within my will and power." This reveals, as Shaw points out, that Julian "has not comprehended the synthesis at all. . . . And since this part is only valid as a constituent of the synthesis, it has no reality when isolated from it." As Julian's world begins to crash around his head, he vows desperately to sacrifice to the gods: "I will sacrifice to this god and that god: I will sacrifice to many. . . . One or other must surely hear me. I must call on something without me and above me."

Earlier, in his discussion of the "twin-natured" representative of the third empire "who shall swallow up both emperor and Galilean," and yet in whom "both shall succumb; but . . . shall not perish," Shaw appended in 1912 a revealing footnote: "Or, as we should now say, the Superman." Julian, however, does not achieve the third empire: "It was something for Julian to have seen that the power which he found stronger than his individual will was itself will; but inasmuch as he conceived it, not as the whole of which his will was but a part, but as a rival will, he was not the man to found the third kingdom. He had felt the godhead in himself, but not in others. Being only able to say, with half conviction, 'The kingdom of heaven is within ME,' he had been utterly vanquished by the Galilean who had been able to say, 'The kingdom of heaven is within YOU.' But he was on the way to that full truth" (pp. 592–593). The ultimate synthesis of emperor and Galilean, of Pan and Logos, of world will and self-conscious intellect, is still in the future. Julian is not Superman; and as Shaw concluded: "The third empire was not yet, and is not yet."

In writing about some of the later plays, Shaw made use of the antitheses he had set up in his discussion of *Emperor and Galilean*—as in his treatment of the opposition between Oswald's pagan joy in life and sunshine and the gloomy idealism Parson Manders tries to impose on Mrs. Alving in *Ghosts*. But his analysis of *Emperor and Galilean* deserves particular attention here, to the virtual exclusion of the other plays, because that play seemed uniquely important to Shaw, and because what seemed important in it was the particular kind of cultural, intellectual, and spiritual evolution he found represented there. In writing about the other plays he discussed primarily the contrasts and conflicts between idealists and realists. But in *Emperor and Galilean* Shaw saw Ibsen searching, as he was searching himself, for a religion in which all the conflicting and seemingly dissociated parts, the idealism and the realism, the intellect and the will, the spirit and the body, without losing their individual legitimacy or reality, could be recognized as part of some larger creative process to which he could give his allegiance.

As we have seen, some kind of evolutionary principle had long been a central part of Shaw's thinking, although it had become increasingly sophisticated as it itself evolved. Butler had reestablished the possibility of mind or intention or purpose in the biological sphere; Mill had never questioned the function of mind in the dimension of social evolution. But what was necessary before the facts or even the theories of biological and social evolution could become a religion for Shaw was a will and purpose outside of the individual that give men a common goal— without falling back on the omniscient and omnipotent deity who put his puppets through their paces as part of some already perfected plan. Schopenhauer offered one component of that missing but essential element: a world will of which the individual was a part, his intellect existing by virtue of, and in order to serve, the larger will. But Shaw simply could not accept what he had characterized as Schopenhauer's "philosophy," with its pessimism and its inability to see the will as driving the evolutionary processes of the universe toward anything "better" than mere animal survival. In Ibsen's particular application of these ideas, however, Shaw found a philosophy that apparently satisfied many of his needs: a world will that worked through man, pushing him from childhood through youth toward maturity, but not in a straight line. It was a dialectic process, from pagan joy in the senses and the things of this world to its negation in Christian asceticism and spirituality, and then beyond both to a third stage uniting body and spirit in a synthesis that transcends at the same time that it subsumes its elements, becoming something better, a new unity that maintains its constituents, and yet is superior to their mere sum.

The process just described was not in fact invented by Ibsen, and in all essential respects it comes very close to representing Hegel's description of the dialectic triad of thesis, antithesis, and synthesis. It is probable that Ibsen was familiar with Hegel's ideas, and quite possibly with his writing.[25] Shaw's analysis of *Emperor and Galilean* casts Ibsen's ideas in Hegelian form, and it is clear that Shaw knew perfectly well what he was doing from a footnote that appears early in the original (1891) edition: "The doctrine of justification, not by works, but by faith, clearly derives its validity from the consideration that no action, taken apart from the will behind it, has any moral character: for example, the acts which make the murderer and incendiary infamous are exactly similar to those which make the patriotic hero famous. 'Original sin' is the will doing mischief. 'Divine grace' is the will doing good. Our fathers, unversed in the

25. See Brian Johnston, "Archetypal Repetition in *Ghosts*," *Scandanavian Studies*, 41 (May 1969), 93–125.

Hegelian dialectic, could not conceive that these two, each the negation of the other, were the same" (p. 552).

The evidence makes clear that in the decade of the 1880s Shaw was suddenly exposed to a large number of new and exciting ideas. With his insatiable intellectual appetite, combined with an intense desire to be accepted by the large world where these ideas were current, he made room for as many as possible, testing and rejecting some, half digesting others, adjusting elements from many sources to the deep resources of his own mind and personality, until by the end of the decade—and most evidently in *The Quintessence of Ibsenism*—he was possessed of a complex and coherent body of thought. It appears, moreover, to have been the ideas he derived from Hegel that provided the catalyst, the vital spark that gave order and sense and point to all the other elements, and pulled the fragmentary pieces together into a dynamic structure that appealed to Shaw's spirit and hopes as well as to his mind. The familiar terminology—of the Life Force and Creative Evolution—came only later, and owe much to the writing of Henri Bergson. But Bergson's book *Creative Evolution* did not appear until 1907 in France and 1910 in England; and there is no evidence that Shaw knew of his work until some years later. The ideas themselves, that the terms were borrowed to describe, first appear in *The Quintessence,* and are developed and articulated in various forms until they find their most complete statement in *Man and Superman,* written between 1901 and 1903. And the key concepts that produce the critical differences between the world will of Schopenhauer and the evolutionism of Butler on the one hand and Shaw's Life Force and Creative Evolution on the other can, I believe, be traced to Hegel. But if the collection of ideas that Shaw dreamed might become the religion of the twentieth century owes such a debt to Hegel, the matter deserves a chapter of its own.

5   *Hegel and the*
Shavian Dialectic

When Max Beerbohm poked fun at Shaw's eclectic intellectual heritage, he pointed explicitly at his debt to contemporary and near contemporary German philosophers. Critics since have enlarged on the elements in Shaw's plays that owe something to Schopenhauer's *The World as Will* or *The Will to Power,* to say nothing of Nietzsche's superman theories. But neither Beerbohm nor later critics have had much to say about the German philosopher who loomed even larger in the skies of nineteenth-century thought, Georg Wilhelm Friedrich Hegel. That Shaw should have been at least superficially familiar with Hegel's ideas is neither surprising nor difficult to prove. Doubtless he had been introduced to Hegel's name and the broad concepts of the dialectic principle in economic and political history by Marx, whose own rationalization of the necessity of a class war culminating in the classless state is explicitly the adaptation of an Hegelian concept. Shaw very soon rejected the Marxist concept of the class war as a valid model for economic and social facts of life, and his vision of the goal of Creative Evolution, as we have seen, goes far beyond the proletarian utopia with which Marx stops dead. But in spite of later assertions that he had "no use for the Marxian dialectic" and that his mind did not "work in Hegelian grooves,"[1] the evidence, not merely of allusions,

1. From a message sent to the *Labour Monthly* in July 1941, quoted in Allan Chappelow, *Shaw—"The Chucker-Out"* (London: George Allen and Unwin, 1969), pp. 227–228.

paraphrases, and occasionally quotations, but of the thought itself, suggests a much deeper influence than Shaw was willing to acknowledge.

There is no reason to suppose, however, that Shaw was in any sense an "authority" on Hegel. The internal evidence suggests that he had read the "Introduction to the Philosophy of History" and perhaps some fragments elsewhere. If Shaw was, as he claimed, a crow who "hopped, hungry and curious, across the fields of philosophy," he appears to have followed Hegel's plow at some distance, and to have picked up many of the kernels at second hand. But little would be gained by trying to identify Hegel as the fountainhead of all Shaw's ideas; that would be too simple and a gross distortion. What is important is that the Hegelian *element* in Shaw's thought, and specifically the theory of the dialectic principle, whether inherited directly or indirectly, or most likely both, provided Shaw's ideas with a significant and coherent pattern, and gives us an intellectually satisfying means of seeing the relationships among those ideas. And coherence and consistency are not virtues for which Shaw is often given credit.

Indeed, from the very beginning of Shaw's dramatic career the favorite accusation of unfriendly critics—and even some friendly ones—has been that he had an extravagant taste for paradox. And the charge has usually carried the implication that this fondness for paradox was simply a part of his general obstreperousness, a form of intellectual *jeu d'esprit* for its own sake. However, the paradox is not only basic to Shaw's wit, it is also an essential part of his thought and underlies the structure of his plays. And paradox, in the sense of a statement or situation where two opposite and contradictory things *both* seem true at the same time, is basic to the principle that lies at the heart of Hegel's philosophy—the principle of the dialectic.

Quite frankly, the Hegelian dialectic is too abstruse to be described adequately in a few words—or in many. Perhaps the best way to bring to mind its main features would be to offer two illustrations, one from Hegel himself, and the other from the work of his disciple, Karl Marx. The first is a logical and metaphysical application of the dialectic, which Hegel illustrates by taking a basic and elemental concept, in this case the concept of "being"—pure and absolute "being," without qualities, definition, or distinctions. Let this, he says, be our *thesis*. But the concept of being also implies and even necessitates the contrary concept of non-being—also absolute and undifferentiated. This is the *antithesis* of being. Since both concepts are without qualities of any sort, and hence are totally featureless, they are conceptually identical; yet being and non-being are also conceptually *contradictory*. They are both "true," and yet the trueness of both at the same time is paradoxical. But, says Hegel, because it *is* paradoxical, the mind that tries to grasp both concepts at the same time, and to reconcile this "opposition in identity," is led irresistibly to a new notion, that of becoming—in other words, we are led to a synthesis that includes both the thesis and antithesis, but is something more, a process of moving from non-being to being.

Hegel saw this dialectic triad of thesis, antithesis, and synthesis as operative in the realms of both mind and matter—in logic, in metaphysics, in human history, and in the spiritual world. Its significant feature is that it represents a dynamic process—working everywhere and at all times—in which each synthesis is not an end, but becomes the thesis in a new triad. In other words, the dialectic is a *process,* always evolving into more and more complete and comprehensive syntheses, progressively higher and higher forms.

Karl Marx adapted Hegel's description of the dialectic process and applied it to what we would call "social dynamics," defining the "class struggle" in dialectic terms. Although his historical analysis goes back to the feudal system, his major and final triad describes the situation in the nineteenth and twentieth centuries, in which the thesis, he says, is represented by the capitalist class, which owns the means of production, but does not itself produce. The capitalist class, he reasons, out of its own needs, has created its antithesis, the proletariat, or laboring class, which produces, but does not possess the means of production. These two classes, says Marx, are both philosophically and economically opposed and contradictory, and must necessarily produce their synthesis of a classless society, which both works *and* possesses the means of production.

Perhaps the major difference between this application of the dialectic and Hegel's is that Marx applies the principle only to social history, where the process has a final goal immediately in view: the emergence of the classless communist state, for him the ultimate synthesis. But for Hegel the dialectic process is at work in most of the processes of the universe; and although in metaphysical terms it has a theoretic end, in purely human terms it is an unending process of *becoming,* in which each step, each new synthesis, is always better, more "real," than the preceding one, always moving toward the ultimate reality of total self-consciousness, what he called the Absolute Idea. The total process could be summed up by Hegel's formula: Potential Idea (thesis)/Matter (antithesis)/Realized (or Absolute) Idea (synthesis). Shaw was much closer to Hegel than to Marx in his use of the dialectic principle—perhaps most clearly in the extent to which he applied it in different ways to a variety of spheres, not merely the economic or social.

It is appropriate that what seems to be Shaw's first printed reference to Hegel should be in defense of socialism in terms that are not narrowly Marxist. In the essay "Transition" in the 1889 volume of *Fabian Essays,* Shaw was commenting on "the Whig doctrinaires who accepted . . . incompetence and corruption . . . as permanent inherent State qualities." "Not," he reasoned, "that the Socialists were not doctrinaires too; but outside economics they were pupils of Hegel, whilst the Whigs were pupils of Bentham and . . . Bentham's was not the school in which men learned to solve problems to which history alone could give the key, or to form conceptions which belonged to the evolutional order. Hegel, on the other hand, expressly taught the conception of the perfect State; and his pupils saw that nothing in the nature of things made it impossible."[2]

Shaw's first major extended use of Hegelian concepts was, as

2. *Fabian Essays in Socialism,* ed. G. B. Shaw (London: 1889; rpt. New York: Doubleday, n.d.), pp. 222–223.

we have already seen, in *The Quintessence of Ibsenism.* The notions of a world will evolving dialectically in human history, of the force behind the universe, or "godhead," realizing itself through and in man, of the dialectic triad of pagan sensualism and Christian asceticism emerging as a synthesis that partakes of but transcends both the forces that created it, all emerge clearly in the discussion of *Emperor and Galilean.* The Hegelianism was in part Ibsen's, for the principles are indeed implicit in the text of the play. But Shaw recognized them, emphasized them, developed the concepts in his discussion, and ultimately made them part of his own thinking. The book was, after all, by his own confession about himself.

It is perhaps worth mentioning that later in the *Quintessence,* in the section "The Technical Novelty" of Ibsen, Shaw enunciated another characteristically Hegelian idea. "In the new plays," he wrote, "the drama arises through a conflict of unsettled ideals rather than through [situations] to which no moral question is raised. The conflict is not between clear right and wrong: the villain is as conscientious as the hero, if not more so: in fact, the question which makes the play interesting . . . is which is the villain and which the hero. Or, to put it another way, there are no villains and no heroes" (pp. 679–680). The idea suggested here was applied more specifically to tragedy in the Preface to *Saint Joan:* "There are no villains in the piece, . . . it is what men do at their best, with good intentions; . . . the tragedy of such murders as Joan's is that they are not committed by murderers" (*Plays,* II, 312–313). This sounds very much like Hegel's view of tragedy as summarized by A. C. Bradley in his important lecture on Hegel (1909): "The essentially tragic fact is the self-division and intestinal warfare of the ethical substance, not so much the war of good with evil as the war of good with good."[3]

3. *Hegel on Tragedy,* ed. Anne and Henry Paolucci (New York: Doubleday, 1962), p. 369. For a more detailed discussion of the Hegelian tragedy of *Saint Joan* see Louis Crompton, *Shaw the Dramatist* (Lincoln: University of Nebraska Press, 1969), pp. 208 ff. Crompton, unaware of the more direct influences, speaks of the "natural Hegelianism of Shaw's mind."

Shaw's second major ideological statement was *The Perfect Wagnerite,* which appeared in 1898, seven years after *The Quintessence of Ibsenism,* and after his ideas had begun to find dramatic embodiment in his plays. The book might appropriately be called "The Perfect Shavian," for as in the Ibsen book he found what he wanted to find in his subject. There is no question but what Wagner himself had been influenced directly by both Schopenhauer and Hegel; but the overt Hegelianism that permeates Shaw's symbolic interpretation of the Ring Cycle appears at times somewhat more than the text will bear.

In *The Perfect Wagnerite* Shaw treated the Ring Cycle, a discussion of which occupies most of the volume, rather like a kind of Germanic *Emperor and Galilean,* with Wotan, the "Godhead," an incomplete and partial embodiment of the World Spirit, aspiring to a Third Kingdom that will at once transcend and destroy him. The allegory begins, however, at the human level, with Alberic, the dwarf. With his "brutish narrowness of intelligence and selfishness of imagination: too stupid to see that his own welfare can only be compassed as part of the welfare of the world, too full of brute force not to grasp vigorously at his own gain," Alberic becomes the prototype of the capitalist, extorting the world's wealth, exploiting its labor, for his own profit: "If there were no higher power in the world to work against Alberic, the end of it would be utter destruction. Such a force there is, however; and it is called Godhead. The mysterious thing we call life organizes itself into all living shapes, bird, beast, beetle and fish, rising to the human, . . . and these higher powers are called into existence by the same self-organization of life still more wonderfully into rare persons who may by comparison be called gods, creatures capable of thought, whose aims extend far beyond the satisfaction of their bodily appetites."[4] The development is not smooth, however, for these reasonable beings come up against the limitations of matter, represented by the brutishness of the giants and dwarfs: "Godhead, face to face with Stu-

4. *The Perfect Wagernite* (New York: Brentano's, 1909), pp. 10–11, hereafter cited in the text.

pidity, must compromise. Unable to enforce on the world the
pure law of thought, it must resort to a mechanical law" (p.
11). "Wotan, . . . with all his aspirations to establish a reign
of noble thought, of righteousness, order, and justice," has found
that the world as it is is not equal to his dream, and "he himself
has found how far short Godhead falls of the thing it conceives"
(p. 25). But Wotan is driven by "the energy of life [which] is
still carrying human nature to higher and higher levels" (p. 78),
and "with his heart stirring towards higher forces than himself,
turns with disgust from . . . lower forces" (p. 24). That is, in
its reliance on "mechanical law" Godhead has violated and ne-
gated its own nature. "Thus Godhead's resort to law finally costs
it half its integrity—as if a spiritual king, to gain temporal
power, had plucked out one of his eyes [as Wotan had in fact
done]—and it finally begins secretly to long for the advent of
some power higher than itself which will destroy its artificial
empire of law, and establish a true republic of free thought"
(p. 12).

Brynhild is introduced as a representation of the World Spirit
as it operates through Wotan, for she is at once part of him and
at the same time standing over against him, in opposition to
him: "Brynhild is the inner thought and will of Godhead, the
aspiration from the high life to the higher life that is its divine
element, and only becomes separated from it when its resort to
kingship and priestcraft for the sake of temporal power has
made it false to itself" (p. 41). The first impulse of Godhead is
to defend itself and the status quo: "How is the rebel to be dis-
armed? Slain it cannot be by Godhead, since it is still Godhead's
own very dearest soul. But hidden, stifled, silenced it must be;
or it will wreck the State and leave the Church defenceless"
(p. 44). The resistance cannot last: "Life itself, with its accomplished marvels and its infinite potentialities, is the only force
Godhead can worship," and Wotan must acknowledge "the seed
perhaps of something higher even than himself, that shall one
day supersede him" (p. 23). Wotan himself, in other words,
"must long in his inmost soul for the advent of that greater power

whose first work . . . must be his own undoing" (p. 33). But that day will not come until the World Spirit or Will "passes completely away from Godhead, and is reborn as the soul of the hero," the hero being Siegfried, the next stage in the evolution of the Spirit or Force of Life.

Not very far behind Shaw's allegorical reading of the Ring Cycle, with his vision of its dialectic evolution from God to Hero, stands the figure of Hegel. "We are concerned," Hegel says, "with the Spirit's development, its progression and ascent to an ever higher concept of itself. But this development is connected with the . . . annihilation of the preceding mode of actuality which the concept of the Spirit had evolved" (*Reason*, pp. 38–39). Shaw's identification of the "will of Godhead" with "the aspiration from the high life to the higher life that is its divine element, [which] only becomes separated from it" when it is "false to itself" (p. 41), seems to reflect the Hegelian idea that "since the divine thought progresses according to its own laws, which are the laws of the world, . . . what is real in existence is only that which is divine in it. Only this it is which develops. Everything else is contingent and must perish" (*Reason*, p. xvii). The dialectic relationship between Wotan and Siegfried is perhaps most explicit in still another passage in Hegel: "The Spirit, devouring its worldly envelope, not only passes into another envelope, not only arises rejuvenated from the ashes of its embodiment, but it emerges from them exalted, transfigured, a purer Spirit. It is true that it acts against itself, devours its own existence. But in so doing it elaborates upon this existence; its embodiment becomes material for its work to elevate itself to a new embodiment" (*Reason*, p. 89). For Shaw the paradigm for the dialectic relationship lies in the confrontation, in Act Three of *Siegfried*, in which the hero, now become totally "alienated," taunts his disguised father, who observes darkly that one of the eyes looking out from the young man's head is his own (p. 60). That which was created by Godhead, out of its urge to create something better than itself, has now become its enemy, in Hegel's terms an "other," and at the same time carries with it part of its source, its eye, its vision of aspiration toward something better yet. The hero triumphs over the God; and yet in that event Godhead fulfills itself in something higher.

This process of Godhead transcending itself, and in the process transcending the forms and moral laws it had established as part of its compromise with the world, is by definition immoral within the framework of those laws. As Shaw says: "However carefully these laws are framed to represent the highest thoughts of the framers at the moment of their promulgation, before a day has elapsed that thought has grown and widened by the ceaseless evolution of life; and lo! yesterday's law already fallen out with today's thought" (p. 11). Later he speaks of "life itself as a tireless power which is continually driving onward and upward . . . into higher and higher forms of organization, the strengths and the needs of which are continually superseding the institutions which were made to fit our former requirements" (pp. 77–78). Similarly, Hegel claims that "the history of the world moves on a higher level than that proper to morality," and hence the generally accepted rules of any given society are, in terms of this upward movement, a negative force. "The demands and accomplishments of the absolute and final aim of Spirit . . . lie above the obligations, responsibilities, and liabilities which are incumbent on the individuals in regard to their morality. (An individual may for moral reasons resist and for immoral reasons advance the course of history). . . . It is therefore only a formal right, forsaken both by the living spirit and by God, which the defenders of ancient right and order (no matter how moral) maintain" (*Reason*, p. 82). It seems hardly necessary to point out, although more will be said about it later, that most of Shaw's plays are in one way or another dramatic illustrations of the conflict between spirit and morality.

For Shaw the hero represents the temporal fulfillment of the Life Force, climbing "from toad and serpent to dwarf, from bear and elephant to giant, from dwarf and giant to a god with thoughts, with comprehension of the world, with ideals. Why should it stop there? Why should it not rise from the god to the Hero? to the creature in whom the god's unavailing thought

shall have become effective will and life, who shall make his
way straight to truth and reality" (pp. 25–26). For Hegel too
"it is the heroic man who pushes history forward. On the other
hand, the . . . hero is completely guided by the World Spirit,
and the World Spirit uses him, cunningly, for its own ends"
(*Reason,* p. xxxvi).

But for both Hegel and Shaw "the hero" is simply a metaphor for the man who rises above what man *is,* or as Shaw put
it: "The world is waiting for Man to redeem it from the lame
and cramped government of the gods" (p. 32). Of course, the
man who is more than Man is the Superman; and while Wagner's concept of the Hero unquestionably owes something to
Nietzsche, Shaw chose to do little more than mention the fact
in passing. This was not out of ignorance; for when a reader of
The Quintessence had informed him that he had taken his ideas
from Nietzsche, Shaw, who at that time had never heard the
name, began to read the works of his German contemporary
with considerable interest. But while Shaw found the brash irreverence of *Thus Spake Zarathustra* refreshing and stimulating,
there was behind the German's desperate gaiety an essential pessimism regarding the purpose of nature and the universe that
Shaw did not find congenial. Certainly Nietzsche's influence on
the formulation of the basic elements of his religion of the Life
Force is far less important than Hegel's. In the footnote Shaw
added to the 1912 edition of *The Quintessence,* in which he
told of the reader's attribution of his ideas to Nietzsche, he drew
a moral: "I mention this fact, not with the ridiculous object of
vindicating my 'originality,' . . . but because I attach great
importance to the evidence that the movement voiced by Schopenhauer, Wagner, Ibsen, Nietzsche, and Strindberg, was a
world movement, and would have found expression if every one
of these writers had perished in his cradle" (*Q.Ib.,* p. 568)—
would have found expression, presumably, in the writings of
Bernard Shaw. That statement was itself characteristically Hegelian; and Shaw doubtless conceived of his own role as being
not unlike that of the Hegelian hero.

Although the emergence of some Hegelian ideas in a discussion of playwrights influenced by his work is not in itself surprising, the consistency with which Shaw focused his attention on those elements is, and it offers a clue to the way in which the process of writing the books on Ibsen and Wagner played a critical role in how Shaw organized his ideas about the Life Force. And it was important that the Hegelian view of reality should have reached him incarnate in theatrically effective drama as well as in the more explicit formulations of philosophic discourse. Furthermore, the Hegelian dimension of Shaw's thought was no less evident when he talked about his own ideas in his own voice, most notably in some of the prefaces, in a group of speeches given in public halls in London between 1906 and 1912, already cited, and in the work of which he later said: "I put all my intellectual goods in the shop window under the sign of Man and Superman."[5]

The idea that the Will or Force that lies behind the universe and all existence finds its highest manifestation and realization in man was central to both Shaw and Hegel. Shaw put it: "The strongest, fiercest force in nature is human will. It is the highest organization we know of the will that has created the whole universe."[6] In other words, what Hegel called variously the Spirit or Idea, and Shaw called the Life Force, needed and indeed created human mind and body in order to achieve self-consciousness and fulfillment in the "real" world, that is in history. When discussing his personal theology, Shaw was careful to make clear that his Life Force had nothing to do with the conventional deity of Christianity, but was a will, struggling upward, making "material organs with which to grapple with material things," the goal, not the designer, of the universe: "The object of the whole evolutionary process is to realize God."[7]

For Hegel, what he called "the Absolute becomes conscious

5. "Preface" to *Back to Methuselah*, *Plays*, II, lxxxix.
6. "Parents and Children," *Plays*, IV, 64.
7. *The Religious Speeches of Bernard Shaw*, ed. Warren S. Smith (University Park, Pa.: The Pennsylvania State University Press, 1963), p. 6.

only in evolution, and above all in man."[8] "One may have all sorts of ideas about the Kingdom of God," he acknowledged, "but it is always a realm of Spirit to be realized and brought about in man" (*Reason,* p. 20). His language was not Shaw's language, but the ideas were very close: "World history begins its general aim—to realize the idea of Spirit—only in an implicit form, namely, as Nature—as an innnermost, unconscious instinct. And the whole business of history . . . is to bring it into consciousness" (*Reason,* p. 30). In this process, however, "the universal must be actualized through the particular"; and "the Spirit's . . . ascent to an ever higher concept of itself . . . is the result, on the one hand, of the inner development of the Idea and, on the other, of the activity of individuals, who are its agents and bring about its actualization" (*Reason,* pp. 35, 39). The similarity to Shaw's ideas is particularly clear in this summary: "Nature develops, after the stages of the mineral and vegetable kingdom, into man, in whose consciousness the Idea becomes conscious of itself. This self-consciousness of the Idea is Spirit, the synthesis of Idea and Nature, and the development of this consciousness is History" (*Reason,* p. xxi).

"We are all experiments," Shaw said, "in the direction of making God";[9] but not all experiments are equally successful. At any given point in time the highest achievement, the most complete synthesis, the most successful experiment, that which is better than what has been, is the Superman. Shaw acknowledged that "the precise formula for the Superman . . . has not yet been discovered. Until it is, every birth is an experiment in the Great Research which is being conducted by the Life Force to discover that formula."[10] But the vital impulse of the Life Force, what Hegel called "the infinite elan of the World Spirit, its irresistible urge," is to achieve an ever higher stage (*Reason,* p. 67). Juan, himself a Superman, puts it thus: "Life is a force

8. Frank Thilly, *History of Philosophy* (New York: Holt, 1914; rpt. 1945), p. 471.
9. *Religious Speeches,* p. 35.
10. "Parents and Children," *Plays,* IV, 49.

which has made innumerable experiments in organizing itself; that the mammoth and the man, the mouse and the megatherium, the flies and the fleas and the Fathers of the Church, are all more or less successful attempts to build up that raw force into higher and higher individuals" (III, 626). Hegel conceived of a similar fecundity in life's vitality:

The Spirit . . . experiments in a multitude of dimensions and directions, developing itself, exercising itself, enjoying itself in inexhaustible abundance, . . . differentiating its powers in all the directions of its plenitude. . . . Though involved with the conditions of nature, . . . it not only meets in them opposition and hindrance, but often failure and defeat through the complications into which it becomes involved through them or through itself. But even when it perishes it does so in the course of its function and destiny. [*Reason,* p. 89]

And "these vast congeries of volitions, interests, and activities constitute the tools and means of the World Spirit for attaining its purpose, bringing it to consciousness, and realizing it . . . coming to itself . . . in concrete actuality" (*Reason,* p. 31).

But, as the earlier Hegel passage implied, mere fecundity of natural vitality, even with consciousness, is not enough to achieve the World Spirit's purpose. Juan is very explicit on this point:

Life was driving at brains—at its darling object: an organ by which it can attain not only self-consciousness but self-understanding. . . . To Life, the force behind Man, intellect is a necessity, because without it he blunders into death. Just as Life, after ages of struggle, evolved that wonderful bodily organ the eye, so that the living organism could see where it was going . . . so it is evolving today a mind's eye that shall see, not the physical world, but the purpose of life. [Pp. 627–628]

Echoing Hegel's statement that the Spirit finds in mere natural proliferation "opposition and hindrance, . . . failure and defeat," Juan, who possesses this "mind's eye," can say: "In the heaven I seek [there is] no other joy than the work of helping Life in its struggle upward. Think of how it wastes and scatters itself, how it raises up obstacles to itself and destroys itself in its ignorance and blindness. It needs a brain, this irresistible force, lest in its ignorance it should resist itself" (p. 618).

For Hegel too the mind, as organ of self-knowledge, was essential to the self-realization of Spirit: "World history is the exhibition of spirit striving to attain knowledge of its own nature" (*Reason,* p. 23), or again: "The highest achievement of the spirit . . . is self-knowledge, not only intuitive but rational cognizance of itself" (*Reason,* p. 87).

Juan's, and Shaw's, view of the Life Force was based on the premise that intelligence, self-consciousness, purpose, are superior, in a sense more *real,* than blind chance. Or, as Hegel said: "One ought to have the firm and invincible faith that there is Reason in history and to believe that the world of intelligence and of self-conscious willing is not abandoned to mere chance"; and indeed, the *Lectures on the Philosophy of History* were devoted to demonstrating the reasonableness of just that faith (*Reason,* p. 12).

It is, of course, the Devil who reflects the vision of futility and purposelessness Shaw found in Schopenhauer and Nietzsche: "An epoch is but the swing of the pendulum; and each generation thinks the world is progressing because it is always moving. . . . Where you now see reform, progress, fulfillment of upward tendency, . . . you will see nothing but an infinite comedy of illusion. You will discover the profound truth of the saying . . . that there is nothing new under the sun" (pp. 644–645). Juan replies that he *is* possessed of a purpose beyond his own, which is to help the Life Force to "know itself and its destination." Hegel opened Chapter Four of his *Philosophy of History* with this point: "Change in nature, no matter how infinitely varied it is, shows only a cycle of constant repetition. In nature nothing new happens under the sun, and in this respect the multiform play of her products leads to boredom. . . . Only the changes in the realm of Spirit create the new. This characteristic of Spirit suggested to man a feature entirely different from that of nature —the desire toward perfectibility" (*Reason,* p. 68). As Juan says: "I would think more; therefore I must be more"; and Hegel: "His consciousness makes the individual comprehend himself as a person, . . . hence understanding himself as inherently infinite" (*Reason,* p. 86). Or, put another way: "The essentiality of self-consciousness for existence is part of the . . . dialectic. For how else could each natural thing 'seek' to transcend itself?" And it is only in the human realm that this "striving" emerges in self-consciousness (*Reason,* p. xxvi).

Juan is Shaw's Superman, "the philosophic man: he who seeks in contemplation to discover the inner will of the world, in invention to discover the means of fulfilling that will, and in action to do that will by the so-discovered means" (p. 628). Hegel would have called him one of the "world-historical individuals, . . . who grasp just such a higher universal, make it their own purpose, and realize this purpose in accordance with the higher law of the spirit" (*Reason,* p. 39). The Superman is inspired and driven in his thrust upward by something Shaw called "the moral passion"; Hegel used the term too, where "the term 'passion' [means] the particularity of a character insofar as its individual volitions not only have a particular content but also supply the impelling and actuating force for deeds of universal scope" (*Reason,* p. 30). "It is the same with all great historical individuals: their own particular purposes contain the substantial will of the World Spirit." He says again: "One can indeed apply the term 'passion' to the phenomenon of the great men and can judge them morally by saying that passion has driven them. They were indeed men of passion: they had the passion of their conviction and put their whole character, genius, and energy into it." "But . . . they were not what is commonly called happy, nor did they want to be. They wanted to achieve their aim, and they achieved it by their toil and labor. They succeeded in finding their satisfaction in bringing about their purpose, the universal purpose. With such a grand aim they had the boldness to challenge all the opinions of men" (*Reason,* pp. 40–41). World-historical men are, like Juan, subject to what Hegel called "moral discontent," because "they

contrast things as they are with their ideal of things as they
ought to be" (*Reason,* p. 46)'.

Juan demonstrates his right to the title of world-historical man
when he responds to the Devil's efforts to tempt him with the
happiness of hell, in what is probably the most magnificent speech
in Shaw's most poetic play:

> I tell you that as long as I can conceive something better than myself
> I cannot be easy unless I am striving to bring it into existence or
> clearing the way for it. That is the law of my life. That is the
> working within me of Life's incessant aspiration to higher organiza-
> tion, wider, deeper, intenser, self-consciousness, and clearer self-
> understanding. It was the supremacy of this purpose that reduced
> . . . religion for me to a mere excuse for laziness, since it had set
> up a God who looked at the world and saw that it was good, against
> the instinct in me that looked through my eyes at the world, and
> saw that it could be improved. I tell you that in the pursuit of my
> own pleasure . . . I have never known happiness. [Pp. 641–642]

"Hell," after all, "is the home . . . of the seekers for happiness," and Shaw, like Juan, seeks "no other joy . . . [than] the
work of helping Life in its struggle upward."

It is in the world-historical individual and in the Superman
that we can see most clearly the operation of the dialectic. Juan's
speeches make it evident that in Shaw's system the Superman is
a product of the "fusion in opposition" of nature—the element
of the Life Force that is described as "an irresistible force which
. . . in its ignorance would resist itself"—and the directive self-
consciousness of the philosopher's mind.

For Hegel, too, of course, the movement toward self-consciousness was dialectic: "Actualization in the world does something
to the eternal Idea. Man's spirit, the synthesis of the divine Idea
and Nature, makes the indeterminate reality of the Idea deter-
minate in existence" (*Reason,* p. xvii). The development of
natural organisms "proceeds in an immediate, direct (undialec-
tic), unhindered manner;" Spirit is "dissatisfied" with this,
because "the transition of its potentiality into actuality is medi-
ated through consciousness and will" (*Reason,* p. 69). This

mediation, however, implies opposition and struggle: "Freedom, like Spirit, is dynamic; it progresses dialectically against its own obstacles. It is never given; it must always be fought for. Every slackening of Spirit means falling back into the inertia of Matter, which means the destruction of Freedom: either when men are subject to Matter—as in poverty, sickness, cold, famine—or when they are subject to other men and used by them like things" (*Reason*, p. xxvi). Following that line of thinking, it is hard to see how Hegel could have helped being a socialist; but he wasn't, although he helped father the movement. Shaw, who was, made the absolute opposition between poverty and the fulfillment of the Life Force in man the central doctrine of his political thought.

Shaw too saw an essentially dialectic relationship between spirit and matter, and all his writing about the Life Force is permeated with the sense of struggle between it and blind, material nature, which it seeks to impregnate, and inform, and which without it would destroy itself, would "stumble into death." "This wonderful will of the universe," he says, "struggling and struggling." Elsewhere he speaks of will "having a tremendous struggle with a great whirling mass of matter"; and again: "This tremendous power is continually struggling with what we call external nature and is getting hold of external nature and organizing it."[11]

Although written ten years and more after most of the texts we have been considering, Lilith's speech at the end of *Back to Methuselah* is too pregnant with dialectic implications not to be quoted here. As she looks into the infinite distance of time, sweeping out beyond even that parable of the future, "As Far as Thought Can Reach," she speaks with the voice of the Life Force, imagining the final apotheosis when mankind has passed on "to the goal of redemption from the flesh, to the vortex freed from matter, to the whirlpool in pure intelligence that, when the world began, was a whirlpool in pure force. . . . I brought life into the whirlpool of force, and compelled my enemy, Matter, to obey a living soul. But in enslaving Life's enemy I made him

11. *Religious Speeches,* pp. 34 and 49.

Life's master; for that is the end of all slavery; and now I shall
see the slave set free and the enemy reconciled, the whirlpool
become all life . . . although I know well that when they attain
it they shall become one with me and supersede me" (II, 262).

Hegel, on his part, summed up the operation of the dialectic
in these terms:

Let us . . . repeat here that the first stage is the immersion of
Spirit in natural life, the second its stepping out into the consciousness of its freedom. . . . The third stage is the rising out of this still
particular form of freedom into pure universality of freedom, where
the spiritual essence attains the consciousness and feeling of itself.
. . . Then and only then has Spirit attained its reality. Thus, in
existence, progress appears as an advance from the imperfect to the
more perfect. . . . The imperfect, thus, as the opposite of itself in
itself, is its own antithesis, which on the one hand exists, but, on the
other, is annulled and resolved. It is the urge, the impulse of spiritual
life in itself, to break through the hull of nature, of sensuousness, of
its own self-alienation, and to attain the light of consciousness,
namely, its own self. [*Reason*, pp. 70–71]

Shaw not only viewed political and economic history in Marxian terms, but also saw cultural and literary history as a dialectic
process. His review, in 1897, of Musset's play, *Lorenzaccio,* and
the Preface to *Three Plays by Brieux,* ten years later, include
brief histories of the Romantic Movement and the rise of Nat-
uralism set in clearly dialectic terms.[12] Both are too long to quote,
but their implicit assumptions are reflected in a very Hegelian
passage in the Preface (1898) to the second volume of *Plays:
Pleasant and Unpleasant:* "To distill the quintessential drama
from pre-Raphaelitism, medieval or modern, it must be shewn
at its best in conflict with the first broken, nervous, stumbling
attempts to formulate its own revolt against itself as it develops
into something higher" (III, 111).

Since it is "the identification of the artist's purpose with the

---

12. *Shaw's Dramatic Criticism,* ed. J. F. Matthews (New York: Hill
and Wang, 1959), p. 240; and "Preface" to *Three Plays by Brieux* (New
York: Brentano's, 1913), p. xii ff.

purpose of the universe, which alone makes an artist great,"[13] Shaw saw himself playing an important role in the dialectic evolution of both art and the spirit that it embodied: "When I am not potboiling for myself or others I am being driven by my evolutionary appetite to write these fictions. Even when I have the box office in view . . . evolution keeps creeping in." In true artists, among whom he counts himself, "the Life Force is struggling towards its goal of godhead by incarnating itself in creatures with knowledge and power enough to control nature and circumstances."[14]

Identifying himself with the Life Force, as Shaw did in many more flamboyant assertions than that, was probably not sheer bravado or self-dramatization, but part of his most elemental self-image. In a letter to Ellen Terry he warned: "My capers are part of a bigger design than you think." And in the same letter, in a more pensive mood, he said: "Never stagnate. Life is a constant becoming: all stages lead to the beginning of others"— suggesting as it does how far Hegelian patterns had become a part of his innermost thoughts (*Letters*, I, 722).

In addition to their understanding of the dialectic process by which the Spirit or Life Force realizes itself, one important common view linking Shaw and Hegel is the explicit identification of the ultimate *goal* of this process with God. As Shaw wrote to Tolstoy in 1910: "To me God does not yet exist. . . . The current theory that God already exists in perfection involves the belief that God deliberately created something lower than Himself. . . . To my mind, unless we conceive God as engaged in a continual struggle to surpass himself . . . we are conceiving nothing better than an omnipotent snob" (*Letters*, II, 901). The Life Force, then, is not "god," though it is "often called the Will of God."[15] As we have seen, many of Juan's statements in *Man and Superman* reflect Hegel's idea that the dialectic is to be

13. "Preface" to *Three Plays by Brieux*, p. xxi.
14. "Postscript after 25 Years," to *Back to Methuselah, Plays*, II, xcvi–xcvii.
15. "Parents and Children," *Plays*, IV, 11.

viewed as an eternal process, where each synthesis is simply a stage in the slow evolution from Idea as Potential to Idea as Realized, from pure purpose (similar to the Life Force) to God, where God is equated with absolute reality, absolute self-consciousness. And for Hegel God is not only some abstract goal, He is the *becoming* as well, and becomes himself only in man: "God is God only so far as he knows himself: his self-knowledge is, further, his self-consciousness in man."[16] Hegel's views in this area may be summarized: "Nature and history are necessary stages in the evolution of God into self-consciousness. . . . Without the world, God is not God, he cannot *be* without creating a world, without knowing himself in his 'other.' . . . The Absolute becomes conscious only in evolution, and above all in Man. . . . He is a developing God and becomes fully self-conscious only in the minds of human beings who make explicit the logical-dialectical process."[17]

These ideas are reiterated in a variety of ways in the writings of both men. Shaw repeatedly affirms, as in the Preface to *Androcles:* "The kingdom of God is within us" (V, 382); and Hegel phrases it: "The Kingdom of God . . . is always . . . to be realized and brought about in man" (*Reason,* p. 20). Juan speaks of the fusion of mind and raw force as evolving "higher and higher individuals, the ideal being omnipotent, omniscient, infallible, and withal completely, unilludedly self-conscious: in short, a god" (III, 626). Hegel sees the end of the dialectic of Spirit as "wisdom endowed with infinite power which realizes its own aim, that is, the absolute, rational, final purpose of the world" (*Reason,* p. 15). Shaw the preacher cries out to his congregation: "When you are asked, 'Where is God? Who is God?' stand up and say, 'I am God and here is God, not as yet completed, but still advancing towards completion, just in so much as I am working for the purpose of the universe, working for the

16. *Hegel: Selections,* ed. J. Loewenberg (New York: Scribners, 1957), p. 289.
17. Thilly, *History,* pp. 470–471.

good of the whole of society and the whole world, instead of merely looking after my personal ends.' "[18]

The whole heaven-hell parable of the dream episode in *Man and Superman* is based on an identification of hell as the home of *un*reality, *non*-being, *un*consciousness, while heaven is the place of reality, pure being, and absolute self-consciousness, with earth as the dialectical battleground, in the process of *becoming,* of moving from *non*-being to *being*—which brings us back to Hegel's illustration of the dialectic triad mentioned earlier. In fact the plays, early and late, are rich in Hegelian ideas, but little that Shaw wrote after about 1912, except for his adoption of the term "Creative Evolution" from Bergson, adds significantly to the concepts that were formulated in the works already discussed; and it would be unnecessarily tedious simply to string out more examples here. In refutation, however, of those critics who have claimed that Shaw later became completely disillusioned with his theories of the Life Force and the religion of Creative Evolution, it is perhaps sufficient to cite the "Postscript" that he added to *Back to Methuselah* in 1944: "God . . . is therefore not a Person but an incorporeal Purpose, unable to do anything directly, but mysteriously able to create corporeal organs and agents to accomplish that purpose, which, as far as we can see, is the attainment of infinite wisdom and infinite power. . . . The votary of Creative Evolution goes back to the old and very pregnant lesson that in the beginning was the Thought; and the Thought was with God; and the Thought *was* God. He believes in the thought made flesh as the first step in the main process of Creative Evolution" (II, cii). There could hardly be a more explicit paraphrase of Hegelian thought in a nutshell than this.

Finally, it is worth citing a revealing passage in Shaw's too-often ignored parable, *The Adventures of the Black Girl in Her Search for God* (1932). In this Shavian *Pilgrim's Progress* the author himself appears in the person of a red-bearded Irishman, who is made to say of the deity: "My own belief is that He's not

18. *Religious Speeches,* p. 19.

all that He sets up to be. He's not properly made and finished
yet. There's somethin in us that's dhriven at Him, and somethin
out of us that's dhrivin at Him; . . . we've got to find out [His]
way for [Him] as best we can, you and I."[19] Or, as the Black
Girl, who is often a spokesman for Shaw, says: "To know God
is to be God." And a bit later, speaking for himself in the form
of the "Irishman," Shaw says: "But nothing would ever persuade him that God was anything more solid and satisfactory
than an eternal but as yet unfulfilled purpose, or that it could
ever be fulfilled if the fulfillment were not made reasonably easy
and hopeful by Socialism."

This concluding, and perhaps slightly jarring, assertion may
serve as a reminder that Shaw's thinking was of a piece, that his
social and economic thought was related to his metaphysics, that
while "system" may be too pretentious a word to use to describe
his philosophy, "inconsistent" or "incoherent" are even less appropriate. As we have seen, this body of thought seems to have
taken its form roughly in the decade and a half between hearing
Henry George in 1882 and writing *The Perfect Wagnerite* in
1897, and found its most important expression in the works of
the twenty years between *The Quintessence of Ibsenism* in
1891 and the talks on religion around 1910, although of course
he continued to expound his ideas for the remainder of an extraordinarily productive life.

19. *The Adventures of the Black Girl in Her Search For God* (1933;
rpt. New York: Capricorn, 1959), p. 69.

6 *A Priest of*
Hegelian Mysteries

Hegel is surely one of the most elusive and opaque of philosophers, one who is generally better known by reputation than through first-hand reading. His name and ideas were much in the air during the nineteenth century, but Shaw's uses of both clearly indicate a more detailed understanding than would be provided by what was common knowledge. Shaw's formal education was, as we have seen, anything but sophisticated; and although his record of his early reading reveals a breadth that is certainly precocious, no evidence indicates that it brought him anywhere near Hegel. By the time he joined the Fabians he of course knew the name from his reading of Marx, but the reminiscences of Sydney Olivier, an early colleague in the Society and later a close personal friend, reveal his associates' benign contempt for his attainments in such academic subjects as philosophy: "Needless to say we delighted in Shaw's society—his talk was a continual entertainment; and he regarded it, we tolerantly considered, as his duty to talk wittily, if only for practice. And the transparent generosity and liberality of his character had an irresistible charm. But Webb and I were university graduates, I from Oxford, and we often judged Shaw's education and his appreciation of academically and socially established humanities to be sadly defective."[1] One would gather that Shaw did not

1. Letter from Olivier to Archibald Henderson, quoted by Henderson, p. 212.

discuss the obscurities of Hegel with Olivier. And yet it is entirely
characteristic that, having had his curiosity aroused by Marx,
Shaw should have sought out Hegel's work on his own. This may
in fact be what happened, but even so, Hegel is sufficiently difficult as both thinker and writer to require a guide for anyone
not already initiated into the language and concepts of formal
philosophy.

Shaw had such a guide. In a letter to Archibald Henderson,
who, like Boswell, had decided early in life to become the biographer of one of the giants of his age, Shaw responded with some
asperity to a query about influences on his work. He had, he
acknowledged, "read one book and one play by Strindberg," but
he was much more familiar with "the writings and conversation
of Ernest Belfort Bax, whose essays attacking bourgeois morality
were published here before Strindberg or Nietzsche had been
heard of. Both Stuart Glennie[2] and Belfort Bax were (and are)
Socialists and strenuous opponents of Christianity, basing their
views on a philosophy of history. As I am notoriously a Socialist,
the first authors whose influence might have been traced in my
works by English critics are Stuart Glennie and Bax. But no.
Our critics must run to Strindberg & Nietzsche" (*Letters,* II,
554). No mention is made here of Hegel, and indeed there is a
strong suggestion that domestic rather than Continental influences on his thinking are to be sought. Some months later much
the same complaint was made publicly in the original (1906)
Preface to *Major Barbara*.[3] In what he called "First Aid to
Critics" Shaw offered to clear up certain common confusions
regarding influences on his thinking. He protests again about
critics who, "whenever my view strikes them as being at all outside the range of, say, an ordinary suburban churchwarden,
conclude that I am echoing Schopenhauer, Nietzsche, Ibsen,

2. John Stuart Stuart Glennie, antiquarian, folklorist, historian of
religion (in collaboration with H. T. Buckle), and as deep-dyed a Scot as
his unusual name suggests. See also p. 153.

3. *Plays,* I, 299–339. In several respects, including the passages quoted,
this version differs significantly from the more commonly reprinted revised
version of 1944.

Strindberg, Tolstoy, or some other heresiarch in northern or eastern Europe." The ideas, he acknowledges, may not be wholly original—few men's are; but their geneology is not as simple as some critics think:

> I may and do ask . . . why, if they must give the credit of my plays to a philosopher, they do not give it to an English philosopher? Long before I ever read a word by Schopenhauer, or even knew whether he was a philosopher or a chemist, the Socialist revival of the eighteen-eighties brought me into contact, both literary and personal, with Ernest Belfort Bax, an English Socialist and philosophic essayist, whose handling of modern feminism would provoke romantic protests from Schopenhauer himself, or even Strindberg. . . . Belfort Bax's essays were not confined to the Feminist question. He was a ruthless critic of current morality. [I, 299–303]

As these comments suggest, Belfort Bax was a philosopher, and an admitted influence on Shaw. He was also sufficiently remarkable and important in his own right to have deserved more attention than he has generally received. H. M. Hyndman, founder and driving force of the Social Democratic Federation, in his autobiography speaks of "Belfort Bax—then [1881] as now [1910] the only original philosophic thinker in Great Britain."[4] In a brief biographical study Archibald Robertson affirms that Bax "was a thinker in no way inferior" to "Bradley, ... Schiller, James, Russell and the rest of the leading lights of modern British and American philosophy."[5] Samuel Hobson goes even further by calling Bax "the greatest philosophical mind of his day." And Hobson, who for a time had been on the Fabian "Executive" along with Webb and Shaw, is presumably being objective, for he also calls the aggressively non-Fabian Bax "the soundest judge of Socialist strategy in Great Britain."[6]

4. Henry Mayers Hyndman, *The Record of an Adventurous Life* (New York: Macmillan, 1911), p. 206.

5. Robert Arch (pseud. for Archibald H. M. Robertson), *Ernest Belfort Bax: Thinker and Pioneer* (London: Twentieth Century Press, 1927), p. 5.

6. Samuel Hobson, *Pilgrim to the Left* (New York: Longmans, Green, 1938), pp. 40 and 74.

These tributes are, however, somewhat obscure; and the fact is that Bax gets slight attention in those histories of British philosophy where recognition traditionally constitutes the badge of approval of the academic philosophers. According to Robertson, Bax was ignored by the British intellectual "Establishment" because he was educated in Germany and never held any kind of academic post in England. There, at least, only in belated and posthumous testimonials such as Robertson's, Hobson's, and the *Who Was Who* did Bax finally achieve the recognition and in some measure respect he had so bitterly missed in his life. Shaw characteristically thought the better of him because he was outside the Establishment, and many years later, in 1925, wrote from Aberdeen his regrets at not being able to attend a socialist dinner given in Bax's honor:

You will see by my address that I am too far away to attend in person the celebration of the seventy-somethingth birthday of my old friend and fellow-heretic, Belfort Bax. . . . A disposition to canonize me is already apparent; and if Bax would only write plays about saints instead of treatises on the Roots of Reality, he might share my halo. All respectable political parties nowadays have to keep more or less tame philosophers. The Conservatives boasted of Balfour and the Liberals of Haldane. We Socialists boasted of Bax; but he was not tame. We never knew what he would say next. . . . I cordially wave my glass of water as you drink his health. [Henderson, p. 841]

In his pictures Belfort Bax looks less like a rebel and heretic than the personification of the Mid and Late Victorian, as he called himself in his reminiscences.[7] But he was, as they used to say, a man of parts. In addition to being a philosopher of some importance, if not renown, he was also one of the founders of British socialism, a trained musician and music critic, a foreign newspaper correspondent, and an important historian. Ernest Belfort Bax was born in 1854, two years earlier than Shaw, one of four

7. Ernest Belfort Bax, *Reminiscences and Reflexions of a Mid and Late Victorian* (London: George Allen and Unwin, 1918; rpt. New York: Augustus M. Kelley, 1967).

children of Daniel Bax, descendent of an old Quaker family of Surrey. His early education was, as the family histories say somewhat primly, "private," although later he became barrister-at-law of the Middle Temple. In 1875 he went to Germany to study music theory and composition; but while there he became fascinated by German history and philosophy, and indeed German culture in general. His political consciousness had been awakened by the Franco-Prussian War, and most particularly by its aftermath, the crushing of the Paris Commune of 1871. "Henceforward," he says, "I became convinced that the highest and indeed only true religion for human beings was that which had for its object the devotion to the future social life of Humanity."[8] His initial interest in the individualism of the early Mill, Spencer, and Comte was replaced by clearly socialistic lines of thought, and when he returned to Germany in 1880 as Berlin correspondent for the London *Standard,* he took up the serious study of German philosophy, primarily that of Kant and Hegel, under such significant teacher-philosophers as Eduard von Hartmann.

When Bax returned to England in 1882 he became associated with H. M. Hyndman and William Morris in organizing the socialist movement in England and, as Shaw implied, was recognized as the unofficial philosopher of the Social Democratic Federation. Developing his thesis that politically and metaphysically "the social life of Humanity" constituted the ultimate reality and the only legitimate object of human effort, he wrote *The Religion of Socialism* (1886), *The Ethics of Socialism* (1889), collections of essays on socialism (1891, 1897, 1906, 1912), as well as a history of socialism done with William Morris (1894). In a more narrowly philosophical line, Bax published an edition of Kant's *Prolegomena* (1882), *A Handbook of the History of Philosophy* (1885, and several later editions), *The Problem of Reality* (1893), *The Roots of Reality* (1907), and *The Real, The Rational, and the Alogical* (1920). He was an authority on several major social upheavals that involved strong socialist or communist movements. His first book to be published was *Jean-*

8. Arch, *Bax,* p. 4.

Paul Marat (1878), followed by two more books on the French Revolution, three books on German history—*German Society at the Close of the Middle Ages* (1894), *The Peasants' War in Germany* (1899), and *The Rise and Fall of the Anabaptists* (1903)—and a more general study of *German Culture, Past and Present* (1915). Further contributions to the socialist cause included the editorship, during the 1880s and early 1890s, of at least four well-known socialist journals—*Commonweal,* edited with William Morris, *Justice, To-Day,* and *Time*—as well as being a stalwart as public speaker, debater, roundtable participant, and committee member.

A prolific writer of books highly regarded by many authorities, a man of varied interests, probably very near to being a true genius, Belfort Bax was handicapped by a lifelong, and possibly justified, feeling of alienation from and resentment toward the Establishment as autocratic arbiters of philosophical and historical, as well as political, fashions. In all fairness, though, an opaque and humorless style did little to lighten the burden of obscurity. He was a man who had a great deal to say, not merely in quantity, but with a wisdom that deserved to be heard. As so often happens, pathetically few were there to listen. Shaw was quite right: Bax should have written plays, or used any of the other devices to gain the audience Shaw was far from scorning, instead of writing discourses on the roots of reality. But he had a strong sense of personal dignity, and he could never, like his younger friend, descend to wearing the clown's motley. So it was, in a way, the irreverent Irishman who gave the ideas of the erudite and philosophically much more sophisticated Bax a public voice that he did not find for himself.

As we have seen, Shaw made contact with Hyndman's Democratic Federation—not yet the S.D.F.—some time in 1883, and very probably met Bax, one of its leading lieutenants. The qualities that must have attracted Shaw to this somewhat intimidating figure are evident in his description of his friend's distinctly Shavian fondness for paradox: "Bax would propound some quite undramatic and apparently shabby violation of our commercial law and morality, and not merely defend it with the most disconcerting ingenuity, but actually prove it to be a positive duty that nothing but the certainty of police persecution should prevent every right-minded man from at once doing on principle."[9] Toward the end of 1884 both young men were participants in the Marxist discussion group that later became known as the Hampstead Historic Club, and that had such an important formative influence on the Fabians. Of it, Shaw said: "F. Y. Edgeworth as a Jevonian, and Sidney Webb as a Stuart Millite, fought the Marxian value theory tooth and nail; whilst Belfort Bax and I, in a spirit of transcendent Marxism, held the fort recklessly, and laughed at Mill and Jevons." The controversy raged furiously "until Bax shook the dust of the heath off his boots," and Shaw was himself converted to Jevonian economics.[10] In March 1884, the Socialist monthly *To-Day*, of which Bax was co-editor, began publishing, in serial form, the first of Shaw's novels to reach the public, *The Unsocial Socialist;* and in the course of the year a number of short articles and reviews by Shaw were also published by the journal.

At the same time a lively correspondence seems to have developed between Shaw and Bax, even though they must have been meeting with some frequency. Regrettably, none of Shaw's letters to Bax appears to have survived, but a few long and nearly illegible communications from the latter suggest the content and tone of their friendly arguments.[11] "My Dear Shaw," a letter of May 3, 1884, begins: "Your letter has much moved me—to the extent of answering it by return post." Apparently Shaw had suggested some synthesis of Christianity and Marxism that would

9. "Preface" to *Major Barbara, Plays,* I, 303.

10. "Bluffing the Value Theory," in *Bernard Shaw and Karl Marx: A Symposium,* ed. Richard W. Ellis (New York: Random House, 1930), p. 179.

11. The three letters from Bax to Shaw are temporarily (as of June, 1975) located in Additional MS no. 50510 of the Manuscript Collection of the British Museum. My authorities for saying that none of Shaw's letters to Bax has survived are the Bax family, and Dan Laurence, who knows more about Shaw's correspondence than any man now alive.

"spiritualize" Bax's socialism, to which he replied: "I am sure I shall never recognize that Christianity is anything else than in essence an individualist & anti-socialist system in spite of the ingenuity of your friends the smart parsons [?] who twist certain ambiguous phrases into something they are pleased to think is Socialism, or which bears a remote and superficial resemblance to it." He characterizes the "struggle of Socialism, economic, scientific, religious, ethical, political, against the dead-weight of the old individualist, Christian & bourgeois world," as the "throes of the old world in labor with the new." Shaw, he complains, is getting "maudlin" about Christianity, and he ends by assuring him that "the people who want mock-Christian sauce with their Socialist fare are not the people to do you or us any good." Presumably Shaw argued that outright suppression of widely held beliefs would not be effective, because Bax responds that it *would,* and that one of his primary objects "as a Socialist, is the destruction of dogma. The shortest way I can see to this I take." He acknowledges "the other way may suit" some, that of the "litterateur and polite argumentative 'skeptic,' " but that is not his way. "No, Shaw," he concludes, "I regret to see you still have the bourgeois in your blood. Toasting you a successful purification of your intellectual system." In a letter of September 19, 1884, he is still on the topic, urging Shaw to keep clear in his mind the distinctions between "supernatural religion" and "Socialism, Positivism, Shaw—(or shall we call it) Bernardism, etc." What he calls "theological creeds" that involve a "body of dogma . . . are in their nature anti-social & therefore the death enemies of the true Social religion, viz. Socialism." After responding to a number of Shaw's other points, Bax begins his final argument by observing: "From your last sentence [instance?] you have evidently been reading Von Hartmann," presumably at Bax's own suggestion.

It is frustrating to find that so little of that correspondence has survived, but the fact that Shaw and Bax continued their friendly debate on social, religious, and philosophical subjects, both at public meetings and in private, is apparent from the diaries Shaw began to keep in earnest in 1885.[12] Bax spent considerable time doing research and writing at the British Museum, where Shaw was, in his rare spare moments, getting himself an education. This was, indeed, the heyday of that great and venerable institution, before the pressure for scholarly publication had filled its desks with harried young men, when the silent cavern of its Reading Room became both refuge and intellectual womb for some of the best minds of the nineteenth century. Both Bax and Shaw used it in effect as their personal library and writing room, and they apparently often relaxed from their work by arguing through their ideas with each other.

During the years from 1885 to roughly 1890 Shaw's diaries show meetings with Bax in steadily increasing frequency, at the British Museum, at the Wheatsheaf, the vegetarian restaurant frequented by Shaw, at each other's rooms, at socialist meetings, or just walking and talking. There are times when the repeated entries alluding to Bax give the impression that he sees more of him than almost any other single person—except, of course, Jenny Patterson. "Bax at B. M." "Bax at Wheatsheaf," "talked late with Bax"; sometimes they play duets together, Bax being an accomplished musician; and at other times Bax's presence is obviously intrusive.

The closeness of the friendship is suggested by the role Bax played in furthering Shaw's journalistic career. Shaw had, of course, earned his spurs as polemic essayist in the early Fabian Essays, in the controversy with Wicksteed, and as regular contributor to minor socialist journals; but his introduction to "big time" journalism really began through the agency of his friend William Archer, who in 1885 created an opportunity for Shaw to write some book reviews for the *Pall Mall Gazette*. The next year, again through Archer's good offices, he also was doing art reviews for *The World,* and for the first time since he had left the Dublin real estate office was more or less making his own way financially. Still, the critical pieces were only occasional, and his employment far from regular. In January 1888, Shaw was hired,

12. See Chap. 4 above, n. 9.

on the recommendation of yet another friend, H. W. Massingham, as political writer for a new newspaper, *The Star,* edited by
T. P. O'Connor. It was very soon obvious, from the simple fact
that his pieces did not get printed, that Shaw's socialism, as well
as some strong attacks on government leaders, was incompatible
with O'Connor's rather cautious liberalism. Shaw, who throughout his life was as concerned about his employers' getting their
money's worth as he was rigorous in insisting on his own adequate compensation, resigned as member of the staff, although
he continued to write occasional columns on various subjects.

At the time, Bax was employed as music critic of *The Star,*
and when he went on vacation during August of 1888 he invited
Shaw to act as his replacement. Shaw had had some misgivings
when he began writing art criticism, and later admitted to having
more gall than professional expertise; and his reviews for the *Pall
Mall Gazette* had always been more on social problems, if not
socialism itself, than on the novels in question. But music! He
had grown up with music; it was in his blood. At the very least
he fulfilled his own definition of a good journalist: a "man who
can write a couple of thousand words once a week in such a
manner that everyone will read it for its own sake, whether
specially interested or not in its subject";[13] and at best he "was
one of the few critics of that time who really knew their business."[14] That he should know his business was, characteristically,
only the beginning; and Shaw approached music criticism much
as he did the other convictions that constituted the fabric of
his life:

It is my special merit that I have always seen plainly that . . . a
musical critic, if he is to do any good, must put off the learned com-
mentator and become a propagandist, versed in all the arts that
attract a crowd, and wholly regardless of his personal dignity. I have
propagated my ideas on other subjects at street corners to the music
of a big drum; and I should not hesitate to propagate Wagnerism

13. "H. W. Massingham," Shaw's "Introductory Essay," in *H.W.M.* by
J. J. Massingham (London: Jonathan Cape, 1925), p. 210.
14. "Preface" to *London Music in 1888–89, Prose,* pp. 68–69.

there with a harmonium if I were sufficiently master of that instrument or if the subject were one which lent itself to such treatment.[15]

On the less noisy but more noticeable platform of a weekly column Shaw propagandized not only for Wagner, but more broadly for greater integrity of performance, respect for quality in both musicians and composers, and against cultural snobblishness and provincialism, and he probably had a real impact on English musical tastes during the last decade of the nineteenth century.

When Belfort Bax returned to *The Star,* Shaw stayed on as a kind of second string critic; and when Bax resigned in early 1889 in order to devote himself to his writing, his recommendation that Shaw be given his full-time appointment was warmly received by O'Connor, who really liked Shaw in spite of his aggressive unconventionality. Bax had written his column under the pen name "Musigena," and it was in searching for a suitable replacement that Shaw came up with Corno di Bassetto, "as it sounded like a foreign title, and nobody knew what a corno di bassetto was. . . . If I had ever heard a note of it in 1888 I should not have selected it for a character which I intended to be sparkling. The devil himself could not make a basset horn sparkle."[16] Appropriately or not, Shaw sparkled under the name until mid-1890, when O'Connor sold *The Star,* and Shaw moved to *The World,* where he wrote weekly music reviews as G.B.S. until 1894.

The novel situation of having a regular income from the music column made Shaw less dependent on his occasional criticism of art and fiction. This gave him no regrets, for the efforts of a senior editor to insert "puffs" for personal friends into Shaw's reviews of art shows had led him to resign that post in 1889, and the amount of time he required to "read up" on the subject of a book to be reviewed led the *Pall Mall Gazette* unobtrusively to stop sending him items. But the loss was neither Shaw's nor ours. It was as a music critic that Shaw really came into his own,

15. Quoted in R. F. Rattray, *Bernard Shaw: A Chronicle* (Luton, Eng.: The Leagrave Press, 1951), p. 76.
16. "Preface" to *London Music, Prose,* p. 68.

emerging from the comparative obscurity of socialist meetings and societies and journals, cracking the tough shell of the city he had come to conquer a dozen years before, not socially—he never really achieved that, nor aspired to—but intellectually, as a mind. It meant that *The Quintessence of Ibsenism* was taken seriously when it appeared in 1891, and that when his first play appeared two years after that, he was already a very well known, not to say notorious, figure for whom music criticism, drama criticism, and drama itself, were simply different facets of an incredibly active, bewilderingly voluble, and intellectually abrasive but stimulating personality that had become known as G.B.S.

Belfort Bax, however, may have done Shaw an even more significant service than introducing him to the world of London's professional journalism, into which he must surely have gravitated in any case. When their friendship appears, from the number of entries in Shaw's diaries, to have been at its warmest, Bax asked his friend to read and make comments on his *Handbook of the History of Philosophy,* which had originally appeared in 1885, and which he was revising for a second edition. Shaw noted that he began reading Bax's "History of Philosophy" in December 1886, and he made frequent entries in the diary for 1887 indicating that he was pursuing his study whenever he had a free evening, which was not often, not finishing the book until August.

It is a pity that Shaw was not more communicative in his diary, or communicative about different kinds of things. For the biographer it offers a moderately complete account—although with many lapses and penitent efforts at catching up on several weeks at a time—of his coming and goings, meetings both scheduled and casual, whom he talked with at the British Museum or argued with at the Fabian or romanced with in the evening, but scarcely a word about what was said or what he read or what he thought. For the student of Shaw's ideas it offers a barren exercise in frustration, rich in hypotheses and suppositions and void in statements of belief or even opinion. Since he rarely mentioned what he was reading, although he must have been reading heavily, both professionally and for his own education, the fact that he named Bax's *Handbook* so frequently seems to suggest that it was of particular importance or interest to him. And indeed that may well have been the case, not only because of Bax's friendship, or because his ideas were in many respects unusually congenial, but because this probably represented Shaw's introduction, apart from some early reading in John Stuart Mill and Herbert Spencer, to the work of formal philosophy. Certainly his writing before this time had been almost devoid of references to major thinkers other than those specifically social or economic in their concerns; and in the years following we can find increasing evidence of an awareness of the main currents of European philosophy, particularly that represented by Kant, Hegel, Schopenhauer, Feuerbach, and, later, Nietzsche.

Shaw was, in this matter, too proud to be much of a name dropper and consistently minimized rather than exaggerated his debts to other thinkers. Although he had really never had any pretensions, he was moved to confess, in the 1905 letter to Archibald Henderson, that he felt himself "rather an imposter as a pundit in the philosophies of Schopenhauer and Nietzsche." He went on to ascribe more direct influence to Stuart Glennie and Belfort Bax, although in fact the former's only significant contribution had been the notion that, as Shaw put it, Christianity was a "slave morality." Glennie had also articulated another concept that was central to Shaw's approach to the "drama of ideas": "It is the philosophy, the outlook on life, that changes, not the craft of the playwright, . . . and that is why, as Stuart-Glennie has pointed out, there can be no new drama without a new philosophy."[17] But the materials out of which Shaw fashioned his "new philosophy" came, as much as they came from any single or identifiable source, from Belfort Bax, and a debt to Bax was in fact a debt to Hegel.

The Handbook of the History of Philosophy, which Shaw was reading with great interest during the first half of 1887, was not, in spite of its title and its inclusion in the popular "Bohn's Philosophical Library" series, the usual outline summary of the history

17. "Preface" to *Three Plays for Puritans, Plays,* III, lvi–lvii.

of Western philosophy. Bax was a philosopher himself, and in spite of apparently conscientious efforts at objectivity, the book is heavily slanted. Of course, covering such a tremendous body of material in roughly four hundred pages presented insuperable difficulties, and Bax solved them by discussing with some sophistication of detail works or ideas in which he took a particular interest, or found especially offensive, and ignored aspects of a man's ideas that a more conscientiously complete history might have mentioned. This method could not help but give a highly personal focus to the material. Bax was himself a thoroughgoing Hegelian, having been associated in Germany with men who had done as much as any to extend and develop many of Hegel's central concepts. Although Bax, along with his teachers, disagreed with the master on several basic points, he explicitly considered Hegel the last major step forward in the evolution of Western philosophy, its most complete manifestation to date, and devoted more space in his book to him than to any philosopher except Kant. For Bax the history of philosophy effectively came to an end with Hegel; and although he acknowledged the gradual disintegration of the "Hegelian school" and its influence after Hegel's death in 1831, far from seeing that development as a reflection on either the achievement of the philosopher or the vitality of his philosophy, he treated it as an inevitable manifestation of the dialectic principle at work.

Given the strong bias of both the *History of Philosophy* and of Bax's own thinking, it would be curious if some of the Hegelianism had not rubbed off on Shaw. "Rubbed off," however, is hardly an adequate term, because what in fact happened seems to have been much more essential. Probably Bax's most important contribution was that he had achieved by 1887 what Shaw was still seeking: a thorough and consistent and satisfying basis for the integration of the metaphysical, the religious, and the social dimensions of belief. Social theories and activities were for Bax manifestations in the political sphere of his basically Hegelian metaphysics. The ultimate synthesis that Shaw reached was in many respects very different from Bax's; but the debt he owed

Bax for both form and content went to the very heart of his "religion of the Twentieth Century."

In all probability Bax is the medium through which various ideas having their origin with Hegel reached Shaw, but it is unnecessary to spell out their philosophies in detail or to identify precisely what Shaw owed to each. The important material lies in the rather large area of common ideas. On the other hand, Shaw evidently read in Hegel and in von Hartmann as well as in Bax, and our understanding of Shaw's philosophy may be sharpened if we make some effort to discriminate between ideas that appear to be derived from Hegel and from Hegel *cum* Bax.

If a distinction is made, then Bax's share of the influence is characteristically the social orientation, the secular religion. And it is not hard to find, especially in his earlier books, many statements of ideas that would have been particularly congenial to Shaw. Although Bax, like Shaw, was often accused by those who did not know him of being cold and impersonal and rather "cerebral," his instincts were above all humanitarian. In *Outlooks From The New Standpoint,* he reduced morality to two propositions: "(1) Every act necessarily involving cruelty is *per se* immoral; (2) No act not necessarily involving cruelty is *per se* immoral"; and his social views generally were reared on that foundation.[18] Capitalism, because "the absolute despotism of economic interests and economic processes reduces life itself to an impossibility for some, to an absurdity for all," he found inherently cruel, and believed it would remain so because it perpetuated a view of life in which competitive success was the highest ideal of which man was capable.[19] And since capitalism was by its nature an immoral institution, Bax dedicated himself to the extirpation of its two main props: private property and the individualistic ethic.

The assumption that "the end of man's being is social rather than personal"[20] implies that personal virtue is no longer the

18. Ernest Belfort Bax, *Outlooks from the New Standpoint,* 2d ed. (London: Swan Sonnenschein, 1893), p. 111.

19. Ibid., p. 140.

20. Ernest Belfort Bax, *A Handbook of the History of Philosophy,* 3d ed., revised (London: George Bell, 1904), p. 143.

ultimate criterion, that the highest morality is social rather than private. From this perspective, the ideal of freedom is no longer individual self-fulfillment, but the well-being of the community, which as Bax observed is not necessarily the same thing as the average "happiness" of its constituents. The only true freedom, he believed, is the freedom from want which was, paradoxically, to be found in the "freedom from property" of communism: "Liberty is associated inseparably with property—but no longer with *private* property"; the liberty of all requires that property be held by all.[21]

Like Shaw, Bax was convinced that freedom from deprivation and the satisfaction of physical needs are a precondition of a sound community: "Freedom, which implies the satisfaction of existent want for each and for all—first and foremost the animal wants the introspectivist disdains—is the first condition of that higher social life which is the farthest *visible* summit of progress."[22] A preoccupation with satisfying individual wants "fills the mental horizon of the immense majority of human beings. . . . These conditions [are] unfavorable to the development of a higher life, be it moral, intellectual, artistic," or social.[23]

By a similar logic, Bax shared with Shaw a contempt for the morality of individualism, whether it takes the form of an obsession with personal goodness and salvation, a glorification of self-denial and asceticism, or the dedication to duty or patriotism or philanthropy or any of the other ideals with which men dull their awareness of their true commitments.[24] Self-sacrifice might seem patently a social virtue, but for Bax what he calls "the New Ethic of Socialism . . . grudges the amount of energy required to be expended by the individual in his effort to acquire . . . 'self-discipline.' . . . It despises the introspectionist's love of striking ethical attitudes. The mere discomfort or the sacrifice of

21. Bax, *Outlooks*, p. 81.
22. Bax, *Handbook*, pp. 402–403.
23. Ernest Belfort Bax, *The Ethics of Socialism*, 3d ed. (London: Swan Sonnenschein, 1893), pp. 141–142.
24. Ibid., p. 4 ff.

the individual per se is for it no virtue, but a folly, unless it be part of the means to a *clearly defined* social end."[25] It follows that Bax, like Shaw, would scoff at the "old bourgeois morality . . . according to which individual good men make healthy social conditions, rather than acknowledging the truth that it is healthy social conditions which make good men."[26]

At the farthest reaches of his speculations about the triumph of public over private values, Bax suggested that the ultimate *telos,* or object, of the social ethic would be its absorption of the individual ethic and will and finally intelligence into a kind of "corporate" consciousness.[27] This concept was, he acknowledged regretfully, considerably further "than thought can reach"; and, in the present imperfect stage of human development he found in socialism the best mechanism available for moving society in that direction. He called it the "religion" of socialism because, he claimed, even most Christians instinctively felt that "the old ethical statement has exhausted itself, and is passing over into its opposite, although its *form* may still remain intact. The ethical *telos* is now vaguely or clearly felt to be no longer self-renunciation or self-glorification . . . but the . . . identification of self with humanity."[28] Traditional ethics and religions, he pointed out, look for regeneration from within, but "the religion of modern Socialism, on the contrary, looks for regeneration . . . from material conditions and a higher social life. The ethic and religion of Socialism seek not the ideal society through the ideal individual, but conversely, the ideal individual through the ideal society."[29]

As communism was to provide the "social synthesis," so the religious synthesis lay in the "religion of humanity," which preached the fulfillment of all mankind, rather than merely the "blessed," "not in a hypothetical world to come, but in this

25. Ibid., p. 21.
26. Ernest Belfort Bax, *The Religion of Socialism,* 4th ed. (London: Swan Sonnenschein, 1896), p. x.
27. Bax, *Ethics,* p. 30 ff.
28. Ibid., p. 27.
29. Ibid., p. 19.

world here and now, as the only worthy object of our common endeavor."[30] But when Bax spoke of the absorption of the individual ethic into the social ethic, he did not mean to imply the individual's loss of identity or capacity to will; it was simply that at his best, what man willed for himself was in fact for the good of all. He clearly imagined man, or society, as reaching this stage of communal identity through an evolutionary process in which each new level of development incorporated what was most necessary or "true" from the half-truths of earlier stages. After a discussion of history in terms of a dialectic that is more Hegelian than Marxian, in spite of its social orientation, Bax says: "The essential truth at the basis of primitive Communism will be preserved. The essential truth at the basis of modern Individualism will be preserved . . . in . . . the synthesis of human solidarity and human freedom . . . in Socialism." At that point, he goes on: "The first cycle of human development will be complete. That further contradictions [may] show themselves on another plane, of the nature of which we can at present have no possible conception, is no concern of ours."[31]

In making socialism the finest flower of the dialectic process Bax seems to stand closer to Marx than to Hegel, who made the Prussian state of his own day the consummation of social evolution. Bax defended his master by pointing out that all Hegel had done was to describe a historical fact in a way flattering to his political patrons. Hegel, he says, clearly implied that contemporary Prussia represented merely a stage in the continuing operation of the dialectic in human history. Bax, coming later in time, had a broader view of history and could see what he believed to be the next development, the movement from the imperialist-capitalist stage to socialism. But unlike Marx, and like Shaw, Bax insisted that socialism was not itself the final goal, and indeed that the articulation of such a goal was beyond the capacity of the human mind. He wrote, in terms suggestive of the Life Force, of an evolving will or power manifesting itself in human

30. Quoted in Arch, *Bax,* p. 24.
31. Bax, *Outlooks,* p. 89.

history, and said that "the end of progress is the actualization of the immanent purpose of the world." He acknowledged the circularity of such a definition, but argued that when we try to pin down "this *telos* as absolute finality" we discover that "finality in this sense—a being in which there is no becoming, a form with no material content—involves an abstraction, and therefore no longer possesses the conditions of a real synthesis."[32]

This essentially open-ended conception of the "immanent purpose of the world" and its materialization in history runs all through Bax's writing. In *The Ethics of Socialism* he says: "Below and beyond all actuality, reality or finitude of things is presupposed the infinite potentiality, the Eternal Becoming"; and he defines "the good" as "essentially a process of eternal Becoming which is never complete."[33] Shaw clearly found the concept congenial and thought of the dynamics of the Life Force in terms of an "eternal becoming." When, speaking of the "higher and higher organization" by which "man must become superman, and super-superman, and so on," he asks, "What is to be the end of it all?" he answers his own question: "There need be no end. There is no reason why the process should ever stop."[34]

Bax followed Hegel's lead in considering the dialectic not only as a way of describing man's social history, but also as a principle operating at the most basic levels of the physical and metaphysical universe. The range of its applicability is suggested in his essay "The Practical Significance of Philosophy." In it Bax characterizes "human development" as a "self-contained and highly involved synthesis, and as such, its salient category is 'action and reaction.'" The obscurity of this is somewhat lightened when he outlines "the practical importance of philosophy in general research. Firstly, it indicates the method to which all reality conforms, and which is its highest formula. The presentation of the dialectic of any plane of knowledge is the most comprehensive ex-

32. Bax, *Handbook,* pp. 400–401.
33. Bax, *Ethics,* pp. 214 and 216.
34. *The Religious Speeches of Bernard Shaw,* ed. Warren S. Smith (University Park, Pa.: The Pennsylvania State University Press, 1963), pp. 35 and 39.

pression of its law, its supreme explanation. This method again shows us that the most developed category is that of reciprocity, or action and reaction, rather than cause and effect, and that in the last resort all reality turns upon this category."[35] This is pure Hegelianism; but according to Bax he was more rigorous and consistent than his teacher in his application of these principles, particularly to the question of the relationship between the rational and the irrational.

Since Shaw repeatedly affirmed in his writing his intellectual and artistic debt to the works of John Bunyan, his curiosity must have been especially piqued when Bax, early in his discussion of Hegel in *The History of Philosophy,* called *The Phenomenology of Mind* a "philosophical *Pilgrim's Progress.*"[36] Bax presumably used the allusion to suggest the tortuous path "the natural consciousness takes in its progress towards true knowledge," as it passes through successive "stages of self-purification" from error on its way to "a knowledge of that which it is in itself." Man's progress to the Holy City of self-knowledge, he implies, lies through trials of contradiction and opposition, Vanity Fair and the Valley of the Shadow of Death; but the dialectic pattern is clearer in Bax's more explicit analysis:

The task of the "Phenomenology" is thus to show the progress of knowledge from its lowest to its highest stage; each stage is in its turn shown to involve a contradiction, which necessitates progress to a higher stage. At each of these stages the immediate certitude or truth of the stage is proved to be illusory, to involve a self-deception. This is corrected in the following stage, the certitude is . . . in its turn to be subjected to the same process, until all these stages are seen to be inadequate in themselves.[37]

35. Bax, *Outlooks,* p. 192. See also Northrop Frye's essay, "Old and New Comedy," *Shakespeare Survey,* 22 (1969), 1–5, in which he discusses Shaw's abandoning structures based on cause and effect for those following a movement of action and reaction.

36. Bax, *Handbook,* p. 317. See also Jerome Whalen, "Some Structural Similarities in John Bunyan's *The Pilgrim's Progress* and Selected Narrative and Dramatic Works of George Bernard Shaw," unpublished doctoral dissertation, University of Pittsburgh, 1968.

37. Bax, *Handbook,* p. 318.

This dialectic "pilgrim's progress" applies equally to the individual mind or to "the world-mind, as exhibited on the plane of History." In ordinary usage the operation of the mind here described might be called "reason"; but for Hegel the term applies on the cosmic scale as well: "Reason . . . is Infinite Power. . . . Reason is the *substance* of the Universe; . . . it is the Infinite Energy of the Universe. . . . While it is exclusively its own basis of existence, and absolute final aim, it is also the energizing power realising this aim; developing it not only in the phenomena of the natural, but also of the Spiritual Universe—the History of the World."[38]

This account of the Hegelian "reason," which subsumes both power and material, both goal and impulse, sounds rather like Shaw's Life Force, although as we have seen he would not have accorded such apparent primacy to reason. Neither, however, would Bax—and it is on just this point that he differed most basically and most vehemently from Hegel. "To Hegel," Bax complained, "thought was ultimate, the 'I' itself was merely a form of thought, and, as such, he was bound to reduce the alogical to terms of the logical."[39] As Robertson explains it:

Bax's philosophical writings are, from beginning to end, a protest against the Hegelian conception of the power behind the world as just *thought*. Bax adheres to the doctrine that the world consists of nothing else but manifestations of the same power which, in ourselves, is conscious. But he asks: "Does not consciousness presuppose *that which becomes* conscious?" . . . Consciousness . . . is an attribute, not a substance. There can be no attribute without substance, no form without matter, no thought without something for thought to arise in.[40]

Bax affirms the primacy of Being, "that which thinks"; and, since it "precedes" thought, it is essentially nonrational, or as he terms it, alogical. In dialectic terms it would be the thesis; but, Bax insists, both the Being and the thought, its antithesis, both

38. Ibid., p. 331.
39. Bax, *Outlooks*, p. 184.
40. Arch, *Bax*, p. 6.

the irrational and the rational, survive in the ultimate synthesis we call "reality."[41] This notion of a sustained tension between mutually exclusive yet mutually dependent elements or forces is characteristic of Bax's reading of the dialectic theory: "We must frankly admit then that Being can never be finally absorbed in Knowledge, can never be completely reduced to rationality, although Being apart from Knowledge is as unreal an abstraction as Knowledge apart from Being." Later in the same essay Bax restated the idea: "We may trace . . . in the dialectic process which at once interpenetrates and embraces all reality, a double alogical element underlying the logical."[42]

The distinction made here was of great importance to Bax, for he considered his insistence on the primacy and continued necessary involvement of the alogical in the dialectic to be his personal improvement on the Hegelian model, although as he put it, he was simply being more consistent in applying Hegel's logic than Hegel himself. It is also a distinction that defines one of the significant ways in which Shaw differed from Hegel in his handling of the dialectic principle. Don Juan, in the midst of Shaw's most explicit exposition of Hegelian thought, says: "I had . . . never consciously taken a single step until my reason had examined and approved it. I had come to believe that I was a purely rational creature: . . . I said, with the foolish philosopher, 'I think, therefore I am.' It was Woman who taught me to say 'I am; therefore I think'" (*Plays*, III, 631). It may indeed have been Woman, but the furiously antifeminist Bax must have writhed under the jibe.

In giving primacy to irrational or alogical Being, Bax is making a historical and metaphysical statement, not a value judgment. He views both mankind and the "world-mind" as evolving toward greater and greater rational powers, and greater and greater self-consciousness; and this movement he defines as "good." But the irrational dimension, he is saying, will never be completely "evolved out" of the system: "Mere blind *being* ever

41. Bax, *Outlooks*, p. 187.
42. Ibid., pp. 184 and 190.

recedes before thought, chance before law, impulse before delib-
eration"; but the being, the chance, and the alogical never disappear. Never is a long time, and Bax justified using the word by
arguing that the irrational will always be a necessary part of the
tension that in a sense keeps the dialectic going: "The strictly
dynamical element in the real is always incapable of comprehension under logical forms—it is infinite." He was in effect applying
to the realm of ideas the principle of infinite progression he had
elsewhere applied to the evolution of human history: "The notion of finality in philosophy must be given up. Philosophy must
be no longer regarded, as Hegel regarded it, as a closed circle,
but rather an an endless spiral—a progressive conception of becoming, it is true, more and more adequate to its content, but
never furnishing a solution of the world problem in a formula
valid for all time."[43]

The disagreement with Hegel is once again important here
mainly because Shaw appears to have followed Bax's lead, as
the Shavian "tentativeness" discussed in the next chapter will, I
think, demonstrate. There were, moreover, several other points at
which Shaw was inclined to subscribe to Bax's formulation of a
principle that differs, or seems to differ, from Hegel's. Hegel, for
instance, has little to say about, and according to Bax explicitly
denies, the principle of biological as distinct from metaphysical or
social evolution. Bax called this "one of the most unfortunate
blunders into which Hegel could possibly have fallen," and went
to great pains to demonstrate that, on the contrary, biological
evolution was entirely consistent with Hegel's own statements and
was in fact the manifestation of the dialectic in the world of
physical nature.[44] This particular line of argument made it possible for Shaw to go much further than Hegel, or even Bax, in
identifying biological evolution with the essential principles or
"logic" of the universe—to synthesize, as it were, Hegelian and
Lamarckian concepts, and hence to anticipate Henri Bergson's
"Creative Evolution" by well over a decade.

43. Ibid., pp. 183 and 194–195.
44. Bax, *Handbook*, pp. 327–328.

Finally, there is the enigma that has puzzled the apologists for all theologies that, in offering essentially optimistic views of human destiny, have posited a benevolent deity: the problem of evil and suffering. Shaw, in a variety of contexts, but most explicitly in a talk given at the City Temple in 1906, pointed out the dilemma of the nineteenth-century intellectual, faced on the one hand by "the terrible cruelty in the world, which rather confirmed the idea that the force at the back of things was wicked and cruel," and at the same time "intellectually unable to get away from the conception of God the Designer. . . . There must be what they called God, and yet they could not make him responsible for the good in the world without making him also responsible for the evil, because they never questioned one thing about him: that, being the designer of the universe, he must be necessarily omnipotent." But if we could scrap our notions of perfection and omniscience and omnipotence and conceive instead of "a great purpose, a great will, . . . a force behind the universe . . . working up through imperfection and mistake to a perfect, organized being, . . . we get rid of the old contradiction, we begin to perceive that the evil of the world is a thing that will finally be evolved out of the world."[45]

Bax confronted the problem in a significantly similar way, stating the question as characteristically posed by the atheist: "Granting . . . the existence of your Supreme Being, the mere fact of the presence of evil, misery and pain in the world is incompatible with the moral attributes, if we use the word 'moral' in any intelligible sense, of the Creator and Orderer of such a world. . . . No amount of specious confidence-trick assurances of mysterious 'divine purposes' behind it will divest it of its character as evil." His biographer summarized Bax's response to the challenge in language that is distinctly Shavian: "Once . . . we drop the ascription of personality to the Absolute, and postulate only a 'Life Force,' persistently tending to self-realization in finite personalities, the existence of evil ceases to be a metaphysical prob-

45. *Religious Speeches*, pp. 12–13 and 17–19.

lem at all."[46] In a discussion of the evolution of human society Bax uses his own characteristic terminology: " 'Evil' . . . is necessarily absorbed through the pressure of the Dialectic or Logic of Reality."[47]

On the basis of the evidence, it is difficult to believe that Belfort Bax did not play an important role in transmitting to Shaw Hegel's ideas about the creative dialectic of an evolving world will. Archibald Robertson put it much more strongly: "The high-and-dry Hegelianism which was enthroned in 1885 . . . fell to pieces in the ensuing twenty years. Of this movement Bax was the unacknowledged forerunner. His theory was given to the public in 1885—before Bergson's 'élan vital' and before Mr. Shaw's Life Force appeared on the scene. But I have never yet seen a history of modern philosophy in which honour is given where honour is due."[48] Let us by all means rectify the oversight with due honor and recognition, at least for his impact on Shaw. Particularly in his modifications of "high and dry Hegelianism," Bax seems to have had a significant influence on his friend's formulation of his theories of the Life Force and Creative Evolution, as well as on his socialism. Shaw's careful reading of *The Handbook of a History of Philosophy* is a verifiable fact, and it is at least very probable that in those long conversations at the British Museum and the Wheatsheaf Vegetarian Restaurant and at each other's rooms, Shaw worked through with Bax points in the book that particularly puzzled or interested him. And he evidently read on his own, with Bax's encouragement, in the work of Hegel and the neo-Hegelian, von Hartmann.

Hegelian thought provided a model and method of thinking and a way of seeing reality that, coming at just the time in his development that it did, served some very useful functions for Shaw. It served as a structure or framework into which he could fit, and with which he could relate, all the many new ideas that in this period were suddenly moving into his ken. It offered a way

46. Arch, *Bax,* pp. 7–8.
47. Bax, *Ethics,* p. 219.
48. Arch, *Bax,* p. 8.

to organize and make sense out of the materialistic determinism and class dialectic of Marx, the teleology of Butler, the faith in human perfectibility of Shelley and Mill, and the mystical World Will of Schopenhauer. It permitted and indeed thrived on negation and contradiction and inconsistency, which both flattered his instinctive iconoclasm and made room for a pluralism that appealed to his distrust of dogmatism. It offered an ameliorative evolution in which, as far as human society was concerned, he very much wanted to believe. And it gave him a role, as "the instrument of some purpose in the universe which is a high purpose," that satisfied his desire to be used, and made him important, as a "world-historical" individual, not just to London or Ireland, but to mankind.

7 The Dialectic of Dogmatism and Doubt

We should no longer be shocked by the spectacle of a self-assured Shaw affirming some principle or fact, having elsewhere maintained with equal confidence a position that appears its complete opposite. In a world of relative truths, inconsistency can be intellectually honest—as well as a way of attracting attention. As we have seen, Shaw was not in the least shy about inconsistencies, ranging from wild, blatant contradictions to the subtler nuances of the unstated paradox, where one element of the contradiction is left to the imagination. Or sometimes he turned a conventionally accepted platitude upside down in such a way that the inversion is suddenly recognized to be truer than the truism.

Jack Tanner has been accused of being nothing more than a mouthpiece for Shaw because his "Maxims for Revolutionists," attached to *Man and Superman,* is filled with characteristically Shavian paradoxes. Often the particular effect depends on an implied conventional judgment or platitude, which we are invited to inspect a little more closely: "Charity is the most mischievous sort of pruriency." "The conversion of the savage to Christianity is the conversion of Christianity to savagery." "If you injure your neighbor, better not do it by halves." "Do not give your children moral and religious instruction unless you are quite sure they will not take it too seriously. Better be the mother of Henri Quatre and Nell Gwynne than of Robespierre and Queen Mary Tudor" (*Plays,* III, 733–743).

In the Preface to *Major Barbara,* Shaw defines himself in terms
of a contradiction: "Here am I, for instance, by class a respectable man, by common sense a hater of waste and disorder, by intellectual constitution legally minded to the verge of pedantry,
and by temperament apprehensive . . . to the limit of old-maid-
ishness; yet I am, and have always been, and shall now always
be, a revolutionary writer." He explains the apparent contradiction by a series of paradoxes, "because our laws make law impossible; our liberties destroy all freedom," in which the contrast
between the *principles* of disinterested law and true freedom and
the *facts* of licentiousness and laws protecting special interests is
presumably too obvious to require explicit statement. There follows another proposition, offered with the same air of self-evident-
ness, but in fact depending on the whole structure of socialist economic thought for its rationalization: "Our property is organized
robbery." The series ends with a group of statements that are not
so much paradoxes as affirmations of the incongruities arising
from the gross dislocations created by our political and economic
system: "Our morality is impudent hypocrisy; our wisdom is
administered by inexperienced . . . dupes, our power wielded
by . . . weaklings, and our honor false in all its points" (I, 336).
Shavian paradoxes, in their various forms, were not mere topsy-
turveydom; they had as a common element the yoking together
of implicit or explicit contradictions with the purpose of forcing
the mind to move, if not toward something as absolute as Truth,
at least toward seeing things more clearly. The pleasurable shock
of mere inversion, of the platitude slipping on the banana peel, is
fused with the shock of recognition; through the instrumentality
of wit the artist has, hopefully, "created new mind."

Shaw was from the beginning notorious for his delight in
paradox. Sydney Olivier described his first meeting with Shaw in
1884 in a letter in which he spoke of sitting up late one night
"talking on all manner of subjects with Webb and a man named
Shaw, a very clever and amusing man, who defends the most
atrocious paradoxes with much ability."[1] Belfort Bax, rather

1. Sydney Olivier, *Letters and Selected Writings* (London: George
Allen and Unwin, 1948), p. 64.

significantly, had a good deal to say about paradox in general and Shaw's use of it in particular in his *Reminiscences and Reflections of a Mid and Late Victorian.* He felt, for reasons that suggest at least a touch of professional jealousy, that Shaw overdid it, although he put it graciously enough: "Shaw undoubtedly has the signal merit of having stimulated the mind of the English-speaking peoples to independent thought and Socratic question-ing, but it is doubtful whether the backwash of his influence has not tended to promote a craving for paradoxical fare intellectually . . . which has destroyed all taste intellectually for plain state-ment of fact, not wearing the garb of paradox."[2] In this connec-tion, Bax told a revealing and rather touching anecdote regarding Shaw. A mutual friend, J. L. Joynes, coeditor with Bax of the journal *To-Day,* had remarked to Bax that he would not under any circumstances want Shaw as a companion on a proposed journey. Bax, for reasons of his own, repeated this to Shaw, who responded: "I can't reciprocate the sentiment, for I think Joynes would suit me very well as a travelling companion; but I know what he meant: I dare say I should be always trying to say smart things, and this after a time might tend to become boresome."[3]

But the use of paradox for Shaw was not just another way of saying "smart things"; it was a rhetorical strategy designed first to startle the reader into alertness and then to force him into thought. A typical Shaw formula is to offer us a sequence of con-tradictions that keeps us jumping mentally if we are to stay with him: "Mammon, always mighty, put the Church in his pocket; . . . but Mammon overreached himself when he tried to impose his doctrine of inalienable property on the Church under the guise of indissoluble marriage. For the Church tried to shelter this inhuman doctrine and flat contradiction of the gospel by claiming, and rightly claiming, that marriage is a sacrament. So it is; but that is exactly what makes divorce a duty when the mar-riage has lost the inward and spiritual grace of which the mar-

2. Ernest Belfort Bax, *Reminiscences and Reflexions of a Mid and Late Victorian* (London: George Allen and Unwin, 1918; rpt. New York: Augustus M. Kelley, 1967), p. 262.

3. Ibid., p. 166.

riage ceremony is the outward and visible sign."[4] If we are not exhausted by trying to follow the rapid alternation of implied attitudes toward the Church, we come away not only understanding something of his attitude toward marriage, but also with an enlarged awareness of the sense in which Shaw saw the Church as perennially wrong for the right reasons and right for the wrong ones.

That the elements of shock and surprised illumination should contribute to the humor of his writing obviously served Shaw's larger purpose of bringing himself and his ideas to the public attention; but it came naturally, the comic viewpoint being part of his way of looking at the world. Shaw suggested the role of the comic vision in what he called "a general law of the evolution of ideas. 'Every jest is an earnest in the womb of time' says Peter Keegan in John Bull's Other Island. . . . All very serious revolutionary propositions began as huge jokes. Otherwise they would be stamped out by the lynching of their first exponents" (*Q.Ib.*, pp. 665–666).

The humor, one might suppose, like evil, is gradually evolved out, and only the quintessential truth remains—except that within the framework of the mortal and contingent there is no such thing as quintessential truth. So perhaps, in the end, as Tarleton says in *Misalliance*, "Paradoxes are the only truths." In other words, the paradox is not simply a source of humor, or a way of thinking and writing about the world, although it is both of these; but its value as a source of humor and as a way of writing about the world lies in the fact that it reflects the movement of the essential processes of the World Will, Mind, and the Life Force. A paradox is not a truth; it is only on the way to a truth.

Eric Bentley, in his brilliant book, says that Shaw saw life as "the interaction of opposites";[5] but it would be a mistake to suppose the result of such interaction to be merely mediation or balance. Shaw was clearly fascinated by the phenomenon of con-

4. "Preface" to *Getting Married, Plays*, IV, 383–384.
5. Eric Bentley, *Bernard Shaw* (New York: New Directions, 1957), p. 180.

tradiction and antithesis per se, and often the tension generated by such opposition was represented as the source of vitality. It was most probably William Blake's strong sense of a reality made up of elemental antinomies that led Shaw to identify him as one of those "whose peculiar sense of the world I recognize as more or less akin to my own" (III, 507). From his several allusions, it is evident that he found "The Marriage of Heaven and Hell" most congenial, and there are echoes of this and other poems celebrating the "union of contraries" scattered through Shaw's work. A Blakean inversion of labels is explicit in his comments on his diabolonian figure in *The Devil's Disciple* (III, xlix–l), and implicit in the maxims of "The Revolutionist's Handbook," certainly modeled on and at times echoing Blake's "Proverbs of Hell."[6]

When Dick Dudgeon claims the Devil as his "natural master," Shaw, like Blake, is associating the domain of piety and Heaven with emotional sterility, moral prudery, and a cold, dehumanized rationality, while Hell is identified with energy and exuberance and freedom. But when Blake sets up his "Contraries": "Attraction and Repulsion, Reason and Energy, Love and Hate," he appears to treat Reason and Hate simply as obstacles to freedom, negations for energy to struggle against in order that it *be* energy.[7] For Shaw, on the other hand, as for Hegel, the significant consideration is not merely the contradiction, but that each element in the opposition contributes directly to the "new" truth. Furthermore, in the Shavian dialectic the synthesis of what Hegel had called the opposing "moments" is itself incomplete, unstable, being only "more true" than its earlier stage, and hence providing a new thrust, and new thesis, that will eventually result in a

6. For many additional direct and indirect parallels, see Irving Fiske, *Bernard Shaw's Debt to William Blake* (London: The Shaw Society, 1951). Intellectual influences are developed at some length by J. L. Wisenthal in his important book, *The Marriage of Contraries* (Cambridge, Mass.: Harvard University Press, 1974), especially pp. 83–86.

7. "The Argument," *The Marriage of Heaven and Hell* (Plate 3), *The Complete Writings of William Blake,* ed. Geoffrey Keynes (London: The Nonesuch Press, 1957), p. 149.

still "higher" truth. As Shaw said himself, "Truth is not a mean between extremes but quite the most extreme thing I know of."[8]

When Shaw set up the paradoxes "our laws make law impossible; our liberties destroy all freedom," he was not implying that the ideal resolution lay somewhere in the middle, but was suggesting a dialectic sequence based on a hierarchy of "truth." Our liberty, licentiousness, lack of restraint, creates or makes necessary the antithesis of freedom: mechanical, external laws. Only through the negation of this external law in "true" law, that is inner and self-created law, will the higher synthesis of law and true freedom be achieved.

This sense of development through opposition, the heart of the dialectic, although only implicit here, was explicit in many of Shaw's most characteristic paradoxes. As he said in *The Quintessence of Ibsenism:* "The way to Communism lies through the most resolute and uncompromising Individualism" (p. 639); or at the end of *Major Barbara:* "The way of life lies through the factory of death, . . . through the raising of hell to heaven and of man to God" (I, 445). These, like many of the "Maxims for Revolutionists" and similar Shavian utterances, only appear to be paradoxes from the perspective of our imperfect vision; but the movement is from less perfect to more perfect truth. Pra, himself a prophet with imperfect vision, ends *The Simpleton of the Unexpected Isles:* "I . . . must continue to strive for more knowledge and more power, though the new knowledge always contradicts the old, and the new power is the destruction of the fools who misuse it. . . . All hail, then, the life to come!" (VI, 611). Or, as the Black Girl says, filled with the wisdom of her *Adventures:* "Only the truth of number is eternal, . . . every other truth passes away or becomes error, like the fancies of our childhood."[9]

As all this suggests, the paradox is very closely tied to the principle of the dialectic and could reasonably be called its most

8. *London Music in 1888–89* (London: Constable, 1937), p. 228.
9. *The Adventures of the Black Girl in Her Search for God* (New York: Dodd, Mead, 1933; rpt. New York: Capricorn, 1959), p. 60.

natural form of verbal representation. Hegel described the synthesis reached when the mind tries to grasp and reconcile two
logically antithetical concepts and is forced by the effort to a new
level of truth and understanding. So too the paradox, by yoking
together contradictions—more often in the real than in the logical
world—forces the mind that would understand it to a new level
of awareness. Of course, they are not the same: the paradox
tends to be more particular and limited, to put more emphasis on
the element of mutual exclusiveness, the "either / or," rather than
on the synthesis, the "neither / nor but both / and." Perhaps it
would not be farfetched to call the paradox the first derivative of
the dialectic, marking, as it were, the "instantaneous rate of
change," the dialectic caught, frozen for our contemplation,
amusement, and stimulation.

Although the paradox may well reveal dynamic alternatives to
rigidity, in itself it is essentially static, a verbal formulation that is
in effect self-contained. The dialectic, on the other hand, is inherently dramatic, and it is certainly no accident that Hegel
liberally sprinkles his philosophic discussions with illustrations
from drama, mostly classical. The very essence of drama is conflict, not simply between individuals, but also between principles
or social forces or moral values, though these are often represented
by individuals. And in the resolution of the conflict of opposites,
however tentative it may be, a new order or relationship, what
Northrop Frye characterizes as a "new society," is created. This
resolution is rarely, except perhaps in farce, simply a return to
the *status quo ante bellum;* nor, except in melodrama, does the
conflict issue in a simplistic "victory" of one element over the
other. The dialectic denouement in much of dramatic literature is
neither so one-sided nor so naive; the new society, the new stage
of awareness in some ways includes the most essential or most
dynamic elements of the conflicting forces, but transcends both.
But this resolution may itself, either explicitly or as something we
know in our hearts, be incomplete and unstable and temporary,
one we can well imagine falling apart into new conflict after we
have left the theater.

Even beyond the explicitly dramatic uses of the dialectic principle, it appears to underlie and provide the common ground for seemingly disparate elements in Shaw's thought. The relationship of his socialism to capitalism and Marxism, for instance, was neither one of simple evolutionary replacement nor one of compromise, but that of a genuine synthesis. Just as Marx had described capitalism as the dialectic consequence of feudalism and the economics of the industrial revolution, and communism itself as the final synthesis of the historical process, so Shaw treated Marxism as the antithetical moment created *by* capitalism, destroying capitalism, with Fabian socialism as the new synthesis, containing elements of both the capitalist-parliamentary tradition and the Marxist revolution, yet transcending both. But even Fabianism was only another new stage, a jumping-off place for further dialectic growth.

Similarly, the relationship between idealism and realism, as Shaw conceived them, can be described in dialectic terms without straining any definitions. His "pioneer" with eyes in the back of his head (*Q.Ib.*, p. 545), who invokes ideals of duty and virtue and patriotism to defend the status quo and his own welfare, also possesses a respect for the past and its traditions, for orderly procedures of law and government, which becomes vicious only when it is perverted by self-interest into the form without the substance. So too the farseeing pioneer, the one with the eyes in the front of his head, who can face reality and who seeks to find a goal in the future, may trip fatally on hard facts, or be destroyed by "the vital force that drives men to throw away their lives and those of others in the pursuit of an imaginative impulse. . . . The shallowness of the ideals of men ignorant of history is their destruction" (*Q.Ib.*, pp. 534–535). The synthesis is the artist, who creates new mind, new self-consciousness, new understanding, especially in the sense of a new awareness of the relationship among the future and the present and the past. Shaw himself, particularly the writer of the plays, is the synthesis of idealist and realist.

Finally, Shaw set up a fundamentally dialectic antithesis between mysticism and reason. The dialectic was observable in two ways: in history, where the rationalism of the eighteenth and nineteenth centuries was seen as a reaction against the mysticism of earlier Christianity, and "in process of time the age of reason had to go its way after the age of faith" (*Q.Ib.*, p. 551); and secondly as inherent in the opposition between the first principles each school of thought conceived as ruling the world, a mystical, ineffable will on the one hand, and on the other reason, with its seat in the human mind. Enough has been said already about Shaw's thinking to demonstrate the sense in which much of his writing was, as he told Archer, "a protest against . . . the dread of the Will and the blind faith in the intellect" (*Letters*, I, 317). For Shaw the will was not, as he claimed it was for Schopenhauer, "the very devil"; it was the vital and creative energy of the Life Force. Reason was the opposite and negation of will, and yet had to be created by will to bring the will to an understanding of itself and of the best way of fulfilling itself. The synthesis of will and reason, of mysticism and rationalism, is the religion of Creative Evolution. And both the synthesis and the religion are part of a continuing, ongoing process, for "the notion that inspiration is something that happened thousands of years ago, and was then finished and done with, never to occur again . . . is as silly as it is blasphemous. He who does not believe that revelation is continuous does not believe in revelation at all, however familiar his parrot's tongue and pewsleepy ear may be with the word. There comes a time when the formula 'Also sprach Zarathustra' succeeds to the formula 'Thus saith the Lord' " (*Q.Ib.*, pp. 688–689). And because the age of reason goes the way of the age of faith, and Nietzsche goes the way of the Nazarene, "the result is that we all believe that our religion is on its last legs, whereas the truth is that it is not yet born, though the age walks visibly pregnant with it."[10] And Shaw sincerely hoped that he might be one of its midwives.

The dialectic, then, is an operation, a continuing process, a constant becoming, a principle that is at once dynamic and un-

10. "Preface" to *Getting Married, Plays*, IV, 369.

changing. The incompleteness of God and man and society, all in a condition of dynamic, but for that very reason not unobstructed, evolution toward better forms lies behind almost everything Shaw has to say on social, religious, and metaphysical subjects—and also lies behind his plays. Many of the characteristic qualities of the plays, as we shall see in the following chapters, their lack of finality, the sense of an incomplete or not entirely satisfactory resolution, the frequent suggestion of a new dynamic set in motion, derive in part from their dialectic structure and movement. The dialectic process, as has been said, is fundamentally dramatic; it both requires and creates opposition and tension.

In a way, the basic paradox of the dialectic principle is that, while it resolves the tension of a *particular* thesis-antithesis relationship, the synthesis creates a new opposition, and new tension, and hence tension per se becomes a permanent feature of the process—at least until the final or "Absolute Idea" of Hegel is reached. The tension of being unresolved lies behind the vitality and energy necessary to produce and continue the changes basic to Creative Evolution. As Shaw told Stephen Winsten: "Once things are permitted to settle into a definite system then they cease to be open to the inspiration of the Life Force."[11] In the Preface to *Saint Joan* he affirmed the principle, in fact making it the title of one of the sections: "The Law of Change is the Law of God." Immediately preceding that section he reports having received a letter from a priest who recognized the play as dramatizing the conflict between the laws of the institutionalized State, those of the institutionalized Church, and private inspiration. The priest continues: "To me it is not the victory of any one of them over the others that will bring peace and the Reign of the Saints in the Kingdom of God, but their fruitful interaction in a costly but noble state of tension." "The Pope himself," Shaw observed, "could not put it better; nor can I. We must accept the tension, and maintain it nobly without letting ourselves be tempted to relieve it by burning the thread" (II, 298–299). And "as the law

11. S. Winsten, *Days with Bernard Shaw* (London: Hutchinson, n.d.), p. 55.

of God . . . is the law of evolution," resistance to change, rigidity, habit, are all in opposition to God, are a kind of death.

We are all making a pilgrim's progress along the endless road to the Heavenly City, and no stage until the final unthinkable one is or can be without error and imperfection. But the fact that Shaw equated evil with error, with well-intentioned divine bumbling, the consequences of God's "incompleteness," and hence saw it as something that would ultimately be evolved out of the universe as the dialectic of the Life Force approached its final realization, would seem to suggest that evil is simply a passive force. Critics have suggested, in a variety of ways, that Shaw really had no sense of evil;[12] and it is true that basically he was a philosophical optimist. He had complete faith, in the *long* run, in the Life Force. But that faith by no means included man as such: "Nature holds no brief for the human experiment: it must stand or fall by its results. If Man will not serve, Nature will try another experiment" (II, xvii–xviii). The Life Force has higher ends than mere human welfare, and man's survival depends on the extent to which he makes his ends coincident with rather than antithetical to hers. And so in the short run, man has no assurance of permanence, and within the limited human dimension the conflict between the power of life and that of death can be understood as Manichean. The forces of evil are real, they destroy, and they may triumph, as the ending of *Heartbreak House* acknowledges. For Shaw evil may have been the outgrowth of God's mistakes, or his incompleteness, or associated with the Matter that Lilith says is the Life Force's enemy, but it was not conceived as mere absence of force. It is a substantive and real obstacle, capable of blocking and, in the human realm, of defeating the Life Force. And it takes many forms: the power of the status quo, inflexibility, incapacity for new ideas, cruelty, idleness and unearned income (in the economic sphere)—in a word, intellectual and moral as well as social inertia.

But if evil for Shaw was very real as a force and as a threat to

12. William Irvine, *The Universe of G.B.S.* (New York: McGraw-Hill, 1949), p. 71.

humanity, there is still not much sense in his writings of the *mystery* of evil, and certainly no sense of the diabolist vision that sees the basic principle of the universe as evil and malevolent. Shaw's sense of mystery was reserved for life and its dynamic principle in all its varied manifestations. He might not, being mortally blind, know or understand the good; but he knew the Tempter, in all his guises of happiness, morality, duty—one hesitates to say pride, because the common view of Shaw is that he had yielded himself body and soul to that particular sin. That is not so; and one of the greatest paradoxes of that most paradoxical man is that the Great Egotist was also very humble.

Using the model of Hegel's archetypal illustration of the dialectic principle—being/non-being = becoming—it might be possible to set up a grammatically different but logically analogous epistemological triad: I know/I know nothing = I am learning. Or the same idea could be put into a slightly different triad: absolute dogmatism/absolute doubt (or skepticism) = tentativeness.

In his own day and since, Shaw has widely been accused of being dogmatic and doctrinaire in the extreme, of being incapable of admitting error and intolerant of disagreement. And there have been those, including Ellen Terry and observers of considerably greater intellectual pretensions than she, who have found him without "any real convictions." The truth here, as Shaw insisted, is not simply some mean between extremes. Tentativeness does not mean indecisiveness, nor mere contradiction of anything affirmed by someone else—although in Shaw it sometimes took the appearance of both. It includes *both* dogmatism and absence of conviction. A paradox, a genuine synthesis, "tentativeness" was for Shaw a philosophical principle growing out of his view of the world and the religion of the Life Force. Nor had it anything in common with agnosticism, for which Shaw had undisguised contempt as mere intellectual laziness: putting ignorance on a pedestal, worshiping it, and thereby evading the responsibility to think. That ignorance is a real and necessary aspect of our incompleteness justifies neither our embracing nor our forgetting the fact. Indeed, Shaw's much publicized war with science was based largely on what he felt was inadequate humility before its own limitations: "Science becomes dangerous only when it imagines that it has reached its goal. What is wrong with priests and popes is that instead of being apostles and saints, they are nothing but empirics who say 'I know' instead of 'I am learning,' and pray for credulity and inertia as wise men pray for scepticism and activity." What is needed is "faith that the unknown is greater than the known and is only the As Yet Unknown, and resolution to find a manly highway to it" (I, 77). Until man has achieved omniscience, that is, has become God, or until God is realized and completed in man, truth can only be partial, and what Shaw called "our vain lust for truth" is the worst sort of self-deluding idealism.

Absolutes, and the perfection and completeness they imply, are being evolved toward, not deduced from. All our certitudes are disproved sooner or later, Shaw said, and that was really the point behind his sometimes misunderstood observations in his toast to Albert Einstein in 1930: "Religion is always right. . . . Religion gives us certainty, stability, peace. It gives us absolutes which we so long for. It protects us against that progress which we all dread almost more than anything else. Science is the very opposite of that. Science is always wrong."[13] Even though he expounded his "religion of the twentieth century" fervently and frequently, he could acknowledge: "I do not present my creed of Creative Evolution as anything more than another provisional hypothesis";[14] and again: "We must have a hypothesis as a frame of reference before we can reason; and Creative Evolution, though the best we can devize so far, is basically as hypothetical and provisional as any of the creeds."[15] It represented an advance over "the old Dublin brimstone creed solely in its greater credibility:

13. *The Religious Speeches of Bernard Shaw*, ed. Warren S. Smith (University Park, Pa.: The Pennsylvania State University Press, 1963), p. 83. Archibald Henderson, for one, was confused and upset by the speech; see Henderson, p. 767.
14. "Preface" to *On the Rocks, Plays*, V, 506.
15. "Postscript" to *Back to Methuselah, Plays*, II, cv.

that is, its more exact conformity to the facts alleged by our scientific workers"; but it must not be forgotten that "all the provisional hypotheses may be illusions."[16]

The only unchanging law, then, is "the law of change," because "progress is impossible without change; and those who cannot change their minds cannot change anything. Creeds, articles, and institutes of religious faith ossify our brains and make change impossible."[17] But we can legitimately ask if this means *any* change? Mere random motion, like that of the man lost in the jungle, would most probably carry us in a circle, not toward anything.

The synthesis of the paralyzed inaction of fundamental uncertainty and the impulsive action of practical desperation is tentativeness, which in action takes the form of trial and error. For Shaw the "truth," tentative though it always is, is pragmatic, "that which works," although it must "work" for all mankind and not the interests of some special group. And since what works can be determined, not a priori, but by experiment, trial and error becomes a basic principle of human life. There can be no mistaking Shaw on this point. In one of his early talks on religion, in 1907, he says: "We know that in all the progress we make we proceed by way of trial and error and experiment. Now conceive of the force behind the universe as . . . working up through imperfection and mistake to a perfect, organized being, having the power of fulfilling its highest purposes."[18]

In the Preface to *Misalliance* (1910) Shaw enunciates what he calls the "dogma of Toleration": "The deeper ground for Toleration is the nature of creation, which, as we now know, proceeds by evolution. Evolution finds its way by experiment; and this finding of the way varies according to the stage of development reached, from the blindest groping along the line of least resistance to conscious intellectual speculation, with its routine of

16. "Preface" to *On the Rocks, Plays*, V, 506.
17. *Everybody's Political What's What?* (London: Constable, 1944), p. 330.
18. *Religious Speeches*, pp. 18–19.

hypothesis and verification" (IV, 44). Much later, in *Everybody's Political What's What* (1944), he is even more explicit: "The Creator, . . . the Word (properly the Thought), . . . the *Elan Vital*, the Divine Spark, the Life Force, . . . (call it what you will) is not infallible: it proceeds by trial and error; and its errors are called the Problem of Evil. It is not omnipotent: . . . and can act only through its creations. Its creations are not omniscient: they proceed by guesses."[19] The process, however, does not apply merely to the cosmic and evolutionary plane, for "all moral triumphs, like mechanical triumphs, are reached by trial and error" (*IWG*, p. 459).

All communities must live finally by their ethical values: that is, by their genuine virtues. Living virtuously is an art that can be learnt only by living in full responsibility for our own actions; and as the process is one of trial and error even when seeking the guidance of others' experience, society must, whether it likes it or not, put up with a certain burden of individual error. The man who has never made a mistake will never make anything; and the man who has never done any harm will never do any good.[20]

With a consistency he is not always allowed by his critics, Shaw applied the principle to himself. On the grounds that they both were "the servants and instruments of God," Shaw compared himself to Saint Bernard of Clairvaux. He found some similarities and many contrasts: perhaps the greatest being "the tremendous difference that he conceived God as omnipotent, omniscient, all-righteous and infallible, whereas it is plain to me that creative evolution proceeds by trial and error, which should perhaps be called trial and failure. . . . The advantage of my version of the situation . . . is that there is no danger of my imagining that because I regard myself as an instrument of creative evolution I must therefore be right in my way of doing its work. As it works by trial and error, so must I."[21]

19. *What's What?*, p. 232.
20. "Imprisonment," from *Doctor's Delusions, Crude Criminology, Sham Education, Prose*, p. 919.
21. *What's What?*, pp. 327–328.

Since an inability to entertain doubts or new and strange ideas or to admit error are antithetical to the spirit of trial and error, a certain kind of openmindedness is essential. In spite of a reputation for being dogmatic and unyielding, Shaw insisted that he was not. Early in his playwriting career he wrote to his fellow dramatist, Henry Arthur Jones: "I believe you will see as I go on that the conception of me as a doctrinaire . . . is a wrong one. . . . Life only realises itself by functioning energetically in all directions; . . . my passion, like that of all artists, is for efficiency, which means intensity of life and breadth and variety of experience" (*Letters,* I, 462–463). At the end of his career he said: "When critics and biographers try to classify me as an author I smile. I fit none of their pigeon-holes." He felt constrained to add wryly, that for all that "we cannot do without pigeon-holes." He could call his plays "petty tentatives"; and when he admiringly quotes Ibsen, "I belong to no party: I have within me both Right and Left,"[22] we may recognize that although the intended application to himself could not be literally true, we should also recognize, and I think respect, his effort to tell us that his obvious party affiliations were neither doctrinaire nor self-delusionary.

But how can we reconcile these claims of openmindedness and inclusion of "both Right and Left" with the apparently open and sometimes aggressive dogmatism of so many of Shaw's utterances? For those who were deeply offended by his blunt and seemingly arrogant assertiveness no explanation short of depravity or megalomania would suffice. Shaw was very much aware that openmindedness is only a means to an end, to allow the winds of the Life Force to blow freely through the human spirit; but as an end in itself openmindedness runs the risk of paralysis, undermining the foundation for the actions which make possible the "continual becoming" and the "functioning energetically in all directions" that give life vitality and meaning. He was conscious of the paradox, and in *The Perfect Wagnerite* he acknowledged that, while in the sphere of thought alone "anarchism is an inevitable

22. Ibid., pp. 192 and 162.

condition of progressive evolution," in the practical world of man as political and social animal, "anarchy must always reduce itself speedily to absurdity."[23] The resolution of the paradox—insofar as it has any resolution—is suggested in the Preface to *Androcles and the Lion:* "The open mind never acts: when we have done our utmost to arrive at a reasonable conclusion, we still, when we can reason and investigate no more, must close our minds *for the moment* with a snap, and act dogmatically on our conclusions. The man who waits to make an entirely reasonable will dies intestate. . . . The rule of the negative man who has no convictions means in practice the rule of the positive mob" (V, 421; the italics are mine)'.

In order to escape the anarchy and inactivity of the undecided mind we must, on the basis of the best available evidence, make an affirmation and act *as if* the hypothesis were true. Our ignorance leaves us no alternative. In 1897, Shaw wrote Ellen Terry: "In this world you must know *all* the points of view, and take One, and stick to it. In taking your side, don't trouble about its being the right side—north is no righter or wronger than south— but be sure that it is really yours, and then back it for all you are worth. And never stagnate. Life is a constant becoming: all stages lead to the beginning of others" (*Letters,* I, 722). In this case, at least, Shaw cannot be accused of not heeding his own advice.

Few things aroused Shaw's ire as quickly as what he took to be complacent or self-assured dogmatism. "As an Irish Protestant, I raise the cry of No Popery with hereditary zest. We are overrun with Popes. . . . There are scores of thousands of human insects groping through our darkness by the feeble phosphorescence of their own tails, yet ready at a moment's notice to reveal the will of God on every possible subject."[24] Teachers are the worst offenders in this respect, and "no future education authority, unless it is as badly educated as our present ones, will imagine that it has any final and eternal truths to inculcate: it can only select the

23. *The Perfect Wagnerite* (New York: Brentano's, 1909), p. 79.
24. "Parents and Children," prefaced to *Misalliance, Plays,* IV, 46–47.

most useful working hypotheses."[25] It might be supposed that
Shaw is simply happily damning all dogmatism but his own—
except that there is a very basic difference. If we can believe the
sincerity of statements stretching from references to the evolutional nature of truth and perfection in the *Fabian Essays* of
1889[26] through more explicit development in *The Quintessence of
Ibsenism* and in countless later writings, Shaw was constantly
aware, and was trying his best to make his reader aware, of the
tentative nature of his truth that was never final, never complete,
never true, no matter how dogmatically uttered. Eric Bentley
observes that "Shaw utters half-truths, . . . because he would
never presume to think he could utter The Whole Truth";[27] and
it needs to be added that he keeps reminding us of the fact. But
why the contradiction, why the tone and attitude of dogmatism
joined with the insistence on its incompleteness as truth?

The "half-truth" is basic to the paradox; it is the "truth" of
incomplete man in an incomplete world; it is a way of describing
a stage in the dialectic of Creative Evolution; it is on its *way* to
becoming a full truth. Using the language of the dialectic, the
thesis is the present truth, the truth that is taken for granted;
but revelation is continuous, "the new knowledge always contradicts the old," present truth "passes away or becomes error";
and the passing away of old truth and the birth of new is harsh
and painful. Men do not recognize it or accept it. And so the
contradiction of the old truth must be shouted, must be insisted on
aggressively, not because it is true, but because it is, hopefully,
more true, and because it is resisted. Only when the moral or
spiritual force—or possibly simply the volume—of the new equals
that of the old can mind be freed of its congenial bonds, can
change take place, can mind or spirit or Life Force move one small
step nearer realization and away from untruth.

The philosophical need—it may have been psychological too,

25. "Preface" to *On the Rocks, Plays*, V, 506.
26. *Fabian Essays in Socialism*, ed. G. Bernard Shaw (London: 1889;
rpt. New York: Doubleday, n.d.), p. 223.
27. Bentley, *Shaw*, p. 73.

but that is not my concern here—for insistent and aggressive assertion by an essentially shy man doubtless encouraged Shaw to create his "mask"—the showy, self-assertive and self-confident G.B.S., the clown, the boaster, the dogmatist.

But when Shaw "created" a brazen G.B.S., reality itself was modified. As he himself later admitted, he became more and more "like" the supposed mask. Perhaps in a loose sense what was happening was a dialectic process: the mask was not so much some ill-defined "non-Shaw" as a kind of "anti-Shaw," in some respects a negation of the original Shaw, with a synthesis, continuing elements from each, creating something new—a different "real" Shaw. It is not at all fanciful, I think, to see Shaw's various masks —which changed as he did—as an integral part of a "trial and error" process, as a series of experiments in a developing and growing personality, a tentative way of trying to define his personality in terms of a quasi-fictional "other."

The She-Ancient, near the end of *Back to Methuselah,* tells the group of half-comprehending youngsters: "You use a glass mirror to see your face: you use works of art to see your soul" (II, 250). In the course of his life Shaw created a work of art— farcical, at times profoundly comic, more than merely touched by tragedy: Bernard Shaw. And we, as audiences and readers of plays and biographies, only occasionally catch glimpses behind the set, the characters, the acts and scenes he so carefully arranged. What we see is doubtless only a half-truth; but in questioning it, contradicting it, prodding it with such probes as the dialectic, we may move a little closer to an awareness of its reality.

In his plays too, or rather in creating the characters for them, Shaw created a series of masks, which often bore much the same ambivalent and even antithetical relationship to the "real" Shaw as did his clownish or Mephistophelian social masks. He once told Archibald Henderson, "All my characters are 'Shaws.' But to say that they are all self-portraits is silly. It is what every bad critic said forty years ago. You must not let yourself be overwhelmed by my style" (Henderson, p. 718). Shaw made this observation in response to the charge that his characters are mere mechanical marionettes, responding jerkily to pulled strings, mouths flapping mindlessly while we listen to the single ventriloquist speaking all voices. Henderson in his biography repeats and amplifies this vision of Shaw as "puppetmaster" (pp. 717–723); but as a criticism this overstates the case. Plays by their nature are artificial; and all dramatic characters move and speak at the command of their creator. And suspension of disbelief is not the same thing at all as believing. Obviously, dramatic characters and the actions they engage in are, in terms of our everyday world, one-sided, distorted, and incomplete; and the distortion depends on the nature of the reality the playwright is exploring and seeks to body forth on the stage. For Shaw the central reality, the force that lay behind, and was the expression of, man's slow movement upward, was thought—not reason alone, but mind as agent of the Life Force. His avowed purpose, as we have seen, was to bring mind and thought into the theater—that is, to create something that did not exist.

Dramatic truth and dramatic reality are necessarily partial and incomplete, both because of the nature of the medium and the limitations, conscious or not, of the artist's image of reality. Hence the "truth" of the theater must be tentative; it is an "as if" world, its tentativeness only partially compensated for by the "as if" provided by theatrical conventions, the dramatic hypotheses and assumptions out of which the playwright proceeds to build his own imaginative world. This hypothetical and tentative reality of the play world is a little like Shaw's advice to Ellen Terry: to know all points of view, but to take one that is really yours, and stick to it.

But the incomplete, "as if," hypothetical reality of the theater is not simply a refinement or special case of extratheatrical reality; it is actually a negation of, in the sense of being entirely *other* than, the reality of what we loosely call "the real world." The locations, the characters, even the emotions ("What's he to Hecuba or Hecuba to him?") are inherently false—and without the falsity it would not be a "play." The reality of the play is an "other" in which "we can see our own souls," in which the "real" world creates a negation of itself that it may understand itself. In a different context, the relationship is not unlike Hegel's idea that "without the world God is not God, he cannot be without creating a world, without knowing himself in his other."[28] Perhaps it was this idea that was in Shaw's mind when he said that "what produces all these . . . poems and scriptures of one sort or another is the struggle of Life to become divinely conscious of itself."[29] Just as God, in the process of creating his "other" in the antithetical medium of matter, and incarnating Himself in it, knows Himself better and hence evolves into something higher, moves toward His ultimate realization, so man, in creating a kind of negative reality in the antithetical medium of art and fiction, by incarnating himself in "plays," may become more self-conscious, self-knowing, "lifting life to a higher state of awareness."[30]

The relationship between the "reality" we begin with and its "other," the reality we create, is essentially dialectic: both are inherently incomplete and partial truths, but their dynamic reaction and synthesis results, one hopes, in a "more true" understanding. Shaw's way of putting it was to say that art alone "is of one sex only," whereas the "vital art," the truer reality, is the result of a "cross between art and life."[31]

Some critics, reading the comments of the She-Ancient on art, conclude that Shaw believed art to be merely a consoling make-believe, a substitute for those who cannot face reality. This was, of course, his own criticism of the contemporary theater; but neither in *Methuselah* nor elsewhere does this represent his opinion of his own art. It is true that in the final fulfillment of the Life Force, as metaphorically represented in the Ancients, self-consciousness is already complete and art unnecessary; but at any earlier stage of human incompleteness art is an essential means of

28. Frank Thilly, *History of Philosophy* (New York: Holt, 1914; rpt. 1945), p. 470; the italics are mine.

29. "Epistle Dedicatory" to *Man and Superman, Plays,* III, 500.

30. See C. E. M. Joad's penetrating essay, "Shaw's Philosophy," in *G.B.S. 90,* ed. S. Winsten (New York: Dodd, Mead, 1946); the quotation is from pp. 85–86.

31. Quoted in Bentley, *Shaw,* p. 230.

growth toward understanding, not—at least if by Shaw—a substitute or a distraction.

The goals that Shaw considered of first importance, whether
the immediate one of socialism or the broader vision of advancing
the self-consciousness of the Life Force, were the ends for which
his fictions, both "G.B.S." and the plays, were the means. He
eschewed "great art," not out of anything that could reasonably
be called modesty, but because he believed that all genuine art, all
vital art, is written to confront current problems—as a way of
"playing with" and understanding and perhaps changing present
reality. When he said that "all great Art and Literature is propa-
ganda," he meant that it is and should be a public act with
public consequences.[32] But Shaw was also very much aware that
the causes to which he gave himself so completely, which gave
him his sense of reality and satisfied his need for "continual *becoming,* with a goal in front and not behind"—the Fabianism and
the religion of Creative Evolution, even Man, as presently constituted—were all transient, would all be superseded. Our institutions, our intellectual formulations, our art, even our aspirations
are by their natures incomplete and partial.

Tentativeness, then, was not for Shaw simply an escape from
thought, or even from conviction; it was no rationalization of intellectual laziness—although for someone else it might well have
been. It was, along with the dialectics of Creative Evolution, of
which it was a corollary, the common ground on which Shaw's
thought, life, political activity, and art all came together.

To say that Shaw's drama was at the service of the principle of
tentativeness makes it sound rather bland; but the tensions among
the alternative possibilities are dynamic, and lead to some of the
most characteristic features of the plays. For example, the conflict
in a Shaw play, as we have seen, is rarely between clear-cut good
and evil, at least as conventionally defined, but rather between
antithetical "goods"—in other words, a paradox. But as often is
the case with Shavian paradoxes, the two conflicting elements are
"good" only in terms of very different systems of values. Usually

32. "Preface" to *On the Rocks, Plays,* V, 510.

one of the "goods" turns out to be an illusion created and required by the ideals of a rigid, complacent, self-serving, or insecure society. The unthinking pursuit of this false good produces in some more farsighted individual a violent antithetical reaction, taking the form of an impulse, often not articulated, to destroy the false good and replace it with a truer. In other words, the conflict, and hence the dramatic tension, is between that which helps to move the Life Force upward on its way and the idleness or complacency or drifting that oppose and frustrate it.

The recognition, however, that the same drive or stimulus that at one stage of human evolution advances the Life Force might at a later stage prove an obstacle or counterforce, contributed to another characteristic feature of Shavian drama: the conflict and tension of a play are often not resolved, or they lead to a new tension, or to a resolution that is at best only tentative. As should be evident from what has been said already, Shaw considered uncertainty and irresolution philosophically and intellectually necessary, just as action, even though based on provisional or incomplete knowledge, is practically necessary. Only death is certain and final; and certainty and finality are a kind of intellectual and spiritual death.

By the same token, it is often the most self-assured characters in the plays who are drifting, with no sense of purpose, no desire to reach, for there is no need to reach, and nothing to reach for. And drifting too is death. As Captain Shotover says, in the end the science that counts is "navigation. Learn it and live; or leave it and be damned" (I, 594). The uncertain ones seek a way and are at least trying to steer.

Shaw wanted more than anything else to be a navigator, for himself and for his species. Successful navigation, he knew, lay as much in a need to get someplace as in the skill to find a way. And this was the need of Shaw's life: to find that passion that would give life purpose and meaning. He believed that he had found this sense of purpose, of being used, and hence of reality, in a commitment to the will of the Life Force, whose agent he was. Like Joan, he heard his voices; and his joy in life was to listen to them and to "do their bidding" by bringing them into being in the world of actuality as his plays. And, although he knew, like Joan, that his voices were only his own imagination, the plays remain the true testament of Shaw's religion of the Life Force and Creative Evolution. With so much uncertainty, how could the plays have been written *without* passion?

8 Plays for Realists

In his toast to Albert Einstein, Shaw said that "religion is always right, and . . . science is always wrong." In much the same spirit it might be said that a work of art is always complete, a work of criticism always incomplete. Any particular critical approach is necessarily only a partial truth; and even where the angle of vision is most rewarding, it is still only an angle, not a totality.

This truism is worth keeping in mind when considering Shaw's plays, because from some critical perspectives they can be made to seem almost infinitely rich and suggestive and from others one-dimensional to the point of triviality. But although one still hears an occasional complaint about "platform speeches, pamphlets, and leading articles," the plays have by now established themselves as works of art. On the other hand, Shavian drama is, as the playwright kept insisting, first and last a drama of ideas, and it is reasonable to suppose that any clarification of the intellectual and ideological dimension can, without being simplistic or reductive, make the plays as *wholes* more enjoyable because more comprehensible.

The preceding chapters were devoted to trying to trace and illuminate Shaw's intellectual growth and to define the nature of the "religion" that evolved during the highly charged, highly unsettled decade from 1882 to 1892 and that for the rest of his life was the embodiment and sanctuary of his intellectual and spiritual life. In those chapters relatively little was said about, or quoted from, the plays themselves in order to avoid as far as possible the implication that they should or could be seen simply as biographical or ideological documents. But since the justification for exploring in detail the structure and content of Shaw's thought was the hope of "opening up" the plays, making them more accessible to that synthesis of intellectual and emotional response he appears to have sought from his audience, it seems appropriate now to consider explicitly how the main ideas actually operate in the dramatic context. And since we have been looking specifically at the role played by the working of the dialectic principle, probably derived from Hegel through Belfort Bax, in the concepts of the Life Force and Creative Evolution, these elements can provide the focus for an investigation of the plays.

The tendency to look at all the plays from a single rather intellectual angle of vision may create the impression that this is the only productive way of seeing Shaw. There is of course no formula that will make any play yield up all its secrets—nor would we wish there were. Neither is there any single approach that will prove equally fruitful with every play—perhaps the best argument for a kind of critical pluralism that will both maximize the richness of the literary experience and also sustain the all-important quality of tentativeness. But since Shaw's observation that the completely open mind is incapable of action is as true in criticism as anywhere else, the critic must, at least for the moment, "take one point of view and stick to it" with a dogmatism that is paradoxically also tentative and entirely willing to acknowledge its own incompleteness. Seeing Shaw's plays as varied manifestations of the Life Force and of the dialectic principle operating in artistic structure, in the artificial reality of the stage, or in the relationship of the audience to the work of art, is at best a half-truth. But perhaps it is a half-truth that will move us one step closer to the unreachable whole truth.

Since it is patently impossible to treat every work in the Shavian canon with proper respect for its artistic wholeness, the plays that *are* discussed may appear to have been selected because they support a particular thesis. That, of course, is perfectly true. As Shaw repeatedly observed, no criticism is objective, and any that pretends to be is by that fact made suspect. All of Shaw's plays reveal in some degree or other, either overtly or implicitly, some of the characteristic patterns of thought on which I focused in earlier chapters. Some of them do so better than others; and some are simply better plays than others.

The principle of selecting plays, then, is a compromise between utility and quality; the principle of ordering is by and large chronological. In the earlier chapters Shaw's ideas were treated as a slowly evolving body of thought; and while it is true that his philosophy was well formed before he began writing plays, some of his most characteristic ideas find their clearest expression in clusters of plays that fall very loosely into a chronological sequence. So, while my purpose is to show how various key Shavian ideas operate within several representative plays, and not primarily to demonstrate his development as an artist or a thinker, some sense of that growth may in fact emerge—and need not be suppressed.

In the early plays the dialectic principle does not emerge as a philosophically significant element. In one respect, however, it does provide a structural principle in several works. The essence of the dialectic process as described by Hegel is that its movement is from the less real, because less complete and less self-conscious, to the more real—in other words, from the particular and physical and limited to the more universal and complete. Hegel expressed extreme contempt for all dreamers and romantics—although they may well represent a necessary stage in human development—because, as he put it, they are "putting a veil over self-consciousness, and surrendering all understanding," and can believe anything that flatters their fancy.[1] But Hegel had no more sympathy for the antithesis of the romantic, the complete skeptic and cynic who believes nothing. The Truth, the Absolute Reality, the Idea were for him ultimately knowable by the completed mind, and he

1. "Preface" to *The Phenomenology of Mind*, trans. J. B. Baillie, in *Hegel: Selections*, ed. J. Loewenberg (New York: Scribners, 1957), p. 9.

respected only that human mind that goes beyond the seductive
illusions of romanticism and the stultifying nihilism of skepticism,
and by rigorous thought and self-awareness struggles toward that
reality.

A similar or at least analogous kind of dialectic triad provides
the basic logic and structure for many of Shaw's plays. Some
could fairly be subtitled "the education of a realist," tracing a
movement away from romantic self-delusion, or the kind of
idealism described in *The Quintessence of Ibsenism,* and toward
the cynical disillusionment that is the product of disappointed
idealism. The movement usually carries beyond despair to a
synthesis in the form of a new and firmer grasp on reality.

In *Mrs Warren's Profession* this pattern is somewhat truncated,
for Vivie Warren at least imagines herself to be a realist from the
beginning, and at the end she moves only a little beyond the
cynicism of disillusionment. The hollowness of her initial realism,
with its self-assured repudiation of both conventional values and
the sentimentality of the mother-daughter relationship, is exposed
when the revelation of Mrs. Warren's origins and past life shatter
her complacency. In a reversal of roles, her mother becomes for
the moment the realist leading Vivie to the truth. As a consequence of the new understanding, the daughter does an about-
face and indulges in a thoroughly idealistic and even sentimental
admiration of the courage and realism that led Mrs. Warren to
refuse to submit to the usual forms of slavery imposed by the
capitalist system, to prefer prostitution of the body to that of the
soul. But the new truth is only a half truth. What Vivie does not
see is that in the process of beating the system at its own game
Mrs. Warren has herself become the personification of the capitalist, exploiting both the desperation of poverty and the conflict between sexuality and social mores, thereby having a vested interest
in perpetuating the idealisms of Victorian prudery.

Although not cast in political terms, Vivie's final enlightenment, her comprehension of the most sinister aspects of the
capitalist system, is the stage that for Shaw just precedes the
espousal of socialism. But Vivie does not join anything, and her

principal reaction is a revulsion against her mother's money and values, and all the ideals of duty and romance and beauty that have become corrupted by her profession, her class, and her economic principles. By the end of the play Vivie has passed through several stages of understanding, and finds a kind of desperate relief by immersing herself in the "real" world of making her own way, but it is not clear where her new level of awareness will lead. Vivie is incomplete as a person or as a social force, and we can only guess that for her, as for Shaw, life will be a "constant becoming."

A similar dialectic pattern is treated more lightheartedly in *Arms and the Man*. Under the realistic tutelage of Bluntschli, Raina and Sergius are brought from a halfhearted idealistic search for "the higher love," through a period of disillusionment and cynicism, to a recognition of reality. Their final acceptance of the real is presumably suggested by their impending marriages to the arch-realists, Bluntschli and Louka. This evolution toward more complete understanding and self-awareness, not in a straight line, but through a sequence of action and reaction, becomes one of the basic formulae of Shavian dramaturgy. It appears many times, in different forms and combined with other themes; but the pattern represents for Shaw a model of man's intellectual growth: through contradictory error to relatively greater truth.

In *Candida* the oppositions are more complex, and all three of the central characters pass through a crisis that brings each in his own way to a more realistic appraisal of himself and his relationship with others. Overtly *Candida* is a domestic play; but its subtitle, "A Mystery," while it probably refers to the "secret" in Marchbanks' heart as he departs into the waiting night at the end of the play, may also be intended to evoke echoes of the medieval "mystery" play and its quasi-allegorical embodiments of certain large and central generalizations about human nature. Shaw's classification of the virtues and vices has, of course, little to do with the Seven Deadly Sins and a great deal to do with perception and imperception, truth and hypocrisy, realism and idealism. Perhaps his most explicit division of mankind into generalized categories, at least before he wrote *Man and Super-man,* is the distinction made in *The Quintessence of Ibsenism* between the 29.9 per cent Idealists, the 70 per cent Philistines, and the .1 per cent Realists.

The Reverend James Morell at first glance looks like an idealist, but in fact he is so only in the popular and more usual use of the term; and in his unquestioning and complacent faith in the sanctity of marriage, the supremacy of the male, and the love of his wife reveals himself as a generous and well-meaning Philistine. Candida herself is of course a realist; but it is important to note that her realism is limited in its scope to the domestic relationship. She understands something about Morell and a good deal about their relationship and what makes their marriage work, but she is too much the pragmatist—a bit like Bluntschli—to see very far into the heart. She is unwittingly cruel to her husband in Act Two, and callously flip with Marchbanks at what is for him the crisis of his eighteen years. And she sees nothing more in her husband's dedication to Christian socialism than a prop to his ego and an outlet for his passion for mere talk.

Candida and James Morell are almost archetypes of the vast majority of upper middle class humanity, and Shaw respects both the large limitations and the modest virtues they represent. Both learn something in the course of the play: Morell about the nature of his relationship with Candida, that it depends less on her virtue or his strength than on her freely given love and desire to protect him; and Candida, although a realist from the start, learns something about the nature of James's weakness and of her dependence on his need for her. But while both do indeed come to a truer awareness of reality, that reality is essentially circumscribed by their home and their marriage. Domestic reality is by no means contemptible, but it is no accident that in Shaw's concluding line to the play *neither* of the Morells understands the secret in the poet's heart.

Marchbanks is, as Shaw affirmed, the "hero" of the play, and his education goes far beyond the delicate balance of the Morells' marital happiness. Whatever he may learn about himself and his wife, James is too well protected by the "castle of comfort and indulgence and love" with which Candida surrounds him to learn very much of the harsher realities of the world outside. Marchbanks, possessed of poetic yearnings and dazzled by Shelleyan idealism, at the beginning of the play sees Candida as the object and fulfillment of that idealism, with whom he can sail away in "a tiny shallop, . . . far from the world, where the marble floors are washed by the rain and dried by the sun; where the south wind dusts the beautiful green and purple carpets" (*Plays*, III, 236). James responds to this poetic romanticizing with a kind of Philistine realism: "And where there is nothing to do but to be idle, selfish, and useless." Candida, for all her realism, rather enjoys Marchbanks' pretty world of make-believe and is jarred: "Oh, James! how could you spoil it all?" But Marchbanks comes back with a remark that almost epitomizes the Shavian idealist: "Yes, to be idle, selfish, and useless: that is, to be beautiful and free and happy." The crucial opposition of the play, then, is not really between Morell and Candida, or any qualities they may be supposed to represent, so much as between the practical, domestic virtues of the Morells, taken together, and the romantic fantasies of Marchbanks, which for most of the play are indeed "idle, selfish, and useless."

The opposition between the pragmatic, domestic world of the Morells and the romantic vision of Marchbanks permeates the whole play. Marchbanks sees Morell's messages of moral awareness and social action as the fatuous rhetoric of which self-esteem is made, and Candida's onion peeling and lamp trimming as degrading and disgusting, and neither view need be taken as more unreliable than the other. Similarly, Candida and Morell see the young poet's romantic maunderings respectively as charming and immature, although the main dramatic movement of the play is the gradually increasing necessity they feel to take Marchbanks seriously. The threat appears most real to Morell, because it is he who most seriously misunderstands the nature of his marital relationship; and when the solidity of that relationship is reaffirmed—although in a new light—at the end of the play, Marchbanks ceases to be a threat and leaves. He leaves, however, a different person, with a very different image of himself, from the uncertain, blundering, often rather childish boy of the first two acts, who in his clumsy thrashing about to find himself sets in motion the actions and reactions of the plot. The consequence of the forces he sets in motion is that he *does* find himself, and the reaffirmation of the security of the Morell marriage marks his emancipation from the values and the reality it represents.

Throughout the play "happiness" is closely associated with the values at issue. In Act One Morell tells Marchbanks complacently: "I should like you to see for yourself what a happy thing it is to be married as I am." And a little later he adds: "Some day, I hope and trust, you will be a happy man like me." Marchbanks can only sneer at the value and quality of that happiness compared to that which he himself seeks; and at the end of the act, as he senses the interest and sympathy of his highly idealized Candida, he crows: "I am the happiest of mortals." Caught up in an ecstasy of romantic fantasy, his proclamation that "to be idle, selfish, and useless . . . is to be beautiful and free and happy" comes as a reaction to Morell's pedestrian ethic of duty and work.

It is Marchbanks's salvation that he finds happiness, and that he finds it with a realist like Candida. As he kneels blissfully with his head in her lap, she asks if he is happy:

Marchbanks: Yes, very happy.
Candida: Well, that happiness is the answer to your prayer. Do you want anything more?
Marchbanks: No: I have come into heaven, where want is unknown. [III, 251]

A little later he explains to Morell what happened: "Well, in plain prose, I loved her so exquisitely that I wanted nothing more than the happiness of being in such love"; and the past tense may be significant, for he adds: "I desire nothing now but her happiness." But happiness for Candida lies not in tiny shallops nor in "some beautiful archangel with purple wings," but in protecting

James and in preserving the subtle bonds of their marriage. The dream lingers on almost until the end; but Marchbanks has already recognized that the way *beyond* the Heaven he had reached in the Morells' living room only leads to what is "really the gate of Hell," and that while he may have the capacity to "dwell on the summit for ever," and to sustain the intensity of his awareness of "the silent glory of life," this is not compatible with a Candida who chooses to exist "in a scullery, slicing onions and filling lamps."

It is almost as though Marchbanks, like Raina in *Arms and the Man,* had never been entirely convinced of his own romantic ideals, and he loses them without passing through any very intense reaction of despair or cynicism. His disillusionment is not so great as to justify calling it a loss of faith in Candida, nor is it so trivial as a disenchantment in romantic fantasies. He learns that Candida, the realist, the complete woman, the wife-mother, simply exists in a different world from his own purposes and values. As Candida herself realizes, "He has learnt to live without happiness." This means much more than the mere notion of living with unhappiness, the romantic image of the disappointed lover smiling bravely through his tears. Marchbanks makes Shaw's meaning explicit: "I no longer desire happiness; life is nobler than that. Parson James: I give you my happiness with both hands. I love you because you have filled the heart of the woman I loved." And it is important that this is not seen as in any way a renunciation: "I have a better secret than that in my heart. Let me go now. The night outside grows impatient" (III, 268).

There is a tendency on the part of critics to see this night into which Eugene goes as some kind of "higher" romanticism, the "night of Tristan and Isolde." But he is not seeking another Candida, whose fingers never touch paraffin oil or onions, nor even some more intense happiness. He is going out into the exhilarating cold of the night, turning his back on the warmth and comfort and happiness of the fire-lit, lamp-lit home, and the domestic relationship it enshrines. He turns his back too on the tiny shallops and marbled halls of his romantic dreams. He leaves be-

hind *both* the Morells, not as a disappointed Idealist but as an
eager Realist.

This description of Marchbanks's individual development suggests a broadly dialectic pattern that is parallel to, but not identical with, that of the play as a whole. In the first place, the
"thesis" embodied in, or represented by, the Morells' domestic
union can itself be seen as a kind of synthesis of opposed truths—
or more accurately half-truths. Morell is a champion of the weak,
committed to social justice and masculine defense of Ideal Wo-
manhood, and is kept only by his weakness and egotism from seeing how much his public role is based on a combination of rousing
rhetoric and sex appeal, and his private role is a fiction sustained
by his wife. Candida, on her part, sees only the fact of *her*
strength for *his* defense and is prevented by her self-image and
domestic orientation from perceiving James's public role as anything more than mere talk, although Burgess offers tangible evidence that Morell and the movement he represents are in fact
beginning to have an economic and even political impact on
society. This marriage of opposites constitutes a kind of unstable
synthesis; and yet there is no suggestion at the end of the play that
it will or should evolve into anything higher. It is a balanced and
self-contained system, for Candida needs James's weakness to just
the degree that he needs her strength. The marriage consumes
just that energy needed to sustain itself; and in a sense it is the
vast unused potential that provides the impulse and energy behind
Marchbanks's violently antithetical reaction.

It is precisely the vitality, the vision, the sense of growth and
aspiration that Marchbanks does *not* find in the Morells' relationship that early in the play moves him so violently in an opposite
direction. Rejecting Morell's rhetoric and complacency, rejecting
domestic happiness and Candida's complicity in maintaining it,
Marchbanks's vital drive pushes him to seek an antithetical extreme of romantic idealism. But if the world he rejects is too
limited by pragmatic realities, the one he seeks, though alive with
vision and aspiration, has lost all contact with reality. And it is
Candida, who had provided impulse and direction and energy

for his aspirations, who also brings him to recognize their essential limitation: their divorce from reality. When Marchbanks realizes that in spite of his dreams for her she is a solid part of the pragmatic and domestic and somewhat drab world he thought he had escaped, his trajectory suddenly follows a new vector, in a direction we are to imagine partakes of realism as well as of vision and aspiration. It is, in effect, another synthesis, uniting that which is more true in each of its constituent moments, leaving that which is less true behind. That Shaw should not define the poet's "secret" too exactly is entirely characteristic; but we may well imagine that the "night" into which Marchbanks goes is more vital, more challenging, and, in a cosmic sense, more *real* than the domestic bliss on which he turns his back.

But while Marchbanks may in the end rise above the Morells' domesticity, his success is not dependent on their failure. One characteristic of Shaw's plays is that the victory of the protagonist is not represented in absolute terms, not as the triumph of light over darkness. The half-truth is, after all, opposed by a falsehood that is itself only partial.

In the Preface to *Plays: Pleasant and Unpleasant* (written in 1898) Shaw said: "The obvious conflicts of unmistakeable good with unmistakeable evil can only supply the crude drama of villain and hero, in which some absolute point of view is taken, and the dissentients are treated by the dramatist as enemies to be piously glorified or indignantly vilified. In such cheap wares I do not deal" (III, 111). The value system in terms of which his characters are to be judged is clearly not the conventional one whose poles are defined by "good" and "evil." Only in the final words of the Preface does Shaw indicate the values that will replace them: "To me the tragedy and comedy of life lie in the consequences, sometimes terrible, sometimes ludicrous, of our persistent attempts to found our institutions on the ideals suggested to our imaginations by our half-satisfied passions, instead of on a genuinely scientific natural history. And with that hint as to what I am driving at, I withdraw and ring up the curtain" (III, 121).

Although we are given to understand that the moral scheme of the plays will be based on the antithesis between realism and idealism defined in *Quintessence,* Shaw does not try to pin down the precise implications of the key normative term, "reality." This has, understandably, irritated his critics and convinced some of them of the carelessness of his thinking; but Shaw was leery of being trapped by abstractions and preferred to stick to a notion of "realism" as a *way* of seeing the world, grasped empirically— through the experience of his plays, he hoped—and most clearly defined, if at all, in terms of what it is not.

A study of virtually any one of the early Shaw plays reveals patterns of conflict between realistic and idealistic ways of seeing things, of opposition and synthesis, of development that proceeds along dialectic lines. These patterns represent one of the most important ways in which Shaw's philosophy manifests itself in the plays, and a failure to identify them has led to essential misunderstandings.

There have, for instance, been critics who, when writing about *Caesar and Cleopatra,* have complained that Shaw somehow failed in his representation of Caesar's education of the young queen, in which he presumably raises her up to his level and makes her into a kind of female Caesar. This criticism assumes that Caesar's purpose was to remake Cleopatra in his own image; and whatever Caesar may have intended, that was not Shaw's idea. Caesar and Cleopatra are placed, at the beginning of the play, in the now familiar polar relationship; but while the queen indeed changes and develops in the direction represented by Caesar, there is typically no final resolution in which she becomes "like" him, or indeed anything essentially other than herself.

In *Caesar and Cleopatra* the conflict between realist and idealist has moved to the level of what Hegel called the "world-historical individual," and his characterization of that figure is much to the point. The evolutionary fulfillment of Spirit in History is, according to Hegel, the result

on the one hand, of the inner development of the Idea and, on the other, of the activity of individuals, who are its agents and bring about its actualization. It is at this point that appear those momentous collisions between existing, acknowledged duties, laws, and rights and those possibilities which are adverse to this system, violate it, and even destroy its foundations. . . . These possibilities now become historical fact; they involve a universal of an order different from that upon which depends the permanence of a people or a state. . . . The historical men, world-historical individuals, are those who grasp just such a higher universal, make it their own purpose, and realize this purpose in accordance with the higher law of the spirit. Caesar was such a man. [*Reason,* p. 39]

Neither Shaw's Caesar, however, nor the play about him bears anything more than the most casual relation to historical fact. Shaw's interest lies not with Caesar as an individual, but with the theoretical and dramatic relationship between a *force,* represented in the play by Caesar, and human affairs, with its impact, not on any specific historical moment, but on History. This approach is consistent with Hegel's notion that the characteristic quality of the "world-historical individual" is that he is "the middle term, between the universal Idea, which reposes in the inner recesses of Spirit, and the external world" of historical events.

Although Shaw's emperor expresses a strong sense of identity with what he calls the "constant and immortal part of [his] life," which lies hidden in "the lost regions from which [his] birth into this world exiled [him]" (III, 374–375), he is no mere abstraction or theory. On the contrary, the vitality of the play derives almost entirely from the force of this Caesar figure. This play does not hold us by its action or its suspense. The melodramatic question—will Caesar be able to escape the besieging Egyptians and return to Rome?—is scarcely posed, the answer is so self-evident. And far from using the sexual dimension of the relationship between Caesar and Cleopatra to capture our attention, Shaw goes to great pains to establish that Caesar lacks any sexual appeal but his energy, and that Cleopatra's imagination is preoccupied by the romantic image of Antony. Nor are we asked to take an interest in Caesar's personal development or growth. He simply does not change. And yet he is not static. Indeed, the appeal of the play lies largely in our fascination with the force, the grasp of reality, the sheer vitality incarnate for the moment in a figure called Julius Caesar.

Somewhat surprisingly, Caesar's unyielding and indivertible strength, his quality of an "unmoved mover," far from inhibiting the dramatic element in the play, in fact generates tension and conflict. The energy behind his realistic judgments almost inevitably summons up its own obstacles and evokes opposition from the variety of idealists who surround him. At the very beginning Cleopatra herself is little more than an abstraction, simply the role or "idea" of queenhood, an empty mask whose utterances, as Belzanor wryly observes in the Prologue, reflect the will of her advisors and, notably, Ftatateeta. Though Caesar may not change, Cleopatra does, and her evolution from an almost fatuous caricature of royalty to the reality of ruler of Egypt, under the constant abrasion and hammering of Caesar's realism, provides a major structural element of the play.

The Cleopatra that Caesar finds asleep in the arms of the Sphinx lives in a simple world of priests and nurses, whom it is her duty to obey, of the Romans, who are "bad" and "barbarian," and of the easy evasions of magic. Even the elemental reality of power is absent; and when Caesar first endows her with a sense of her own power, she uses it as do all those who lack any sense of purpose: sadistically, to prove to herself her power over others. Her first exercise of new-found authority is to beat Ftatateeta, and she indulges in fantasies of the slaves she will torture, or the "many young kings, with round, strong arms" whom she will whip to death when they have satisfied her needs. Being a queen, she says, means doing just what she likes; and as the old bug-a-boos of obedience and duty and fear are exposed she is intoxicated with a freedom that has no object but self-indulgence. She loses her fear of Caesar as an idealized deity, and before she has recognized his stature as a human, she assumes an impertinent arrogance toward him: "If you do as I tell you, you will soon learn to govern." But as her experience grows, and as her understanding of what Caesar is deepens, she becomes increasingly aware of the suprapersonal dimensions of responsibility implicit in freedom and power if they are to be anything other than destructive.

Early in Act Four it is evident that Charmian's sneering comment is true: "Cleopatra is no longer a child." Although accused of imitating Caesar, she acknowledges that it is not in her nature to be like him, only to learn from him; and when Pothinus is startled by her grasp of the realities of political life, she points out: "Do you speak with Caesar every day for six months: and *you* will be changed." But it had been easier and pleasanter before: "I did what I liked. . . . Now that Caesar has made me wise, it is no use my liking or disliking: I do what must be done, and have no time to attend to myself. That is not happiness; but it is greatness" (III, 438). It is worth noting that Hegel makes a point of emphasizing the rewards that accrue when the particular will is aligned with the process by which the World Spirit is realized in history. There is, he says, a profound satisfaction in furthering the movement of world history "but it is not the kind that is called happiness, for it is satisfaction of purposes that are above particular interests. . . . The world-historical individuals who have pursued such purposes have satisfied themselves, it is true, but they did not want to be happy" (*Reason,* p. 33).

Although Cleopatra rises above the simple equation of power with doing what she wants—or more accurately, what she wants is no longer pleasure or happiness, but "doing what has to be done"—the Queen of Egypt is not of the same order of being as the emperor of the world, no matter how much she may aspire to his approval. In fact, it is not wholly farfetched to consider Cleopatra representing a whole constellation of idealizations and abstractions—the concepts of rights and duties, of law and social hierarchy, of honor and vengeance, what Hegel had called the "established system"—that are in various ways obstacles to Caesar, and that like Cleopatra are not so much overcome as in some way reshaped through the force of his personality and his realism.

Most of these same abstractions are also embodied in several minor characters and in aspects of the action. Britannus, for instance, first comes to our attention in the act of rephrasing Caesar's words in terms of laws, contracts, and duties. And as he explains why his countrymen paint themselves blue, it is evident that his horizons are circumscribed by the decorums and decencies decreed by "the right people." Britannus is thrall to social proprieties and moral maxims rather than to any individual, and it is quite appropriate that Caesar should mistake this freedman for a slave. But, as Britannus affirms at the end, it is only in Caesar's service that he has found freedom.

Ftatateeta, on the other hand, is not an abstraction or a slave to ideals, but one possessed by passion, by a blind irrational devotion that is too easily used by others—as when she kills Pothinus to satisfy Cleopatra's desire for revenge. Not wholly dissimilar is Rufio's blunt, honest, but somewhat shallow and malleable "common sense." In the very sincerity of his loyalty and the shortsightedness of his vision Rufio can do almost as much damage as an out and out idealist—a Philistine who is dangerously susceptible to the force of such abstractions as vengeance. But he too catches something of his master's vision and is worthy to be left as Roman governor of Egypt, although he will rule "in his own way," not as Caesar would rule.

Vengeance, as retribution, as punishment, as an obligation due to honor, is an abstraction so ubiquitous in the play as to become something more than a motif. Almost every character, minor as well as major, with the exception of Caesar, justifies himself or the actions of others by appeals to the legitimizing and sanctifying power of vengeance. When Cleopatra acknowledges that Pothinus was murdered at her command for daring to insult her, she asks: "Caesar would not avenge me; he spoke him fair and set him free. Was I right to avenge myself?" And Lucius Septimius, Apollodorus, Britannus, and Rufio, each for his own reasons, affirm her right. Not for the first time, nor the last, a Shavian hero is completely misunderstood by those who profess to love or follow him; and Caesar's principles are betrayed by those closest to him through inability to share his vision.

Emboldened by the support she finds for her view, Cleopatra cannot resist exulting in her triumph: "If one man in all Alexandria can be found to say that I did wrong, I swear to have myself crucified on the door of the palace by my own slaves." But Caesar does not see with Alexandria's eyes:

> If one man in all the world can be found, now or forever, to *know* that you did wrong, that man will have either to conquer the world as I have, or be crucified by it. . . . These knockers at your gate are also believers in vengeance and in stabbing. You have slain their leader: it is right that they shall slay you. . . . And then in the name of that *right* shall I not slay them for murdering their Queen? . . . And so, to the end of history, murder shall breed murder, always in the name of right and honor and peace, until the gods are tired of blood and create a race that can understand. [III, 456–457]

In this calculatedly startling paradox, the common ground between the man of Peace and the man of War, the man of the spirit and the man who, ever since Jesus spoke of "the things which are Caesar's," had symbolized the material world, lies in their both being members of this new and lonely race that understands. They know, as Ra says in the Prologue, that "the way of the gods is the way of life."

But Caesar's way is not always the way of life. As a world-historical individual, a builder of empire, a soldier, he knows that conquests are not made without killing. He warns that Pothinus's murder is only a link in an endless chain of blood, vengeance, and counterrevenge, in eternal unbalance; and yet he unblinkingly accepts Rufio's murder of Pothinus's killer, Ftatateeta. The contradiction is something less than a paradox, but more than moral expediency, and the logic is quite clear. The claim that the second killing was done "without punishment; without revenge; without judgment" is not mere rationalization. As Rufio's parable of the lion spells out, self-defense is not a principle or a duty, it is a necessity of life. What made murder horrible to Caesar, and to Shaw, was the trick of making it into a virtue by evoking abstractions like justice and punishment and honor, instead of treating

it as a means to an end in terms of which it must be justified, if
it is to be justified at all.

Caesar's grasp of reality renders him as immune to Cleopatra's
appeals to vengeance and to her attempts to attribute vengeance
to him as he is to her beauty. His realism places him beyond the
comprehension of those who hide, even from themselves, the
meanness of their jealousies and ambitions and self-conceit behind
the labels of honor and duty and respectability. But he is not
above their hatred or their weapons. It is clear, from several allusions to the events of history, that Caesar at the end is leaving
the little men and women of Egypt, in whom he has done his
best to instill his way of seeing things, to be killed by the little
people of Rome.

Caesar, who feels himself exiled into a world in which he finds
"no air native, . . . no man kindred," stands in almost a godlike
relationship to the other characters in the play. Distant, inscru-
table, he inspires a devotion qualified by awe and a humanly unreliable desire to learn his lessons; but he operates at a level of
intellectual and emotional existence that ordinary mortals either
grasp imperfectly or completely misunderstand.

The feeling of almost godlike isolation that characterizes the
lonely heights of the realist is something Caesar shares with other
Shavian heroes, such as Don Juan, Undershaft, Henry Higgins,
or the early longlivers of *Back to Methuselah*. And Cleopatra's
development follows much the same pattern as other "learners":
Barbara Undershaft or Liza Doolittle or Ellie Dunn. They all
start out in almost complete spiritual and intellectual opposition
to a figure possessing superhuman clarity of perception and
strength of purpose, whom they never really understand, but who
in a series of educational confrontations lifts them to higher levels
of self-consciousness and of realism in their awareness of the
world around them. Characterizing these superhumanly perceptive teachers or models as godlike is not mere hyperbole. In a
very real Shavian sense these figures partake of godhead, and
their function, whether in the dimension of "world-historical"
events or on the private and domestic level, is to encourage or

coerce more ordinary mortals into a larger participation in, or exercise of, their own potential divinity. In the Prologue spoken by the god Ra, which he substituted for the original opening scene of *Caesar and Cleopatra,* Shaw not only identifies Caesar as one who fulfills "the will of the gods," but characterizes his role in history, as an agent or representative of the future, in distinctly Hegelian terms.

The Prologue opens with a statement of a favorite Shavian notion: that although human nature changes slowly, if at all, human history and institutions and understanding do evolve. In this context he suggests that ancient Rome, much like England in a later age, once stood on the threshold between an old world and a new one. The old Rome is represented by Pompey, who put his faith in law and duty and the power of the sword. Pompey's way "is the way of death; but the way of the gods is the way of life; and . . . Julius Caesar was on the side of the gods. . . . And the gods smiled on Caesar; for he lived the life they had given him boldly." The symbolic antithesis between the two leaders is made even more explicit:

And thus it fell out between the old Rome and the new, that Caesar said, "Unless I break the law of old Rome, . . . the gift of ruling that the gods gave me will perish without fruit." But Pompey said, "The law is above all; and if thou break it thou shalt die." Then said Caesar, "I will break it: kill me who can." And he broke it. . . . And the gods laughed and approved; and on the field of Pharsalia the impossible came to pass; the blood and iron ye pin your faith on fell before the spirit of man; for the spirit of man is the will of the gods. [III, 359]

But the way of the gods, the way of the future, the way of life is in perpetual conflict with the way of death, and Caesar "battled his way back to Rome to be slain there as Pompey was slain, by men in whom the spirit of Pompey still lived." Ra, one of the gods whose spirit and love of life and vision of something better is incarnate in Caesar, or half a dozen other Shavian characters, tries like them to elevate the vision of ordinary mortals like us. We are, he says, "a dull folk," but his hope lies in a Hegelian conviction that "it is in the nature of a god to struggle for ever with the dust and the darkness, and to drag from them, by the force of his longing for the divine, more life and more light."

The whole concept of the mortal incarnation of the divine principle is handled most explicitly in the play Shaw subtitled "A Comedy and a Philosophy," and of which he remarked later that he had "put all [his] intellectual goods in the shop window under the sign of Man and Superman" (II, lxxxix). He was never shy, then or later, to claim the play as a major repository of his ideas— only, he complained, "the effect was so vertiginous, apparently, that nobody noticed the new religion in the centre of the intellectual whirlpool." The philosophy and the religion are largely crammed into Act Three, where he "took the legend of Don Juan in its Mozartian form and made it a dramatic parable of Creative Evolution." Fantasy is the medium Shaw uses in the self-contained fragment generally known as "Don Juan in Hell." It allows him almost complete freedom from the limitations of human nature, at least in its external and everyday manifestations, making possible a more explicit and easily defined representation of the godlike personality than was possible in the relatively frail mortality of Julius Caesar.

Characteristically, Shaw sets up an opposition between the metaphorical representatives of two antithetical ways of seeing the world and human existence, an opposition identified in the Don Juan episode as "heaven" and "hell." Of course when we hear that hell is the "home of honor, duty, justice," that its inhabitants worship love and beauty, and that life there is "a perpetual romance and universal melodrama," and that on the other hand heaven is, according to the Statue, unbearably dull, we might fall into the same trap as his contemporaries and imagine that he is creating pseudo-paradoxes by merely turning things upside down. But as usual it is not so simple. Hell is indeed a state of damnation, heaven is salvation; but Shaw does not conceive of them as places where people "go" as a reward or a punishment. They are only parables, and "a parable must not be taken literally. The gulf is the difference between the angelic and the diabolic temper-

ament. What more impassable gulf could you have?" (III, 614)'.
On the other hand, as the Statue says when Juan asks the way
to the frontier of hell and heaven: "Oh, the frontier is only the
difference between two ways of looking at things. Any road will
take you across it if you really want to get there." Heaven and
hell, then, stand for states of mind and ways of thinking, not of
the dead but the living.

The frontier between the diabolic and the angelic temperaments, however, is very clearly defined. The Statue, simply because he *prefers* hell to heaven, typifies the diabolic personality.
He characterizes hell to Ana thus: "Written over the gate here
are the words 'Leave every hope behind, ye who enter.' Only think
what a relief that is! For what is hope? A form of moral responsibility. Here there is no hope, and consequently no duty, no work,
nothing to be gained by praying, nothing to be lost by doing what
you like. Hell, in short, is a place where you have nothing to do
but amuse yourself" (III, 610). When Juan tells Ana that "heaven is the home of the masters of reality," she replies: "Thank
you: I am going to heaven for happiness. I have had quite
enough of reality on earth." Juan reiterates his distinction, that
hell is "the home of the unreal and of the seekers for happiness,"
and that he seeks heaven, the "home of the masters of reality,"
in order to "escape at last from lies and from the tedious, vulgar
pursuit of happiness." Near the end of the episode, when the
Statue, with characteristic shallowness, wants to know "What is
the use of knowing?" Juan tells him: "Why, to be able to choose
the line of greatest advantage instead of yielding in the direction
of the least resistance. Does a ship sail to its destination no better
than a log drifts nowhither? The philosopher is Nature's pilot.
And there you have our difference: to be in hell is to drift: to
be in heaven is to steer" (III, 646)'.

This definition provides the key to one of the central oppositions of the play, as well as a point of contact between the heaven-
hell metaphor and Shaw's philosophy of the Life Force and Creative Evolution. Hell is the essence of negation, of denying purpose
to life beyond self-indulgence and personal happiness—and justify-

ing itself in terms of idealistic abstractions like Beauty and Romance and Virtue. It is believing with the Devil that "the power
that governs the earth is not the power of Life but of Death;
and the inner need that has served Life to the effort of organizing
itself into the human being is not the need for higher life but for
a more efficient engine of destruction" (III, 621).

But Juan and Shaw, being of the angelic or godlike persuasion,
think otherwise: "Life is a force which has made innumerable
experiments in organizing itself . . . into higher and higher individuals." Life *is* going somewhere—but precisely where is not
predetermined by abstract eternal laws or by divine fiat, but grows
and evolves along with, and as a part of, the same dialectic processes by which life itself develops. This Life Force, as we have
already seen, has two antithetical dimensions, or moments of
force. On the one hand, it is a "raw force" that "raises up obstacles to itself and destroys itself in its ignorance and blindness,"
while on the other, in its drive toward more and fuller life this
force creates that which can control, organize, and give direction
to its inchoate fecundity and directionless energy. As "Life, after
ages of struggle," evolved the physical eye, so that the organism
may "avoid a thousand dangers that formerly slew it," so it
evolves the mind, "an organ by which it can attain not only
self-consciousness but self-understanding," that it may "be able
to choose the line of greatest advantage instead of yielding in the
direction of the least resistance."

When Juan announces as the law of his life the principle that
as long as he can conceive of something better than himself he
cannot rest unless he is "striving to bring it into existence or clearing the way for it," he defines a significant feature of both the
heavenly or angelic personality and the concept of the Superman
with which they are identified. Shaw's Superman, unlike Nietzsche's, is not a goal or an end product so much as a process or a
stage of development: one step better than what *is;* and heaven
is not a place but a direction, the intuited end of an unending
dynamic called Creative Evolution. There is, in effect, a dialectical
opposition here that is suggestively similar to the basic triad Hegel

had used to illustrate the operation of his principle. Hell, as Shaw represents it, is not merely the realm of the death of the spirit, it is the home of the unreal, a representation of non-existence, non-being, total negation. Its antithesis is a heaven which, though indefinable, is clearly conceived as pure or absolute being. And Juan, superior to but representative of mankind in general, is the middle term, the Hegelian synthesis: becoming—in the process of evolving from hell to heaven, from non-being to being.

Although most of Shaw's critics have outgrown the old complaint that the Don Juan scene of *Man and Superman* is dull because it is all talk and are quite willing to accept it as an intellectual tour de force, they usually imply that brilliance is no substitute for action and that its lack of movement is essentially undramatic. But even beyond the fairly obvious conflict of ideas, which provides an element of drama, the episode also has a clearly defined plot line—in fact, it has two. In characteristic Shavian fashion they both follow the education of major characters to an opening out of vision, and to an awareness of their relationship to a newly perceived reality. One plot is directly related to the hell–heaven–superman dialectic in terms of which Juan is *becoming*, moving from relative non-being to relatively greater being. When he first meets Ana, Juan is a dissatisfied but despairing inhabitant of hell: "You are certainly damned, like myself; and there is nothing for it now but to make the best of it." The first part of the scene belongs largely to the Devil and the Statue, as they try to represent hell in its most favorable light, and it is only as a result of Ana's questioning that Juan learns of the possibility of "going to heaven." This knowledge restores his vitality and vision, and he becomes suddenly articulate, opposing the unreality of hell with the reality of heaven, the Devil's death force with the Life Force, the demonic perception that things are as good as they can be with the angelic perception that things must be better. His revulsion becomes complete: "Here there is nothing but love and beauty. Ugh! . . . Never in my worst moments of superstitious terror on earth did I dream that hell was so horrible" (III, 644). And recognizing in himself the mind of the philosopher, "Nature's pilot," he steers his course across the border into what is indeed his true home, heaven.

There is, however, another dialectical relationship operating in the Don Juan episode that in both its implications and its plot is related to but essentially different from the hell–heaven–superman one. When Juan defines the nature of the "philosophic man," it is in terms of a triadic relationship among pure mind, which "seeks in contemplation to discover the inner will of the world," the physical means to translate ideas into concrete experiments in the real world ("in invention to discover the means of fulfilling that will"), and a movement toward something better ("in action to do that will by the so-discovered means") (III, 628). In that description one essential component is absent, namely, the energy or force necessary to bridge the gap between the conception and the reality. Juan confesses that neither philosophers nor theologians, politicians nor even artists have provided the necessary spark. What he calls his "astounding illumination" came from a very different source: "Up to that moment I had never lost the sense of being my own master; never consciously taken a single step until my reason had examined and approved it. . . . It was woman who taught me to say . . . 'I would think more; therefore I must be more'" (III, 631). As Juan describes the experience, the Apollonian control and restraint and rationality of the philosopher is violently confronted with the overwhelming Dionysian impulse of the woman: "That moment introduced me for the first time to myself, and, through myself, to the world. I saw then how useless it is to attempt to impose conditions on the irresistible force of Life; to preach prudence, careful selection" (III, 632). And yet the need for prudence and careful selection is precisely what Juan has been preaching. The reasonable, directive, ameliorative force of the mind is in opposition to the creative energy of the woman, but both are in the service of a higher will. A little later Juan gives that world will a voice: "'I have done a thousand wonderful things unconsciously by merely willing to live and following the line of least resistance: now I want to know myself and my destination, and choose my path; so I have made a

special brain—a philosopher's brain—to grasp this knowledge for
me as the husbandman's hand grasps the plough for me. And this'
says the Life Force to the philosopher, 'must thou strive to do for
me until thou diest, when I will make another brain and another
philosopher to carry on the work' " (III, 646).

The vision and energy and hence the effectiveness of any particular "philosopher" or mind is necessarily partial and finite; those
of the Life Force are infinite. And it is only the infinite vitality
embodied in the "woman" that makes human history a creative
evolution rather than a static abstraction. Juan admits that "sex-
ually, Man is Woman's contrivance for fulfilling Nature's behest
in the most economical way. She knows by instinct that far back
in the evolutional process she invented him, differentiated him,
created him in order to produce something better than the single-
sexed process can produce" (III, 624). Since the male/female,
consciousness/energy impulses are conceived as metaphysical
rather than merely biological "moments" or antitheses of the Life
Force dialectic, they need not in reality exist in separate individuals or be associated exclusively with one sex or the other; but
the metaphor is a useful and vital one for Shaw, even though it
leads to misunderstanding.

What might be called the "sexual plot" of "Don Juan in Hell"
is evident in the Don Juan plot line, "the education of the superman," and even more significantly in Ana's parallel but different
growth toward understanding. On her arrival in hell, Ana argues
vehemently with the "enemy," Juan, and with her father, who
has recently fled the abode of the blessed, that both virtue and
social standing require her immediate removal to heaven. As the
others enlarge on their definitions of heaven and hell, and Juan
waxes more eloquent, she falls silent. Although her relatively few
utterances, whether practical or idealistic in tone, articulate a
point of view that is thoroughly conventional, she is listening and
learning. She comes to realize that her place is with neither the
complacent narcissists of hell nor the philosophers of heaven. She
has a role in the cosmic scheme more vital than either self-indulgence or contemplation. After Juan has gone off on the heavenly

road, and the others are leaving for the satanic palace of unreality, Ana cries out: "Stop! . . . Tell me: where can I find the Superman?" The Devil tells her: "He is not yet created"; and she cries out: "Not yet created! Then my work is not yet done. [Crossing herself devoutly] I believe in the Life to Come. [crying to the universe] A father! a father for the Superman!" (III, 649).

The sexual terms in which Shaw develops the conflict in both "Don Juan in Hell" and in the autonomous three acts of *Man and Superman* that surround it can be understood either metaphorically or literally. The triad of mother/father = new life is a model for the more cosmic dialectic of the opposition between two antithetical moments or forces associated with the male and female principles, or with the Apollonian and Dionysian impulses, the synthesis partaking of both elements and yet being something new, more complete or self-comprehending, better than what is, a Superman. At the same time these universal forces are manifested in the commonplace world as what is popularly known as the "war between the sexes."

The major themes, and more specifically the two plots, of the dream sequence are reflected in human terms in what, for simplicity's sake, can be called the "frame" play. For example, the conflict between two ways of looking at things made explicit in the counterclaims of heaven and hell in Act Three is implicit in the characterizations of the frame. Roebuck Ramsden is a self-styled liberal whose mind has been incapable of entertaining a new idea for over forty years, and whose speech, like his thinking, is circumscribed by clichés about duty and respectability and manliness. It is entirely appropriate that he should be resurrected in the dream sequence with the petrified brains of the Statue. Neither as the Statue nor as Ramsden does he represent much of a force in the play, but seems rather a deadweight of non-insight and nonbeing, an obstacle to be overcome, in the dream a foil for Juan's argumentativeness and in the frame providing countless opportunities for Jack to demonstrate his "impudence"—or as Shaw would say, his realism. In either shape Ramsden clearly belongs to hell.

Jack, on the other hand, is a mortal, imperfect, and sometimes even foolish, version of Don Juan. His infatuation with his own ideas, which contributes to his impulsive but wasted praise of Violet as an unwed mother, has led some critics to see him as a negligible or even a satiric figure. He possesses, however, a realistic if unconventional way of looking at things and an intellectual incisiveness that he shares with G. B. Shaw, and which is verifiable in their "Revolutionist's Handbook" as well as in the play itself. Juan, to be sure, has moved from non-being to total being, and in his mythic context has fulfilled himself as the intellectual, self-conscious impulse. Obviously, Jack is metaphoric eons behind Juan; but he is on the same path, and he is one of the "heavenly" personalities.

The family likeness between Jack and Juan is in fact not hard to see. In a long conversation with Ann, Jack tries to explain what has happened to their youthful camaraderie. She suggests that they were both becoming aware of their sexual natures, and he replies: "Are you sure it was not that we were beginning to be something more? . . . The change that came to me was the birth in me of moral passion; and I declare that according to my experience moral passion is the only real passion. . . . The moral passion has taken my destructiveness in hand and directed it to moral ends. . . . I no longer break cucumber frames and burn gorse bushes: I shatter creeds and demolish idols" (III, 550).

In an even more manifestly "angelic" speech Jack says of Tavy's romantic conviction that yielding his will to Ann's represents his highest fulfillment: "Yes, of her purpose; and that purpose is neither her happiness nor yours, but Nature's. Vitality in a woman is a blind fury of creation. . . . Because they have a purpose which is not their own purpose, but that of the whole universe, a man is nothing to them but an instrument of that purpose." Jack then lectures Tavy that it is his moral and social responsibility as an artist to keep the open independence of the free spirit who follows his purpose in splendid isolation:

The artist's work is to shew us ourselves as we really are. Our minds are nothing but this knowledge of ourselves; and he who adds a jot to such knowledge creates new mind as surely as any woman creates new men. In the rage of that creation he is as ruthless as the woman, as dangerous to her as she to him, and as horribly fascinating. Of all human struggles there is none so treacherous and remorseless as the struggle between the artist man and the mother woman. Which shall use up the other? that is the issue between them. And it is all the deadlier because, in your romanticist cant, they love one another. [III, 538]

This clearly sets up the sexual dialectic that underlies both the frame play and the dream sequence of Act Three, the metaphor of the latter being foreshadowed in Jack's response to Tavy's complaint that his friend is trying to save him from his "highest happiness": "If it were only the first half hour's happiness, Tavy, I would buy it for you with my last penny. But a lifetime of happiness! No man alive could bear it: it would be hell on earth."

Although Jack evidently has the instincts and even some of the self-conscious understanding of Juan, he has a long way to go and much to learn. A significant epiphany is provided by the man of the future, the technologically advanced man, the pragmatic product of the Polytechnic Institute, when the mechanic Straker suggests that it is obviously Jack, not Tavy, whom Ann has marked as her prey. The revelation brings home to Jack what we presumably have recognized during his lecture to Tavy on the eternal opposition of poet and woman: that he, Jack Tanner, is the artist of his own definition, dedicated to showing us ourselves as we really are, and not his sentimental young friend.

Octavius Robinson does not reappear as one of the *personae* of the Don Juan scene, but his Mozartian counterpart, Ottavio, is mentioned as a resident of hell, and it is quite clear that Tavy has all the characteristics of the demonic personality. He is idealistic, romantic, a seeker after happiness. In the last act Jack describes him as someone "who sees nothing in nature but romantic scenery for love duets! Tavy, the chivalrous, the faithful, the tenderhearted." Ann continues the portrait; "Men like that always live in comfortable bachelor lodgings with broken hearts, and are adored by their landladies, and never get married. . . . The poetic temperament's a very nice temperament, very amiable, very harmless and poetic, I daresay; but it's an old maid's temperament." Jack concludes: "Barren. The Life Force passes it by" (III, 681–682).

The second and more important stage in Jack's education is accomplished through the agency of his dreams of hell in the high air of the Sierras and is reflected in his recognition that the Life Force passes by the Tavies of this world. And that awareness carries as a corollary the recognition that he is himself a principal in the "remorseless struggle between the artist man and the mother woman."

At the end of the Don Juan episode Donna Ana chooses not to remain in either heaven or hell, for she seeks neither happiness nor self-understanding. For her, both are irrelevant, and her instinct is to return to the "real" world, the world in which the struggle of evolution from nothing to everything, from less-than-man to more-than-man still goes on: "I believe in the Life to Come. A father! a father for the Superman!" She rushes off the stage, to reappear shortly after as Ann Whitefield, in the final stages of her pursuit of Jack. She does not understand precisely why it is Jack that she must have—although she acknowledges that his impulse to escape, which Tavy lacks, has something to do with it—but have him she must. And she will use any means, appeals to duty and propriety and romance, to an idealism in which she is too much of a realist to believe, to get him. She is in no way rational; but she possesses the higher understanding of instinct.

Tanner understands; but his understanding is powerless. "Why me?" he asks, "me of all men! Marriage is to me apostasy, profanation of the sanctuary of my soul, violation of my manhood, sale of my birthright, shameful surrender." But he can answer his own question: "We do the world's will, not our own. I have a frightful feeling that I shall let myself be married because it is the world's will that you should have a husband. . . . The Life Force. I am in the grip of the Life Force." This is the elemental struggle between the force that creates new mind and the force that creates new men: "I am fighting for my freedom, for my honor, for my self, one and indivisible." But even in his agony Jack knows that the isolated self, free and indivisible, is not enough. He accuses Ann of seeking happiness, but she protests: "It will not be all happiness for me. Perhaps death." And Jack groans: "What have you grasped in me? Is there a father's heart as well as a mother's?" (III, 680–683).

Jack Tanner has learned the lesson of his dream and knows, at least instinctively, that the free autonomous rational mind, no matter how clearly it sees the past or the future, is of itself sterile, futureless, a handful of dust, that to have life, to create, it must embrace its antithesis and engender something unattainable by each alone. It is more than romantic hyperbole for Jack to exclaim that in Ann he holds the whole world and its future in his arms.

Jack is "trapped" and "defeated," and critics ever since the play first appeared have made much of the fact. But the defeat, if any, is a private one. Nothing is lost but some pride, perhaps, and a little freedom; but self-sufficiency, we have learned, is only another form of self-indulgence. Ann and Jack are in the grip of the Life Force, and its will is their will: to create new mind in the only abode where it can create a better world—in new men and women. Jack has lost the cause of male liberation; but he has won the cause of the Life Force and of the future. In his final speech Jack announces that they have both forever renounced happiness, freedom, tranquillity, and "the romantic possibilities of an unknown future," and that the wedding presents will all be sold in order to pay for circulating free copies of the "Revolutionist's Handbook." Ann, characteristically, has no idea what he is talking about, but urges him to "go on talking." But the universe understands; and the "universal laughter" at the end is not of derision, as some have imagined—Shaw's laughter is rarely derisive—but rather of sympathy and joy: sympathy with the defeat of the Apollonian sterility of pure intellection, joy at the fulfillment of the Life Force, and through it of the world's will.

Man and Superman may succeed as a philosophy, but while a very few daring, if not suicidal, producers have tried to stage the play as written, as a whole, the simple fact is that including all four acts makes it unsittably long. The frame play and the "Don Juan in Hell" have been done frequently, and successfully, as autonomous plays; and yet there is an important symbiotic relationship between the two that makes the enforced divorce mutually damaging.

As he had done in several earlier plays, Shaw in the frame play takes a number of well-known conventions, characters, and patterns of action from the romantic comedies and melodramas of his day and gives them a new point, and a new seriousness, by disappointing expectations. We have, for instance, the wise, kindly old guardian; his beautiful and nubile young ward; a handsome and high-minded young man who worships the ground she walks on; a wealthy ne'er-do-well who provides romantic complications by trying to seduce the naive heroine; with a fallen sister thrown in to provide a sentimental tear or two. The "set-up" is as old as Rome, and Shaw neatly deflates each cliché by pulling the rug from under it and turning it on its head. But if the frame play were all there was it would be legitimate to conclude that the point of the play was to invert yet another convention and demonstrate the unfortunate but probably valid point that, in spite of the traditions of Courtly Love and the Romance, women hunt men rather than vice versa.

The "Don Juan in Hell" episode offers an important new dimension to the whole by putting the inversions of the frame play, and its exposé of conventional character types, into a philosophical framework. The conventionality of Roebuck Ramsden, the impudence of Jack Tanner, the romanticism of Tavy and the tough-minded manipulation of others by Ann, all become negative and positive forces in a comprehensive and dynamic view of life in which a sense of direction is more important than the drifting of self-indulgence, where knowing and satisfying the needs of the world will is more rewarding than personal happiness or personal salvation.

The episode is much more self-sufficient philosophically than the frame play, and yet in its very density of ideas it needs the action of the surrounding drama to tie its abstractions to the level of ordinary human experience. Both Shaw and the Devil call the dream a "parable" in which the ideas implicit in the frame are made explicit; and yet in another sense it is the frame play that is the parable, in which the metaphysical realities of Juan's Life Force philosophy are translated into immediately comprehensible human terms. As man needs his extension of himself in art in order to understand himself, so each part of *Man and Superman* contributes a kind of reality and truth to the other. The relationship is almost dialectic, analogous perhaps to the abstract will of the Life Force and its recalcitrant human incarnations; and when we are denied the synthesis of the play as a whole something irretrievable is lost. Shaw was not unaware of the difficulties his enthusiasm for explaining himself had made, and he tried thereafter to make both his discussions of ideas (*Getting Married*, 1908) and his incarnation of those ideas in action (as in his next play, *Major Barbara*, 1905) clearly self-contained.

9   *God's Wavering*
       Warriors

Major Barbara is perhaps Shaw's most successful effort at making both his ideas and the dialectic oppositions immanent in the action rather than explicit, as they had been in "Don Juan in Hell." The play was written in 1905, two years after *Man and Superman,* and was produced in the same year as part of the Barker-Vedrenne experiment in Shaw matinees at the Court Theatre. Shaw later made some revisions, involving short additional scenes, for the Gabriel Pascal film of 1940–1941.

Although it was a modest success at its first appearance, *Major Barbara* has met with considerable critical resistance and is perhaps one of the playwright's most widely misunderstood plays. Then and now critics have put on it such disparaging labels as an "incoherent farrago of ideas," "an irreligious play," and "a cynical representation of the triumph of materialism over spirituality." As a result of the play, Shaw was called a communist by the conservatives, a counterrevolutionary by the Marxists, and an atheist by everyone except the Salvation Army, who understood. Shaw was presumably delighted with the brickbats, not because they were true, but because they were evidence that he had stirred people out of their lethargy. But too often the most violent epithets were hurled by the Lady Britomarts of the world, to whom he replied through Andrew Undershaft: "You are the incarnation of morality. Your conscience is clear and your duty done when you have called everybody names" (*Plays,* I, 438).

The play is in fact revolutionary, religious, and coherent.

Several familiar Shavian patterns are to be found in the play, the most obvious being one we have noted before, in which a major character passes from naive illusion to total disenchantment and then beyond both to a more clear-sighted vision of reality. Barbara herself moves from an idealistic faith in the integrity and ideals of the Salvation Army to complete disillusionment with both. When the Army accepts money from the purveyors of drunkenness and death, Bodger and Undershaft, she resigns her commission with a cry that contemporary critics found blasphemous: "My God: why hast thou forsaken me?" But by the end of the play she has transcended her despair and found a new, more realistic faith, working with what exists in the real world to create something better. She will raise "hell to heaven and . . . man to God" by following the "way of life" even into the Valley of the Shadow.

The central conflicts of the play grow out of an antithesis that is stated in a variety of ways. Metaphorically, the opposition is between two armies, the Salvation Army, the Army of God with its spiritual weapons, and the literal armies of guns and high explosives. Each is represented by a specific character, Barbara and Andrew Undershaft, who are also in conflict.

There seems to be little problem with how the audience is intended to "take" Barbara, for she is in all respects a thoroughly sympathetic figure, in spite of, or perhaps because of, the ease with which her father destroys her faith in her Army. Audiences, readers, and critics, however, have never been able to come up with any common point of view regarding Andrew Undershaft. And we may well wonder whether the man Cusins calls Mephistopheles and "devil incarnate" for his temptation of Barbara would inhabit the heaven or the hell of *Man and Superman*. Shaw provides a substantial clue in the Preface to the play, where he discusses "Froissart's medieval hero, who saw that 'to rob and pill' was a good life": "Froissart's knight, in placing the achievement of a good life before all other duties—which indeed are not duties at all when they conflict with it, but plain wickednesses—behaved bravely, admirably, and in the final analysis public-spiritedly. Medieval society, on the other hand, behaved very badly indeed in organizing itself so stupidly that a good life could be achieved by robbing and pilling" (I, 309). Undershaft expresses much the same attitude when his wife accuses him of having been selfish and unscrupulous in his rise to the status of munitions tycoon: "Not at all. I had the strongest scruples about poverty and starvation. Your moralists are quite unscrupulous about both: they make virtues of them. I had rather be a thief than a pauper. I had rather be a murderer than a slave. I dont want to be either; but if you force the alternative on me, then, by Heaven, I'll choose the braver and more moral one" (I, 435). Undershaft, the supercapitalist, is "right" in terms of a society and a social morality Shaw believes to be wrong, where strength and wealth are virtues, and where theft and murder may be the only means for a man to keep his self-respect. But the implication is, of course, that were society to organize itself more intelligently Undershaft would be an impossibility.

As he is treated in the play, however, Undershaft is clearly an ambiguous figure, a paradox, "right" and "wrong" at the same time, and yet beyond such distinctions; and he is one moment or pole in the dialectic of the play. He is aggressively dedicated to his own welfare, and yet his welfare is not happiness, nor is it wholly his own. When Cusins asks him what power drives his munitions plant he replies enigmatically: "A will of which I am a part." He is clearly a realist who scorns the pious platitudes and ideals by which a virtue is made of economic piracy. Like Tanner in his impudence, Undershaft is "Unashamed" of himself, his behavior, and his values. And he recognizes the importance of being able to tell the past from the future: "If your old religion broke down yesterday, get a newer and a better one for tomorrow."

In *Man and Superman* the underlying dialectic antithesis between the creative and life-giving impulse and the limiting, self-conscious, and direction-giving impulse is represented in terms of sexual conflict. In *Major Barbara* the central opposition is expressed in terms of religion. On the one hand is Barbara's Salva-

tion Army, representing traditional institutionalized Christianity
at its most Christian, and on the other is what Undershaft claims
is his religion. When Barbara asks him about it he says: "I am
a Millionaire. That is my religion"; and when Cusins poses the
same question, he replies: "Money and gunpowder; freedom and
power; command of life and command of death." But Undershaft
has created his own antithesis, both literally and in the sense that
Barbara's Christian idealism and sense of purpose are a reaction
against the materialism and "drive for power" of her father. At
the same time, *his* drive for wealth and power are in conscious
opposition to the doctrine of Christian acceptance and humility
represented by his daughter at the beginning of the play. In the
opening scene, added when Shaw revised the play, Barbara tells
the audience at the Salvation Army shelter: "Some of you turn
away from God in bitterness at the hardship of your lives, saying
that you do not want God: you want happiness and beauty. God
will give you both. . . . The rich are not happy. The poor have
only to reach out their hands for God's happiness and take it.
. . . It is the easiest thing in the world."[1]

Undershaft's reaction to Barbara's doctrine is explicit and
thoroughly Shavian: "Leave it to the poor to pretend that poverty
is a blessing: leave it to the coward to make a religion of his
cowardice by preaching humility." The opposition between the
two ways of seeing things permeates every aspect of the play, but
perhaps it rises to its most explicit symbolic statement when
Undershaft asks his daughter, "Where is your shelter?" and she
answers, "In West Ham. At the sign of the cross. Ask anybody
in Canning Town. Where are your works?" To which he replies,
"In Perivale St. Andrews. At the sign of the sword. Ask anybody
in Europe" (I, 362).

The great failing of the Salvation Army, and by implication of
Christianity in general, is that it teaches passivity, acceptance,
doing what is "easy," and hence, indirectly, the "getting something for nothing" philosophy that Shaw saw as the bane of human society. It is a view of life that perpetuates poverty by breed-

1. *Major Barbara: A Screen Version* (Baltimore: Penguin, 1951), p. 39.

ing weakness and rendering the poor impotent. When Cusins says to Undershaft, "I don't think you quite know what the Army does for the poor," he replies, "Oh yes I do. It draws their teeth: that is enough for me as a man of business." In the West Ham shelter we witness the practical effects of the Army's work, encouraging dishonesty and hypocrisy in those who, like Rummy Mitchens and Snobby Price, have lost all sense of pride and personal dignity, and contempt in those who have not, like Bill Walker. The failing of Undershaft's religion, on the other hand, is that all his money and gunpowder have no purpose, no goal, except to create themselves and perpetuate themselves. And it carries in itself the seeds of its own destruction.

In Hegelian terms, the force that can be called the thesis is here identified with power, pure power, without the limitations of any idea of purpose or direction. As Undershaft says, he will sell "arms to all men who offer an honest price for them, without respect of persons or principles; . . . I will take an order from a good man as cheerfully as from a bad one" (I, 430–432). But pure power creates a need for a direction and a purpose to which it can be put, lest, like the female principle of the Life Force, "in its ignorance it should destroy itself." And because direction necessarily implies restriction and limitation, it is to that extent an antithesis. The antithesis is represented in *Major Barbara* by the Christian idealism of Barbara and the humanistic values of Cusins, who possess an awareness of purpose, in terms of human good and aspirations for a better world, but have no power to make their vision a reality. Both the power and the sense of purpose are incomplete and impotent by themselves—and each needs the other.

The necessary synthesis is achieved only when the power is given a direction and a purpose beyond itself, that is, for human improvement; or, to put it the other way around, when idealism comes to grips with reality and is willing to *use* power: "Society cannot be saved until either the Professors of Greek take to making gunpowder, or else the makers of gunpowder become professors of Greek" (I, 439). Cusins finds the prospect of power

offered by Undershaft both fascinating and abhorrent. The munitions magnate points out: "Poverty and slavery have stood up
for centuries to your sermons and speeches and leading articles:
they will not stand up to my machine guns." Cusins bursts out:
"I repudiate your sentiments. I abhor your nature. I defy you in
every possible way. Still, it is true. But it ought not to be true."
Undershaft replies: "Ought! ought! ought! ought! Are you going
to spend your life saying ought, like the rest of our moralists? Turn
your oughts to shalls, man. Come and make explosives with me"
(I, 436). Cusins accepts the proffered synthesis and assures
Barbara: "It is not for myself alone. I want to make power for
the world." She protests, "I want to make power for the world
too; but it must be spiritual power"; to which Cusins replies, "I
think all power is spiritual: these cannons will not go off by themselves. . . . You cannot have power for good without having
power for evil too."

Barbara also has learned that good will alone is not enough, and
that no money or power is wholly innocent: "There is no wicked
side: life is all one. And I never wanted to shirk my share in whatever evil must be endured." She recognizes that God's work must
be done with the tools He has given us: "Turning our backs on
Bodger and Undershaft is turning our backs on life." The synthesis of power and directive vision is most explicit, appropriately,
in Barbara's climactic cry of conversion: "I have got rid of the
bribe of bread. I have got rid of the bribe of heaven. Let God's
work be done for its own sake: the work he had to create us to
do because it cannot be done except by living men and women.
When I die, let him be in my debt, not I in his" (I, 444). If man
wants a better world, he has got to create it himself, not sit back
and "let God do it"; and the end of human existence is not to be
"good" and be rewarded in Heaven, but to create heaven on
earth. Cusins responds to Barbara's speech with some surprise:
"Then the way of life lies through the factory of death?" And
she replies: "Yes, through raising of hell to heaven and of man
to God."

The similarities between *Major Barbara* and *Man and Super-*

man are quite obvious. As if to demonstrate that his symbolic identification of the two antithetical impulses of the Life Force with a man and a woman has no sexist implications, Shaw in the later play identifies raw undirected vitality and power with the man, and attributes to Barbara, even more than to Cusins, the self-conscious sense of aspirations toward something better that is associated with the Superman. On the other hand, Undershaft is, like Caesar or Jack Tanner, a thoroughgoing realist. He does not see very far, perhaps; and as an arch-capitalist his realism is dedicated to exploiting the follies and idealisms of society. But it is his realism that "educates" Barbara, and it may well be that unlike Cleopatra she will leave her tutor far behind. But while she is the most vocal about her new-found vision, the play ends with a kind of equilibrium among the three principals, a kind of trinitarian synthesis of mind and spirit and Life Force vitality, collectively carrying the fate of society into the future.

The future too will follow the dialectic pattern, and Undershaft's technocratic utopia, so various, so beautiful, so new, will in time be overborne. Those who find in the model village of the munitions factory a prototype for the Shavian utopia cannot have read the play very carefully. It may be the best that is possible under a capitalist dispensation, but essentially it represents a society based like ours on snobbery, complacency, illusions of freedom, and all the Deadly Virtues of the idealists. It too must pass away, and although Shaw does not suggest how, we may hope that under the guidance of generations of Barbaras and Cusins it will evolve, painfully perhaps, into something much better.

Far from being an "incoherent farrago of ideas," *Major Barbara* appears to have a carefully worked out intellectual and dramatic structure based in part on the idea of a dialectical opposition. The synthesis provides the climax of the plot and subsumes the best elements of the antitheses to create something better than either. The synthesis in turn provides the base for yet another step upward toward heaven, toward God, toward the fulfillment of the Life Force and the realization of the Hegelian Idea.

By the same token, far from being a "cynical representation of the triumph of materialism over spirituality," the play seems a somewhat quixotic vision of worldly power acquiring a spiritual dimension that gives it a point, a purpose, and a future. And far from being an irreligious play, Barbara's articulation of her newly found vision, "Let God's work be done for its own sake: the work He had to create us to do because it cannot be done except by living men and women," is a profoundly religious statement. The only religion it disparages is the one mentioned by Juan when he protests that "religion for me [was reduced] to a mere excuse for laziness, since it had set up a God who looked at the world and saw that it was good, against the instinct in me that looked through my eyes at the world and saw that it could be improved" (III, 641–642).

Both Barbara and Juan are clearly preachers of the Shavian religion, but Juan has already achieved the synthesis of the realist with the visionary philosopher, while Barbara is only beginning to learn to reconcile her sense of what might be with her father's realistic awareness of what is. The difference is significant in that Juan's development in the dream sequence is primarily an intellectual process, whereas Barbara is dynamically and dramatically involved with the forces and obstacles of the "real" world. Many of the plays that followed tend to vacillate between a dramatic focus on characters whose spiritual growth is reflected, like Juan's, through a flow of words that is simply amazing and one on those whose development is a function of action.

Recognizing the dramatic imponderability of *Man and Superman*, Shaw in the next few years did his best, when he could no longer suppress the urge to project his seemingly endless internal dialogues onto the stage, to isolate the discussion pieces and offer them as separate plays. But while such plays as *Getting Married* (1908), *Misalliance* (1910), and *Heartbreak House* (1913–1919) appear to contain little more than long arguments on various topics, the "plays of action" are not significantly devoid of discussion, and *The Shewing-Up of Blanco Posnet* (1909) and *Androcles and the Lion* (1912) are among the most explicitly polemic plays Shaw wrote. Indeed, a comparison of plays in the two categories reveals that the "action" plays, the melodramas and romances and fables, tend to develop the Life Force philosophy further, and more explicitly, than the "talk" plays. With the obvious exception of the Don Juan episode the discussion is rarely even by implication about Creative Evolution, which is appropriately better manifested in action than in conversation.

The *Shewing-Up of Blanco Posnet* is notable more as a *cause célèbre* in Shaw's running battle with the authorities than as a dramatic success, but the offense the Lord Chamberlain took at the play is at least a tribute to its effectiveness in raising basic religious issues. And however foolish the censor may have been in forbidding the play, the deletions he required as a condition of licensing obviously went right to the heart of Shaw's purposes in writing it. Shaw wrote to Lady Gregory while the furor was still boiling:

My doctrine is that God proceeds by the method of "trial and error." . . . To me the sole hope of human salvation lies in teaching Man to regard himself as an experiment in the realization of God, to regard his hand as God's hand, his brain as God's brain, his purpose as God's purpose. . . . You will find it all in Man & Superman, as you will find it all behind Blanco Posnet. Take it out of my play, and the play becomes nothing but the old cry of despair—Shakespear's "As flies to wanton boys so we are to the gods: they kill us for their sport"—the most frightful blasphemy ever uttered, and the one from which it is my mission to deliver the world. [*Letters,* II, 858–859]

In keeping with this sense of mission, Shaw subtitled the play "A sermon in crude melodrama"; but the literal sermon only occupies the final few minutes, and the remaining melodrama largely takes place before the play begins.

A true melodramatist would have provided the whole story: Blanco's escape with the stolen horse, the fugitive's impetuous act, when he gives up his horse to the strange woman with the dying child, his capture and trial as a horse thief, and his last-minute rescue from certain death. A modern absurdist, on the other hand, might well suggest in the death of the child, which renders the sacrifice futile, the ironic brutality of an indifferent or empty universe. But Shaw arranges the material to focus on a quite different dimension: the question that nags its way into the center of Blanco's consciousness, and hence into ours. Like Dick Dudgeon of a century earlier, in *The Devil's Disciple*, he asks himself why he, a sinner, social outcast, and drifter, by constitution a defier of both convention and authority, and by all available standards a lost soul, should have chosen to put his neck in a noose to save someone else. His initial explanation is that a malevolent God is "getting even" with him for his former defiance. But when the local whore Feemy, in spite of her evident viciousness, her brutal taunts at the bereaved mother, or even the contumely Blanco has heaped on her, "goes soft" and tells the lie that saves his life, he recognizes an alternative possibility. The power that has moved them works from the inside: "Softy! . . . Landed like me! Doing what you never intended!" (V, 271). And the power that works from the inside may in fact be powerless to control external events, powerless against the infection that kills the child, powerless against death, unless it moves a human spirit to work for life on its behalf.

Blanco's final speech, his "sermon," is in tone and content not unlike Barbara's—an almost ecstatic statement of discovery and recognition, the consequence of being "shewn-up" to himself. As a miserable sinner and a bad man he is "a fraud and a failure," and so is Feemy. In fact, "theres no good and bad; but by Jiminy, gents, theres a rotten game, and theres a great game," the game that works against life and the game that works for it. The rotten game is the game of "the boys," who are eager to kill for the sake of killing, or "the girls," whose concern for comfort and propriety is stronger than their concern for life. It is the game of the life-deniers, like Elder Daniels, who soothe their terror with pious religious palliatives, accepting death by disease as the Hand of God. But in the great game it is not so accepted: "It was early days when He made the croup, I guess. It was the best He could think of then; but when it turned out wrong on His hands He made you and me to fight the croup for him. . . . He wouldn't have made us at all if He could have done His work without us. By Gum, that must be what we're for!" (V, 274). In one of his rare, but apparently sincere, acknowledgments of the value of medical science in general or vaccination in particular, Shaw explained to Lady Gregory: "God has tried lots of machines—the diptheria bacillus, the tiger, the cockroach; and he cannot extirpate them except by making something that can shoot them or walk on them, or cleverer still, devise vaccines & anti toxins to prey on them."

Blanco Posnet is the familiar Shavian figure, the disillusioned or imperceptive person who is taken in hand by one of the realists, one of the "god-like" characters, who wrestles for the soul and brings it, often painfully, to a new awareness of reality and vitality. Blanco is educated to abandon the game of death and play for life: "And now I'm for the great game every time." Although there seems to be no realist in the play, no educator, to show Blanco the way, Shaw explains the omission, in case it is necessary, to Lady Gregory: "The real protagonist in my play, who does not appear in person on the stage at all, is God" (*Letters*, II, 864).

The Shewing-Up of Blanco Posnet represents as explicit a statement as can be found in any of the plays of Shaw's "religion," based on the essentially Hegelian concept of a Spirit, here called God, that slowly evolves and realizes itself by incarnating itself in and making use of its antithesis, matter, with the highest development of the synthesis at the moment being Man. The parable used to put across this piece of twentieth-century theology is, however, neither convincing nor attractive in the sense that the stories of *Arms and the Man* and *The Devil's Disciple* have an inherent popular appeal, no matter how Shaw may have tampered with the melodramatic spirit. In his next effort of the same kind he turned to a tale that, he observed, had delighted children for centuries, the Roman legend of Androclus, or Androcles, and the lion.

The legend itself only provides a comic frame for the rest of the play, and once we have gotten by the regrettable prologue, the language of which is tolerable only to the very young, the waltzing lion is pushed into the background and Shaw is able to develop some further thoughts about religion. Making Androcles, an escaped slave in the original story, one of a group of persecuted Christians on their way to martyrs' deaths at the Coliseum permits Shaw to turn the play into a study of various manifestations of primitive Christianity. The sacramental, sacerdotal, and institutional sides of Christianity are dealt with at length in the Preface, but are largely ignored in the play, except possibly in the figure of Spintho. The fact that Spintho is the most contemptible person in the play reflects Shaw's feelings about what he called "salvationists." Spintho is cowardly, corrupt, and vicious, concerned only with his personal salvation, and rationalizes his gross self-centeredness on the grounds that no matter how great the depravity, a last-minute repentance wipes all slates clean: the magic of martyrdom is a certain ticket to eternal bliss, "no matter what I have done."

The central opposition in *Androcles and the Lion* is not, as Shaw points out in a note to the play, "the conflict of a false theology with a true," but of religion and no religion. Spintho's, for all his talk of martyrdom, is no religion, but a justification for greed in this life and a scheme for buying happiness in the next. Lavinia, the principal "Christian" of the play, is not concerned with mere labels. As she tells the Roman captain, who has urged her to save herself by dropping a pinch of incense on the altar of the Roman gods: "If Diana meant to you what Christ means to me . . . we should kneel side by side before her altar like two children. But . . . men who believe neither in my god nor in their own—men who do not know the meaning of the word religion— . . . these men drag me to the foot of an iron statue that has become the symbol of the terror and darkness through which they walk, of their cruelty and greed, of their hatred of God" (V, 439–440). Hatred of God is for her the same as hatred of life, and she is physically incapable of forcing her body to so betray her nature as to make an act of worship.

Rome, both in the play and in the Preface, is identified with non-religion: the religion of death. In the Preface, which is devoted largely to drawing various distinctions between the Christianity of Jesus and that of Paul, Shaw describes the latter as "more Roman than the Romans," and "an inveterate Roman Rationalist" who was "always hopelessly in the toils of Sin, Death, and Logic, which had no power over Jesus." Paul's conversion to Christianity was, Shaw claims, "no conversion at all: it was Paul who converted the religion that had raised one man above sin and death into a religion that delivered millions of men so completely into their dominion that their own common nature became a horror to them, and the religious life became a denial of life" (V, 396). This aspect of Paul's legacy lives in the play in the salvationist Spintho and in the Romans, with their iron hearts and false logic. The play focuses on the Coliseum, where Romans from the emperor to the slave meet in the worship of death.

Christianity, on the other hand, is the religion of life. In the Preface Shaw observes that "the aim of Jesus is not only that the people should have life, but that they should have it 'more abundantly.' " When the Roman captain scoffs at the Christians' faith in another world, Lavinia replies: "What does that matter? Do you think I am only running away from the terrors of life into the comfort of heaven? If there were no future, or if the future were one of torment, I should have to go just the same. The hand of God is upon me." Lavinia is not running away from anything; she is committed to life, to reality, and hence to God. As her own entrance into the Coliseum of death approaches, she draws an explicit contrast between her own instincts and Spintho's dreams of eternal happiness:

A man cannot die for a story and a dream. None of us believed the stories and the dreams more devoutly than poor Spintho; but he could not face the great reality. What he would have called my faith has been oozing away minute by minute whilst Ive been sitting here, with death coming nearer and nearer, with reality becoming realler and realler, with stories and dreams fading away into nothing. . . .

I have now no doubt at all that I must die for something greater than dreams or stories. I think I am going to die for God. Nothing else is real enough to die for. [V, 462–463]

And when the captain challenges the paradox, "What is God?" Lavinia comes back with an often-repeated Shavian idea, "When we know that, Captain, we shall be gods ourselves."

Dying for God—and for life—means more to Lavinia than being "a good Christian." Ferrovius, the giant "muscular Christian," who carries a somewhat overdeveloped sense of the sinfulness of his quick temper, is shocked when she expresses the hope that he will flatten his gladiatorial opponent: "Woman: you are no Christian." But when she replies, "I am not always a Christian," Shaw implies that she is not always a Pauline abstraction, but a vital reality. Indeed, neither Lavinia nor the barely restrainable Ferrovius nor the meek Androcles fits a formula; but each in his own way is on the side of life.

In a finale that borders on wildest farce, Ferrovius's very unChristian slaughter of six fully armed gladiators and Androcles' triumphal waltz around the no longer deadly Coliseum awe and terrify the Emperor into converting to a Christianity as superficial and sterile as his Roman paganism. Ferrovius accepts the limitation to his own faith, recognizing that "the Christian god is not yet. He will come; . . . but meanwhile I must serve the gods that are not the God that will be. Until then I accept service in the Guard, Caesar." Caesar approves, observing that the way the world moves is "to make the best of both dispensations," the wise man being neither bigoted in clinging to the old nor impractical in "keeping an open mind for the new."

The wise and the pragmatic may take the middle road, more for convenience than from conviction; but to move the world off dead center requires something more. The only sense of sin Shaw will admit to is his dissatisfaction with the status quo, and he asserts in the Preface that "the fundamental condition of evolution . . . is, that life, including human life, is continually evolving, and must therefore be continually ashamed of itself and its present and past" (V, 398).

Christianity, Shaw also says in the Preface, is "a step in moral evolution which is independent of any individual preacher" (V, 325). And this evolution too is pushed forward by the constant pressure of the life-affirmers, those with a faith in "a creative spirit in ourselves called by [Jesus] the Heavenly Father and by us Evolution, . . . Life Force and other names." This is opposed by the immovable obstacle of greed and laziness, an obsession with the need for law, and a disrespect for life: "People who are shewn by their inner light the possibility of a better world based on the demand of the spirit for a nobler and more abundant life, not for themselves at the expense of others, but for everybody, are naturally dreaded and therefore hated by the Have-and-Holders" (V, 471). Christianity itself, being a step in human evolution, has become in time the fortress of the "Have-and-Holders," the status quo. But there is still the Life Force, the supermen and superwomen who, with Lavinia, will still "strive for the coming of the God who is not yet."

The faith in the God who is not yet that sustains Lavinia in her refusal to accept the gods that are, a faith that is more or less explicit in *Blanco Posnet* and *Major Barbara* and lies behind most of the early plays, is less clearly articulated in *Heartbreak House*— and according to many critics is wholly absent. The harsh and violent reality of the First World War, during which the play was written, could not but have taken its toll. It was evident to Shaw, from both the origins of the conflict and the behavior of his countrymen, that this was not to be, in Cusins's phrase, a case of making war on war, for all the propagandists' cant, nor were Barbara's dreams of a better world even at issue. But although the play was finished before it was possible to tell what way the world was heading, it was clear that the old order was disappearing in a moral and economic and political cataclysm. *Heartbreak House* is about the end of an era.

Although subtitled "A fantasy in the Russian manner on English themes," *Heartbreak House* could just as accurately be called a symphony on various Shavian themes. Many of the familiar motifs hold this seemingly diffuse play together: the education of a realist; the opposition of diabolic and angelic natures, with the associated alternatives between drifting and steering; a metaphoric handling of the sexual dialectic; and an ending so tentative as to have been misread as despair. The Chekhovian parallels suggested in the subtitle range from the arbitrary to the essential, and Shaw points to the most important in the Preface, where he characterizes the representatives of the cultured, educated Englishman in his play as being "helpless wasters of their inheritance, like the people in Tchekov's Cherry Orchard," a play he had already identified as one of Chekhov's "four fascinating dramatic studies of Heartbreak House" (I, 449).

The distinction, argued by William Irvine, between the two playwrights' methods of characterization—the "allegorical," "ethical abstractions" of Shaw and the "typical," "human beings" of Chekhov—is legitimate but misleading.[2] Chekhov, it is true, seems more interested in the reactions of his characters to the rapid flux of historical and social change than in making broad generalizations about human nature. And Shaw is, as usual, making a generalized comment, but not by reducing his characters to ethical abstractions. In effect, he is writing another history play—like the *Caesar and Cleopatra* of some years before, or the still-to-come *Saint Joan*—except that in *Heartbreak House* the historical event is contemporary: the coming of war to England. The characters, although not maintaining even the fiction of historicity, are no more allegories than Caesar or Joan, and like them they embody, in sometimes incongruous combinations, qualities Shaw thought important to the way humans of any era, as individuals and as social groups, defy or direct the flow of history.

Drifting on the torrent might more aptly describe the occupants of Heartbreak House; and like the inhabitants of hell in *Man and Superman* "it is the fact that they are . . . drifting with [the Devil's] want of will, instead of doing their own, that makes them the uncomfortable, false, restless, artificial, petulant, wretched

2. William Irvine, *The Universe of G.B.S.* (New York: McGraw-Hill, 1949), p. 294.

creatures they are" (III, 642). The passengers on this rudderless
"ship . . . this soul's prison we call England," are not wholly
damned, for they *are* restless and dissatisfied with both themselves
and their habitation. But their will to discover alternatives to
either seems paralyzed by a profound confusion as to who they
are or why they are there. This inner disharmony, growing out of
unresolved internal contradictions, creates a pervasive sense of
dislocation, uselessness, and futility; the dominant character trait
is inertia, with a forced cheerfulness hiding something very close
to despair.

As we have seen, Shaw's characters do not on the whole fall into neat categories called "good" and "bad." Those in *Heartbreak
House* are no exception, having their virtues and vices, as Hesione
Hushabye says, "anyhow: all mixed." Each character seems to be
caught in a kind of dialectic struggle between two antithetical
"sides" or impulses of the personality, one potentially fruitful, the
other tending to negate or frustrate that creativity. And because
we may feel very differently about these impulses, it is often
difficult to know how to "take" some of the characters, or to
guess what Shaw's attitude toward them may have been.

Hector Hushabye is one of several ambiguous characters in the
play. As Marcus Darnley, mysterious foundling, veteran of the
barricades, rescuer of ladies and tigers, whose "life has been one
long romance," he is a fraud who looks suspiciously like an inhabitant of hell. As amorous pursuer of the beautiful but shallow
Lady Utterword, he is a fatuous gigolo made available by his
wife's generosity, and yet he can acknowledge that he is "playing
the fool, out of sheer worthlessness." It is Hector who stands up
to Captain Shotover: "I must believe that my spark, small as it
is, is divine, and that the red light over the door [of "the Mangans
and Randalls and Billie Dunns"] is hell fire." And to Hector,
Shaw gives one of his most passionately held convictions: "We are
members one of another." Erroneously attributing it to St. John,
Shaw had used the passage on several occasions to describe the
unity of mankind in its common divinity, its collective possession

of Godhead. Hector's spark may be small, but it is still glowing. As the Captain warns him at the end, his courage may be of no use, but it proves his soul is still alive.

Hesione is alive too, fascinatingly so. To a great degree it is the very intensity of her vitality that has made what Ellie calls "a household pet" out of her husband. At her best Hesione is generous, intelligent, and perceptive. She understands the men and how to handle them, but not herself and her limitations, nor does she have the vision to cope with the world except in her sexual role as wife and mother-figure. When Ellie is in the first stage of her "heartbreak" she turns on Hesione in a fury: "I suppose you think you're being sympathetic. . . . You see me getting a smasher right in the face that kills a whole part of my life: . . . and you think you can help me over it by a little coaxing and kissing." These are indeed Hesione's most effective ways of dealing with the world, but they have their limits: "When I am neither coaxing and kissing nor laughing, I am just wondering how much longer I can stand living in this cruel, damnable world" (I, 546). In the sense that her intellectual and moral nature is circumscribed by her role as a woman, Hesione is not unlike Ann Whitefield—the Ann likened to a boa constrictor by Jack Tanner.

Ariadne Utterword has her sister's overpowering fascination—"diabolic," Hector calls it. This sexuality is contradicted and restrained in Ariadne by an almost obsessive need for propriety and decorum, and the price of this inner contradiction is emotional sterility. Romantic relationships, as Ariadne frankly admits, are for her nothing more than a game at which she is an expert player, a game played out in the pathetic hope that somewhere she may find that which will evoke a spark of true love.

What in Ariadne appears as sexual magnetism is in Mangan a kind of commercial vitality, an exceptional ability to manipulate others financially. He hopes to marry Ellie because a wife is a social, sexual, ego-gratifying convenience. She is, however, a very small counter in the intricate economic game he is playing, in which the only reward is the illusion of power, for it emerges that

Mangan in fact possesses nothing but the entrepreneurial skill to make the capitalist machinery work. Stripped of his imposing facade as the captain of industry, Mangan is pathetically insecure, a whimpering child with a tender ego.

Mazzini Dunn is characterized as the complete antithesis of Boss Mangan: he is a world-improver rather than a world-destroyer, a "soldier of freedom" rather than a captain of industry, socialist rather than capitalist, visionary rather than visionless, a bit complacent rather than restless and dissatisfied, and, as the world goes, a failure. Although Ellie's epithet, "the soul of goodness," is both sincere and accurate as far as it goes, his very innocence, impracticality, and good nature render him impotent in bringing about change in the world of human affairs.

Randall Utterword is too minor, and perhaps too contemptible, to have much attention lavished on his contrarieties, but he has them nonetheless. In him all the so-called advantages of civilization, money and education and the freedom of the "right" society, have been squandered on a shallow, petulant nonentity. And whatever effectiveness he may have as a human being has been rendered impotent by his romantic infatuation for Ariadne.

Captain Shotover is certainly the most obviously equivocal of all the characters in *Heartbreak House,* and most of the critics have in one way or another recognized him as "half dotard and half seer."[3] In this ambiguity, at least, he bears a distinct similarity to Andrew Undershaft, for while the Captain utters sentiments and represents a view of life that are in some ways distinctly Shavian, it is difficult to believe that Shaw could make his hero or spokesman an alcoholic any more than a capitalist. But Shotover's vision is clearer on three bottles of rum than the other characters' on none. Like that of John Tarleton in *Misalliance,* his is a still young spirit yoked to an aging body. And that may provide the key to his split personality. The internal conflict is in various ways that of the active, inquiring mind confronted with the decay of the machinery of life. The vitality that found fulfill-

3. Louis Crompton, *Shaw the Dramatist* (Lincoln: University of Nebraska Press, 1969), p. 162.

ment "on the bridge in the typhoon, or frozen into Arctic ice for months in darkness," and that led him to look for "hardship, danger, horror, and death, that [he] might feel the life in [him] more intensely," is confronted with the lure of happiness. The passion for navigation, worn down by the demands of the life it guides, is tempted by the ease of drifting into oblivion. The price of energy is exhaustion, and life consumes itself—but is no less life for that.

Insofar as the play is about the opposition between the impulses of life—curiosity, daring, resistance, the effort of seeking something better—and the impulses of death—comfort and happiness, cynical self-serving, and dreams of ease—the play is about Captain Shotover. These antithetical forces may momentarily cancel one another out and produce stasis, but they are not static, and the Captain's vital force is running down. His vitality has, as the Devil in *Man and Superman* predicted, been turned to the cause of destruction; his resistance to dreams of peace must be artificially bolstered by rum; and the effort of seeking has exhausted him. He is a once noble institution, with many of the lendings of his prime still about him, suffering inevitable deterioration, and yet having a will that refuses to yield without a struggle.

As we have seen looking at other plays, the inner divisions between and within characters often reflect larger moral and metaphysical contradictions inherent in human nature, or in the cosmos itself. And while Shaw had little use for such simplistic labels as Good and Bad, and openly scoffed at Virtue, his repeated insistence on his belief in the reality of sin suggests that one of the basic antitheses of his thinking was between sin and its opposite, whatever that might be called. Actually it is quite clear that the opposite is the Life Force, and that sin for Shaw was any element or quality that thwarts life. This might be, at one extreme, apathy, complacency, living in the past, anything that leads to impotence or sterility, and at the other, cruelty and hatred of life.

In most of the characters in *Heartbreak House* the impulses toward life and power and self-consciousness are set against, and indeed seem to generate, counter impulses, obstacles, oppositions; and characteristically the most basic contradictions seem to grow out of the most paradoxical of human experiences: love. In fact most of Shaw's plays, from *The Philanderer* to *The Millionairess*, are about love. That has, of course, been the single most popular subject of literature, and Shaw was never shy about seeking an audience. But beyond that, he found in the love relationship a model or symbol for both the dynamics and the most elemental polarities of human nature. In this respect, *Heartbreak House* is in both theme and central metaphor very much in the tradition of *Man and Superman*.

In *Man and Superman* sexual love, embodied in Ann White-field, was identified with the vitality and creativity of the Life Force. At the same time it was clear that while procreation is necessary for the perpetuation of vessels for the Life Force, it is not sufficient for its fulfillment. For the woman, "vitality . . . is a blind fury of creation," and "a man is nothing to [her] but an instrument of that purpose" (III, 537); she offers a man happiness and mothering because of his sexual, not his intellectual, contributions. Relieved of the "exhausting labor of gestation," man's "superfluous energy has gone to his brain and to his muscle" (III, 625). But brain and muscle, without purpose and vision, can become destructive. As Juan said of life: "Think of how it wastes and scatters itself, how it raises up obstacles to itself and destroys itself in its ignorance and blindness" (III, 618).

Love is necessary for life; but when it becomes an end in itself, it can be an obstruction to life, for which love is a beginning and not an end. For Hector a love that has already served its pro-creative purpose becomes a kind of prison. He is dominated by Hesione, has become her "lapdog," because with her he "had one real go at least." "That was a confounded madness," he reflects. "It has left its mark on me. I believe that is why I have never been able to repeat it" (I, 524). He tries to repeat it in the romantic poses of Marcus Darnley; but as Captain Shotover comments: "She has used you up, and left you nothing but dreams."

From Hesione's point of view, however, she has simply been

fulfilling her function of making her man happy. This maternal impulse to protect, and ultimately overwhelm, the vitality that had once seemed so attractive, is implicit in her complaint: "What do men want? They have their food, their firesides, their clothes mended, and our love at the end of the day. Why are they not satisfied?" (I, 529). Her anger at the unreasonableness of men, who will not be satisfied with happiness and love and comfort, breaks out again in Act Three, under the night sky from which the bombs will soon descend. When Ellie announces her marriage to Captain Shotover, Hesione turns to Mangan: "Dont you feel how lovely this marriage night is, made in heaven? Arnt you happy, you and Hector? Open your eyes: Addy and Ellie look beautiful enough to please the most fastidious men: we live and have not a care in the world. We women have managed all that for you. Why in the name of common sense do you go on as if you were two miserable wretches?" (I, 587). The Captain supplies the answer: "I tell you happiness is no good. You can be happy when you are only half alive."

The world Hesione wants is unchanging, womblike, a world of peace and security sustained by the satisfaction of the need for food and love and comfort. But Hesione at least has had love, and children. Her sister Ariadne has had neither, and the vitality manifest in her efforts "to fall in head over ears" with almost anyone, has been frustrated and turned awry by her need for the security of a rigid social structure. For her the "natural, wholesome, contented, and really nice English people" are what she calls "the equestrian classes," whose lives are given purpose and discipline by riding. Her need for order is revolted by the instability and confusion of her father's house: "Oh, this house, this house! . . . no regular meals, nobody ever hungry because they are always gnawing bread and butter or munching apples, and, what is worse, the same disorder in ideas, in talk, in feeling. When I was a child . . . I was unhappy, and longed all the time—oh, how I longed!—to be respectable, to be a lady, to live as others did, not to have to think of everything for myself" (I, 495).

Ariadne has escaped from disorder into the well-regulated world of Sir Hastings Utterword, who has been governor of all the crown colonies in succession, and she has found happiness— though not fulfillment—as mistress of Government House. Her husband, at least, knows how to keep order: "Get rid of your ridiculous sham democracy; and give Hastings the necessary power, and a good supply of bamboo to bring the British native to his senses: he will save the country with the greatest of ease."

Boss Mangan is as obsessed as Ariadne by a need for the security of order and propriety, and his complaint about Heartbreak House echoes hers: "What shame is there in this house? . . . I tell you I cant bear this. I was brought up to be respectable. . . . How are we to have any self-respect if we dont keep it up that we're better than we really are?" (I, 584). For him too love has been reduced to a game that has much to do with keeping up appearances and nothing to do with life. He possesses power, in London at least, but paradoxically the cynical pragmatism that gives him that power renders it empty and purposeless.

Mazzini Dunn is too broad-minded to fear new ideas, but even more than Hector he has lost his vitality and sense of purpose in the quagmires of memory and complacency. He is, he tells Hesione, "quite safe," because "it wouldn't be natural" to try to re-create the grand passion he had experienced with Ellie's mother. He has been moved by human injustice and suffering; but when Hector asks him why he didn't *do* anything, he explains: "But I did. I joined societies and made speeches and wrote pamphlets. That was all I could do. . . . Every year I expected a revolution, or some frightful smash-up: it seemed impossible that we could blunder and muddle on any longer. But nothing ever happened, except, of course, the usual poverty and crime and drink that we are used to. Nothing ever does happen. It's amazing how well we get along, all things considered" (I, 592). Mazzini's potency and vision, like his love, belong to the past. He has been lulled into a deathlike passivity by the reassurance that there is "an overruling Providence, after all," who like Hastings will keep things in order. His parents, who were poets, "gave him the noblest ideas"; but their passion is spent.

The passion to fight free of peace and security and complacency, to keep the freedom of what he calls "God's open sea," steadies Captain Shotover's will even though "the last shot was fired years ago." He knows his physical vitality has consumed itself: "The dreams are conquering. . . . I am too weary to resist or too weak. I feel nothing but the accursed happiness I have dreaded all my life long: the happiness that comes as life goes, the happiness of yielding and dreaming instead of resisting and doing, the sweetness of the fruit that is going rotten" (I, 568). But with what strength he has, and with the help of rum, he resists the temptation to passivity offered by the other half-real figures who haunt Heartbreak House.

Hesione's search for happiness is no good for Captain Shotover: "I am happier now I am half dead than ever I was in my prime. But there is no blessing on my happiness." Mangan, with his obsession for the security of respectability, is to him only "a dog barking to keep the truth out." For Hastings's and Ariadne's need for law and order he has only contempt: "Any fool can govern with a stick in his hand. . . . It is not God's way." And of Mazzini's faith in Providence, Shotover says: "Every drunken skipper trusts to Providence. But one of the ways of Providence with drunken skippers is to run them on the rocks." When Ellie challenges this with his own rum drinking, he expands the metaphor: "Let a man drink ten barrels of rum a day, he is not a drunken skipper until he is a drifting skipper. Whilst he can lay his course and stand on his bridge and steer it, he is no drunkard. It is the man who lies drinking in his bunk and trusts to Providence that I call the drunken skipper, though he drank nothing but the waters of the River Jordan" (I, 593). The alternatives are clear: "Navigation. Learn it and live; or leave it and be damned." Juan had put it: "To be in hell is to drift: to be in heaven is to steer."

Although *Heartbreak House* is manifestly an allegory of England and Europe drifting toward the catastrophe of the First World War, it only becomes explicit in the Captain's reply to Hector's question about "this ship that we are all in? This soul's prison we call England?" "The captain is in his bunk, drinking bottled ditchwater; and the crew is gambling in the forecastle. She will strike and sink and split. Do you think the laws of God will be suspended in favor of England because you were born in it?" (I, 594).

For all that it may be the English ship of state that is heading on the rocks, the play's structure does not provide a political allegory. The characters, with the possible exception of Mangan, do not represent any specific political elements, and no political or social solutions are even hinted at. The forces or impulses at work are both metaphysical and spiritual, and although they have their corresponding manifestations on the social and political level, within the play they are represented as essentially internal contradictions. There is a natural tendency to externalize these conflicting forces and see them as the powers of good and evil operating in and through the world of overt human action. Captain Shotover justifies his work with dynamite and death rays in terms of just such an external mortal combat between those who, like himself, seek something better, what he calls "the seventh degree of concentration," and the hoggish Mangans and lovesick Randalls, the forces of greed and self-indulgence and lusting after happiness. It is the struggle of life against death, of heaven against hell, and the Captain would find an eternal "enmity between our seed and their seed." But, as Hector observes, "It is the same seed"; and he adds the Biblical words: "We are members one of another."

There are several Shakespearean echoes in *Heartbreak House,* but none more important than in the representation of the commanding, strong-willed old man in whom the battle between life and death is running down. Like Captain Shotover, Lear would like to externalize the inner dichotomies and see his daughters as representatives of forces of evil for which he bears no responsibility. He is near to madness, and hence to a truer vision of things, when he recognizes Goneril: "My flesh, my blood, my daughter; . . . thou art a boil. / A plague-sore, an embossed carbuncle, / In my corrupted blood" (II, iv, 224–228). Without making an allegory of *King Lear,* it is appropriate for us to see many of its characters as in one way or another concrete dramatic projections of the king's own nature. Most importantly, his various kinds of blindness are not resolved into understanding until, having already condemned himself, on the heath, for the evil of two daughters, he understands that Cordelia too is of and in his blood.

Captain Shotover, in much the same way as Lear, can be seen as a kind of Mankind-figure, embodying in his private drama the quintessential oppositions and paradoxes of our divided being: a mind that can invent ingenious new ways of destruction in a body that once was filled with vitality and daring and love, a mind that could aspire to the Superman in a body that seeks comfort and happiness and death. Heartbreak House and its inhabitants, then, are in some respects an extension of the inner life and contradictions of the Captain. Within and among them are to be found the various antitheses that are at once a curse and the source of the dynamics of human evolution. Where antithetical moments or forces cancel each other, the result is stasis; for the process to become dialectical requires an input of energy and will, of what Shaw—and Hegel—called "passion." The Captain's disappointment at the running down of the dialectical momentum emerges poignantly in the almost ritualistic chant at the end of Act One: "I builded a house for my daughters, and opened the doors thereof, / That men might come for their choosing, and their betters spring from their love." But love alone is not enough, and for each daughter in her own way it becomes an obstacle to vitality, and so betrays his aspirations.

Captain Shotover, however, has a third daughter—or at least Ellie Dunn, near the end of the play, calls him her "spiritual husband and second father." And Ellie is different from the other characters. In them opposing impulses seem to have reached a stand-off, while she changes significantly in the course of the play.

Ellie's development follows a familiar Shavian dialectic: from idealism to disillusioned cynicism to a state containing something of both, a realistic view of the world united with a knowledge that it could be better.

When she first arrives at Heartbreak House, Ellie is a little like Raina Petkoff, full of noble ideas about a higher love, and convinced that "the world is really a glorious world for women who can see its glory and men who can act its romance!" Marcus Darnley seems, like Sergius, to represent the "unspeakable fulfilment" of these romantic aspirations; and when he too turns out to be a fraud, playing the role because it is successful with women, her world is demolished. But the breaking of so small a thing makes an almost inaudible crack, and indeed is not so much an event as a process. Ellie says: "I have a horrible fear that my heart is broken, but that heartbreak is not like what I thought it must be." Hesione's explanation is that "it's only life educating you"; and the education occupies the rest of the play.

Ellie's first response to heartbreak is to cauterize her feelings against further damage: "Unless I can be hard— as hard as nails —I shall go mad." Sergius, disillusioned in war and heroism, had dismissed "the dream of patriots and heroes" as "a fraud. . . . A hollow sham, like love." Ellie, learning that even Hesione's lovely black hair, which had ensnared Hector, is false, cries out in despair: "Everything false!"

In her newfound hardness and cynical practicality, Ellie announces that she will indeed marry the despicable Mangan, making a convenience out of him as he had made a convenience of her father, hoping to find in his money a guarantee of comfort and peace if not of happiness. Captain Shotover recognizes what is happening, and warns her that selling the soul for comfort and peace is the way of death: "Your reward will be that you will eat, but you will not live" (I, 567).

Ellie at first is not sure she wants to be "educated" by Shotover: "I like you to dream," she tells him. "You must never be in the real world when we talk together." When he tells her that it is precisely the "happiness of yielding and dreaming" that is at once possessing him and the thing in life he most fears, she muses: "You dread it almost as much as I used to dread losing my dreams and having to fight and do things. But that is all over for me: *my* dreams are dashed to pieces" (I, 568). But with Shotover's help she discovers it is *not* all over, that cynicism and selfishness are not the only alternatives to romantic idealism: "I feel now as if there was nothing I could not do, because I want nothing." And the Captain responds: "Thats the only real strength."

Captain Shotover is the source of a new vitality for Ellie that carries her beyond the paralysis of disillusionment and despair, and in return she symbolically dedicates her "broken heart and . . . strong sound soul to its natural captain, my spiritual husband and second father." When Ariadne accuses her of being "the most conceited young woman [she has] met," Ellie replies, "I know my strength now."

Exactly where this strength, self-assurance, and realism will lead Ellie is, characteristically, far from clear. The aimless drifting of this house full of "heartbroken imbeciles," who, as Hector says, "sit . . . talking, and leave everything to Mangan and to chance and to the devil," is not enough for her: "It cant go on for ever. I'm always expecting something. I dont know what it is; but life must come to a point sometime." Although Ariadne suggests that "the point" for a young woman of her age is a baby, Ellie has in mind some larger change. It is in response to the assurance that drifting, under the guidance of Providence, is perfectly safe that the Captain states the case for "Navigation. Learn it and live; or leave it and be damned." The disillusioned idealist, Mazzini, says, "I thought all that once, Captain; but I assure you nothing will happen," and with symbolic appropriateness the first distant explosions of the approaching air raid are heard.

The bombs from the unidentified aircraft are quite evidently the "point" toward which life has been moving—but they have been much misunderstood by the critics. It is almost a commonplace to regard *Heartbreak House* as Shaw's testament to his own disillusionment and despair, during and following World War

One, at what he took to be the destruction of all his own hopes for a socialist order and the reaffirmation, both at home and abroad, of the power of the capitalist establishment. From this point of view the bombs at the end might suggest Armageddon, in which a feckless humanity drifts into well-deserved extinction, and the enthusiasm of Hector and Ellie for the excitement of the raid is the final evidence of the failure of the will in an open expression of a death-wish.

Shaw was indeed profoundly distressed by the war, seeing in it the direct consequences of the greed of the Mangans, the power politics of the militarists, and the drifting of everyone else. But ever since his earliest explicit exegesis of his religion of the future in *Man and Superman,* Shaw had made it quite clear that he had serious misgivings about the capacity of the human species, as presently constituted, to carry on the process he called Creative Evolution. He had affirmed that unless substantial changes took place in human nature the Life Force would find a more adequate vehicle than man. In this context it is doubtful that the folly and futility of the First World War made any profound change in this thinking.

At the end of the play we indeed have a strong sense that "life is coming to a point." The aimless drifting, the refusal to face reality, the retreat into romantic ideals, and into the desperate hope that love and security and happiness would be enough, have carried man as far as they can, and have proven inadequate. Much that was pleasant, familiar, and reassuring would surely be swept away in the storm that was approaching, just as the rectory is left a pile of rubble. Billie Dunn, the moral pirate, and Mangan, the economic pirate, are destroyed by the bombs that Captain Shotover likens to the Day of Judgment; and we do not know what new judgments other bombs on other nights may bring. The note of excitement and exhilaration with which the play ends, with Hector and Ellie "hoping" the bombers will return, and their willingness to burn down Heartbreak House to guide them on their way, scarcely seems appropriate to despair, unless Shaw is indulging in a perfect ecstasy of nihilistic irony.

In *The Cherry Orchard* Chekhov introduces a kind of audible symbol when, in the scene in the cherry orchard in Act Two and again at the end of the play, "a distant sound is heard. It seems to come from the sky and is the sound of a breaking string. It dies away sadly."[4] At its first appearance, someone speculates that it sounds like a lift cable breaking in a far-off mine shaft; and Firs says the same noise was heard at the time of "the troubles," when the serfs were given their freedom. At the end of the play, the same noise accompanies the sound of the axes cutting down the orchard. It is evident from the context that the snapped string suggests the breaking of the golden chain, the rigid hierarchies of the old aristocratic system. The bonds of the social structure are giving way; but the only actual destruction is the clearing away of the beautiful but useless orchard.

Shaw, in his Russian fantasy, explicitly echoes Chekhov's symbol. Early in Act Three, as the characters are engaged in idle conversation (much as they are in Act Two of *The Cherry Orchard*), Hesione calls attention to "a sort of splendid drumming in the sky. . . . It came from a distance and then died away." There is some speculation that it might be a train, but Hector announces that it must be "Heaven's threatening growl of disgust at us useless futile creatures. I tell you, one of two things must happen. Either out of that darkness some new creation will come to supplant us as we have supplanted the animals, or the heavens will fall in thunder and destroy us." Torn between a protective romanticism and the impulses of realism, the frustrated Hector sees himself as "useless and dangerous," along with the house as something that "ought to be abolished." The mysterious sound from the sky, which here too symbolizes the end of a worn-out order, appears again at the end as the sound of aircraft; but the destruction they bring is by no means total. They bring an end to the church, but the man of God survives; they blow up the capitalist thieves, but the other inhabitants of Heartbreak House remain. They mark the failure of drifting, of self-indul-

4. Chekhov, *"Uncle Vanya" and "The Cherry Orchard,"* trans. Ronald Hingley (London: Oxford University Press, 1965), p. 85.

gence, and of mindless greed—but we do not know what will happen when they come again. Ellie and Hector hope they will return to destroy Heartbreak House—a place characterized earlier as "the soul's prison."

Ellie knows at the end that there is no blessing on the romantic search for happiness, or on Mangan's money, or on Ariadne's faith in order and propriety, but that there is a blessing on her broken heart, on the Captain's spirit, and on their "marriage." Something of the Captain's failing vision and vitality, embodied in his passion for navigation, the science of steering rather than drifting, finds new life and energy in her. It lifts Ellie above the self-defeating paralysis, the forces counter to life, of the other characters; and in that possibility, in the fact that her soul is still alive, and that she has recognized the will of the Life Force in the Captain as *her* will, lies a hope for the future.

Support for the idea that the possibility of destruction at the conclusion to *Heartbreak House* need not reflect Shaw's personal despair over contemporary events may be found in a document already cited for its apparent contributions to his thinking: Hegel's essay *Reason in History*. As we saw, Hegel considered what he calls "passion" the source of energy and vitality in the operation of the dialectic. To whatever is merely potential or implicit, "a second element must be added for it to become reality, namely . . . [the] passion of man" (p. 28). In the affairs of men, "two elements therefore enter into our investigation: first, the Idea, secondly, the . . . passions" (p. 29). This power is close to Shaw's "moral passion," or as Hegel describes it, "the whole energy of will and character." In this sense passion may not yet have a specific goal, "a particular content," but can still "supply the impelling and actuating force for deeds of universal scope. Passion is thus the subjective and therefore the formal aspect of energy, will, and activity, whose content and aim are at this point still undetermined" (p. 30). The important point is that these passions are primary among the elements that "constitute the tools and means of the World Spirit for attaining its purpose, bringing it to consciousness and realizing it" (p. 31).

In Hegel's system, the passion and energy necessary to move the Spirit from potentiality to reality in history necessarily confronts obstacles and opposition: "It is at this point that appear those momentous collisions between existing, acknowledged duties, laws, and rights and those possibilities which are adverse to this system, violate it, and even destroy its foundations and existence." As "these possibilities . . . become historical fact, they involve a universal of an order different from that on which depends the permanence of a people or a state" (p. 39). The counterforce to change has as its ideal what Hegel calls "the preservation of ethical life," that is, "the preservation of a people, a state, of the well-ordered spheres of life" (p. 38). At a time of "transition from one spiritual pattern to the next, . . . the later universal, so to speak, the next higher genus of the preceding species, [being] potentially but not yet actually present in the preceding one . . . makes all existing reality unstable and disunited." In spite of a powerful impulse to maintain the status quo, passion overbalances inertia, and "the existence of a national spirit is broken when it has used up and exhausted itself. World history, the World Spirit, continues on its course. . . . The Spirit's development, its progression and ascent to an ever higher concept of itself . . . is connected with the degradation, destruction, annihilation of the preceding mode of actuality which the concept of the Spirit had evolved" (pp. 38–39).

It is in this passage that Hegel articulates the proposition that it is the "world-historical individual" who furthers the evolution of the World Spirit in defiance of "the well-ordered spheres of life." For him Caesar had performed such a function; and for Shaw the role would also be assigned to Joan. In *Heartbreak House* Ellie Dunn observes, but does not cause, just such a historical crisis as Hegel describes, yet she clearly would fight free of a society that "has used up and exhausted itself," and at the end she would help destroy a symbol that explicitly represents prewar England.

Vitality and realistic vision and the will to steer are major achievements, and the *sine qua non* for being a vessel for the

Life Force. But what exactly Ellie will do with these powers and whether they are enough in the face of the powers of inertia to save her world is scarcely suggested. What happens to her, what lies beyond, is left a mystery. On the other hand, a failure to answer that question is by no means something novel for Shaw, and it is not in itself adequate grounds for discovering a newly emerged despair in the play.

It is true that in *Heartbreak House* the obstacles to the fulfill-ment of the Life Force and the obscurity of the future loom larger than in most of Shaw's earlier plays, and it is largely this that creates an atmosphere of pessimism. And it is also true that although in the later plays—that is, *Heartbreak House* and after—the dialectic may still be much in evidence, the stress is not so much on a synthesis per se as on its transient, elusive quality, a horizon always retreating before us. But as we have seen, un-certainty was always a part of Shaw's vision, and all triumphs were tentative. The possibility of failure, the possibility that the forces counter to life may in any particular case prevail, provides a tension that is not released by the final curtain. Characters are brought to the threshold of new possibilities; but they are usually much more confident than we as to the path ahead. Vivie War-ren, with her overdeveloped defenses, may be headed for a life of emotional and literal sterility. Marchbanks's night may be one of intellectual as well as emotional darkness. Ann Whitefield's sexual and emotional needs may well overwhelm Jack's artist's impulse to "make new mind," as Hesione has already smothered Hector's spirit. Barbara may lose her way in the Valley of the Shadow; and the need for money and the pressure from his daughters have already persuaded Captain Shotover to put his creative talents to the service of the powers of destruction. Shaw makes no effort to preclude such idle speculations. Even Juan, who except for the Ancients has a firmer grasp on the Life Force than any other of Shaw's characters, confesses that "so far, the result of Life's continual effort not only to maintain itself, but to achieve higher and higher organization and completer self-con-sciousness, is only, at best, a doubtful campaign between its forces and those of Death and Degeneration. The battles in this campaign are mere blunders, mostly won, like actual military battles, in spite of the commanders" (III, 625). When the Statue protests that this is a dig at him, Juan assures him that "it is a dig at a much higher power than you, Commander. . . . The Life Force is stupid; but it is not so stupid as the forces of Death and Degeneration." The margin of victory is at best infinitesimal. The way of evolution is by trial and error, and human life, either individual or collective, may be one of the errors. Mortal eyes cannot always distinguish between success and failure, truth and error, or, as Cauchon says, saints and heretics. Shaw did not claim more than mortal eyes. He was a self-confessed blunderer; and that generally unacknowledged humility lies at the very heart of his plays and his message. But the paralysis of uncertainty is infinitely worse than trying and being wrong, for error itself is an essential part of the dialectic processes of evolution.

10   *Beyond the Horizon*

Back to Methuselah (1921) is the most explicit dramatic statement not only of Shaw's theories, but also of both his optimism and his pessimism. Given this explicitness, we might well expect to find in it, at least, a clearly defined representation of precisely where the whole process of Creative Evolution is going. He takes us as far as his imagination can reach; and many readers and critics have supposed that the last two sections of the five-part play represent his efforts to draw up a blueprint for Utopia, the goal toward which the universe is working. He makes it clear, however, that this "Metabiological Pentateuch" is more a myth than a model, not a history but a metaphor. He is, as always, more interested in defining a process than in making predictions. Moreover, the furthest point his thought could reach in this fanciful legend for some future bible is only a beginning, and Lilith describes the history of man from Eden to Ancients as "the first hour of the infinite work of creation."

There is no reason to see in the world of the Ancients and the Children hatched from eggs a representation of some ideal future any more than the scenes in Eden of Part One are a literal representation of an ideal past. In both cases Shaw is depicting in allegorical fashion the operation or relationship of various forces that seem to him to play the major roles, positive and negative, in man's development; and the method is more speculative than didactic. With the assumption that a will for life, and more specifically a will for a better life, is the basic drive behind the

Life Force, an almost infinite range of possibilities might be
willed: longer necks, to reach better fruit, longer legs, to step
over mountains—or if higher and higher organization and more
complete self-consciousness are indeed Man's goals, if he believes
with Juan, "I would think more, therefore I must be more," he
might will a longer life in which to become more.

In choosing this particular hypothetical example of the way in
which the Life Force works through individual human wills to
control or modify material, biological life so that it may create
the conditions necessary for its own development, Shaw went
directly to the central dialectic of Creative Evolution. According
to him, life invented death to prevent overcrowding and to permit
life the room in which to carry on the widest possible range of
experiments. As the evolutionary process—life working through
matter—evolved at its highest point into the human animal, and
with man created a mind that could become self-conscious and
guide its own way, the goal no longer required the experimental
proliferation of forms so much as the opportunity for that mind
to realize itself to its fullest potential within a single life. As life
gains more and more complete control over itself and over matter,
death loses its creative or positive function and becomes the enemy
of life.

Back to Methuselah, then, is not so much a blueprint for the
future as a glorification of that vitality of will that serves the Life
Force by welcoming change and experimentation as it moves
slowly toward some unimaginable fulfillment. The initial antithesis, set up at the very beginning of the play, is essentially the basic
Hegelian one of being and non-being. In Eden, Adam and Eve
first discover the fact of death. The discovery of the dead deer
evokes profound but conflicting emotions: fear of non-being, and
fear of eternal being. Eve complains of Adam's contrariness:
"You say we must not cease to exist. But you used to complain
of having to exist always and for ever." Adam puzzles over the
accuracy of her criticism and fumbles for a way out of the contradiction: "I do not like myself. I want to be different; to be

better; to begin again and again" (*Plays,* II, 5). He has discovered, in other words, becoming.

The Serpent emerges on the scene almost as the spirit of antithesis, the embodiment of dialectic—and appropriately speaks for
the Life Force. More specifically, she represents the *will* of the
Life Force to "become something more." The Serpent has given
Adam's desire to "be different; to be better; to begin again and
again" a concrete reality by willing the biological process of
birth: "When you and Adam talk, I hear you say 'Why?' Always 'Why?' You see things; and you say 'Why?' But I dream
things that never were; and I say 'Why not?' " (II, 7). Death is
that which is cast off in the process of renewal; "I call that renewal being born." Death is at once a necessity and an obstacle,
the overcoming of which creates new life. Imagination conceives
the goals that give new life a purpose: "Imagination is the beginning of creation. You imagine what you desire; you will what
you imagine; and at last you create what you will."

The spirit of contrariety, however, rules in the Serpent. Her
imagination inspires the will to extend life, and because of her
Adam desires to reproduce himself and find eternal life in individual death; but at the same time she makes propagation of
his kind an escape from responsibility. Of the nettles and briars
that threaten to take over the garden without his constant care,
she whispers seductively: "They will not overrun the whole garden
for a long time: not until you have laid down your burden and
gone to sleep for ever. Why should you trouble yourself? Let the
new Adams clear a place for themselves."

The resolution of the original antithesis of being and non-being,
called becoming or birth or renewal, leads to a multiplication
not only of life but of contradictions. The desire for more life
carries with it a desire for relief from the exhaustions of effort
and responsibility. The Serpent exults in the possibilities now accessible to the couple whose eyes she has opened: "You will invent things every day now that the burden of immortality is
lifted from you." But as she leads her friends into the brave new

world, each new discovery brings into existence its own opposite. Desire brings hate as the sting in its tail. The remedy for fear is hope; but the blessing of hope makes possible the curse of despair. Adam discovers in love the seeds of jealousy. The Serpent, with her gift of imagination and the infinite possibilities it opens up, also brings the knowledge of good and evil. Adam complains that his "old trouble was heavy; but it was simple. These wonders that you promise to do may tangle up my being before they bring me the gift of death. I was troubled with the burden of eternal being; but I was not confused in my mind."

The contradictions and paradoxes of existence seem to Adam a dubious gift: "Life has become uncertain"; but by choosing a particular day for the end of life and the end of love, he will escape uncertainty: "I will bind the future. I will be delivered from fear." The Serpent, the spirit of the Life Force in all its creative contradiction, accepts the fears of freedom: "I fear certainty as you fear uncertainty. It means that nothing is certain but uncertainty. If I bind the future I bind my will. If I bind my will I strangle creation" (II, 18). I think Shaw saw himself as a serpent: stimulating the imagination, encouraging the will, opening eyes to both possibilities and paradoxes, with no desire to strangle the future with anything more binding than a metaphor.

The synthesis of being and non-being suggested by the serpent, the discovery of renewal through procreation, brings forth Cain. When he appears in Act Two of "In the Beginning," Cain has already murdered Abel and is characterized as the rebel, the soldier, the destroyer. He embodies some of the aspirations for "something better" Adam had expressed earlier: "Am I not better than you?" he asks his father, "stronger, happier, freer?" But it is aspiration turned sour, quite willing to kill to keep the fruits of its power. In Act One, Adam had speculated that the "Voice in the garden" would be man's defense against the impulse to murder. When the Serpent suggests that the voice is only his own voice, he replies: "It is; and it is not. It is something greater than me: I am only a part of it." On the other hand, Cain sneers that he is "not a child to be afraid of a Voice." Rather, he

listens to a different "Voice": "I call yours the Devil. Mine I
call the Voice of God." Adam gives them different names:
"Mine is the Voice of Life: yours the Voice of Death." Cain
boasts that the urge within him is to be "something higher than
man. There is hero and superman." But to Eve he is no superman, only "Anti-Man."

The impulse that drives Cain into his role as antiman, however, is
not Adam's old fear of life, but dissatisfaction. "I revolt against
the clay," he tells Eve, "I revolt against the food. . . .I do not
know what I want, except that I want to be something higher
and nobler than this stupid old digger whom Lilith made to help
you to bring me into the world" (II, 30). Without a goal or
purpose beyond himself, without a voice that speaks for a "something" of which he is a part, without the vision of the Life Force,
these vague aspirations degenerate into self-indulgence. Cain is
the first idealist, justifying the pursuit of power and freedom and
pleasure with concepts such as honor and nobility, beauty and
eternal bliss. And yet this "revolt against the clay," this dream of
"a life infinitely splendid and intense," provides the energy the
Life Force needs to move toward "something better."

At the end of Part One, Eve, exhausted and discouraged
though she is, glimpses a hope that she shares with Cain, a hope
"of the coming true of your dreams and mine," she tells him, "of
newly created things. Of better things." It is a hope for sons who
both dream and work, who create that which has not been, who
"never want to die, because they are always learning and always
creating either things or wisdom, or at least dreaming of them."
It is a hope of grandsons, like Enoch, "who . . . hears the Voice
continually, and has given up his will to do the will of the Voice,
and has some of the Voice's greatness" (II, 32).

To realize such a hope involves a perpetual struggle, however,
a struggle that was for Shaw closely associated with the central
paradox of his metabiological theories. In Hegelian terms it is
the paradox that the concept of becoming should partake of and
subsume the concepts of both being and non-being. In Shavian
terms it is the paradox that the evolving reality of life partakes of

and indeed requires death as well as life. Cain, created by Adam and Eve and rebel against both, embodies the obstacles to the Life Force. Idealist, egotist, killer, one that "loves death more than life," it is "through him and his like [that] death is gaining on life" in the delicately balanced opposition. And yet Eve says that the impulse and will toward something better depends on *his* dreams as well as hers. The dissatisfaction implicit in the fictions of the idealist, the energy of the egotist and the passions of the fighter contribute positively as well as negatively to the total vitality of the process; and, as Cain tells Eve, even "death plays its part in life." Cain, the enemy, the antiman, in a paradox that has its parallel in the Bible story, is at once rejected and embraced, and from the tension between the two comes the power that drives the dialectic.

Adam, of the earth, unimaginative, Philistine, is satisfied with what is, without struggle or tension or aspiration: "Life is still long enough to learn to dig." Eve, in part echoing Cain, sees beyond what is: "Yes, to dig. And to fight. But is it long enough for the other things, the great things? . . . Will they learn all the ways of all the stars in their little time?" (II, 34). Part One of the play ends on a note that characteristically combines hope with a sense of inadequate vision, as Eve continues: "There is something else. We do not yet know what it is; but some day we shall find out; and then . . . there shall be no more digging nor spinning, nor fighting nor killing."

How the Life Force, operating through the will of individual men and women, struggled with the death impulse and slowly evolved a longer and longer life span that man might learn more and more is the business of the middle three parts of the play. In the last section, "As Far as Thought Can Reach," Shaw offers a figurative representation of a point far along the continuum of evolution where life, after eons of struggle and countless infinitesimal defeats and slightly less infinitesimal victories appears on the verge of triumph over death. Man, in the form of the Ancients, has willed his own longevity virtually to the point of immortality, and contemplates the dissolution of the last remaining vestige of the old obstacles, the old enemy, his physical body.

For the Ancients the body is only appearance, illusion, associated with dolls, statues, works of art, all subject to the forming power of will. They have long since discovered that the will can form the body into a thousand fantastic forms, with hundreds of legs and a dozen heads; they have also learned that the only power of the will that is important is over itself—over thought and mind, that is, "themselves": "It came into my mind that this monstrous machinery of heads and limbs was no more me than my statues had been me, and that it was only an automaton that I have enslaved" (II, 253). Yet the slave is also a master, and the magistrate becomes a prisoner in his own prison. The Ancients are on the verge of that last unimaginable effort of life to overcome the last obstacle that is also the source of its force and vitality. One of the Ancients expresses it as a will to become a vortex. When one of the Children objects that "even a vortex is a vortex in something," the Ancient observes that the vortex is not *in* the thing, but "is a power over these things." Pure power, however, with nothing to move, becomes eternal immobility. The shriveled Ancients were not Shaw's ideal for mankind, nor did he dream of some utopian future in which man would be reduced to disembodied abstract thought. He was concerned with defining, not the future, but a dynamic and evolving relationship of forces. When all oppositions are resolved, the dynamic ceases; but this "event" occurs in a future as theoretical and abstract as the realization of Hegel's "Idea," and in the same way had a philosophical but scarcely a human reality for Shaw.

The drive of *Back to Methuselah* is generated by the tension between the antithetical impulses, the will for more life and the will for less, the way of life and the way of death. As the force of life approaches final triumph, as the Idea, or what Shaw calls God, nears realization, and as all the dialectic oppositions are resolved, the energy necessarily dwindles. The common criticism that the play as a whole is essentially undramatic is in fact justified by the ending. Although several quasi-dramatic contrasts are established, demonstrating the distance between the

Ancients and the Children and then the even greater abyss between the Children and their embarrassing resurrections of
twentieth-century man, the case is too loaded to be called a conflict. At the end the Ancients, bored by their confrontation with
the Children, simply drift away, and the play subsides into a
quiescent and visionary epilogue. Adam and Eve reappear to
comment, a little sadly, on the long road mankind has traveled
since the beginning. Cain, the embodiment of man at his most
material and physical, observes that "there is no place for [him]
on earth any longer," although it was a "splendid game while it
lasted."

It is Lilith, the embodiment of the Life Force, looking out over
the vast expanse of past and future, who has the final word. The
burden of her valedictory to the world of man is the triumph of
life and spirit over their antithesis: matter. It is, in fact, worth
quoting again her essentially Hegelian summary of the history
of the world. Of mankind she says: "After passing a million goals
they press on to the goal of redemption from the flesh, to the
vortex freed from matter, to the whirlpool in pure intelligence
that, when the world began, was a whirlpool in pure force. . . .
I brought life into the whirlpool of force, and compelled my
enemy, Matter, to obey a living soul. But in enslaving Life's
enemy I made him Life's master; for that is the end of all slavery;
and now I shall see the slave set free and the enemy reconciled,
the whirlpool become all life and no matter" (II, 261–262).

Critics have tended to distort the implications of this passage
by reading "intelligence" as though it were "intellect," and to
see it as some kind of cold and rigorous rationality, and thus as a
testament to Shaw's faith in the mind. Mind is never mentioned, and the emphasis is on the antithesis of matter and *life*.
And even then he is only stating a symbolic relationship and
fantasizing on an ultimate apotheosis. The beginning and the
end are, in a sense, of largely theoretical significance. Only what
comes between is of direct human significance; and it is important
to remember that in the evolution from pure force, pure unful-

filled will, to pure life, matter provides the means, the bridge, the necessary though not sufficient middle term of the equation.

Matter and flesh may be the "enemy," but the processes of life, the realization of the Life Force, can only proceed in a dialectic fashion. Evolution is a relationship between life and matter. Redemption *from* the flesh can only take place *through* the flesh. Lilith speaks of the beginning: "I tore myself asunder; I lost my life, to make of my one flesh these twain, man and woman. And this is what has come of it." The restless curiosity and impatient dissatisfaction of maternal Eve and materialist Cain are, as it were, the visible manifestations of that eternal tension between flesh and spirit that has made the whole process possible: "Best of all," says Lilith, "they are still not satisfied: the impulse I gave them in that day when I sundered myself in twain and launched Man and Woman on the earth still urges them. . . . I gave the woman the greatest of gifts: curiosity. By that her seed has been saved from my wrath; . . . I say, let them dread, of all things, stagnation; for from the moment I, Lilith, lose hope and faith in them, they are doomed."

Man still "reaches out," and although his whole history is "but the first hour of the infinite work of creation," Lilith "will not supersede them until they have forded this last stream that lies between flesh and spirit, and disentangled their life from the matter that has always mocked it." At that final fulfillment and realization of life and spirit, she says, "They shall become one with me and supersede me, and Lilith will be only a legend and a lay that has lost its meaning." But even that seemingly ultimate synthesis may only become the starting place for some inconceivable dialectic by which life will evolve and spread through all "its million starry mansions"; for though "many are empty and many still unbuilt, and though its vast domain is as yet unbearably desert, my seed shall one day fill it and master its matter to its uttermost confines. And for what may be beyond, the eyesight of Lilith is too short" (II, 262).

Her final statement, "It is enough that there is a beyond,"

perhaps is *not* enough, and begs the question; but it needs to be emphasized again that the last part of *Back to Methuselah,* like the first, is only a symbolic representation of the relationship between elements in the dialectic of life, or between will and matter. The tone, it is true, becomes almost ecstatic at the contemplation of the disembodied purity and simplicity of unadulterated spirit; but Shaw is in fact only performing the function attributed by the Ancients to the artist, that of creating fanciful models of a world which, if it is worthy, may then, and only then, be willed into existence. In Part Three, "The Thing Happens," we learn that the first two "longlivers" were introduced to the concept or model of longevity by a work of fantasy, and while their conscious minds dismissed the idea, their wills grasped it and made it real. Shaw had no illusions that his particular model would be the one the Life Force would choose to follow; he would not bind the future by pretending to powers of prophecy. *Back to Methuselah* is only one of what Shaw hoped would be a multitude of possibilities created by God's still uncertain voice, the imagination, and made into reality by the energy of the will. It is not *the* future, it is *a* future; and although Shaw is as tentative as ever, the comprehensive optimism—not for man in the short run but for Life in the long run—is still strong.

Shaw may perfectly well not have believed specifically that man could suddenly will himself into long life or that the cerebral Ancients represented the man of the future. The fact that there is a future, in which the Life Force will find its own way, probably *was* enough for him. But it has not been enough for his critics, who often find in the tenuous fantasies of "As Far as Thought Can Reach" a failure of will and courage and vision. Shaw's faith, however, was not so much in any religion or social program or metaphysical view as in a *process.* Hegel himself could not follow the dialectic of history much beyond the Prussian state of his day, but the central dynamic of his philosophy required a further evolution into a certain but undefined future. Both Hegel and Shaw are in a sense caught in a symbolically appropriate paradox. They seem to be concerned more with means than with ends; but a process implies an end, a goal toward which it is moving and in terms of which it has meaning. The source of the difficulty lies in the fact that the end of the dialectic, the resolution of all antitheses, implies stasis, and with it an end to all tension or vitality or even life—in other words, to everything in which Hegel or Shaw or we have any abiding interest.

In what is for all practical purposes the epilogue to *Back to Methuselah* Shaw tries to deal with this paradox. On the one hand, he makes an effort, in Lilith's speech, to confirm that there *is* a goal, and hence a purpose, behind the activities of the Life Force, but at the same time he suggests that in human terms the process is an infinite one. In the more formal epilogue to *Saint Joan* (1923) he is at once more specific and less precise—and he succeeds better.

In the Preface to *Back to Methuselah* Shaw speaks of *Man and Superman* as his "dramatic parable of Creative Evolution," but claims that he "decorated it too brilliantly and lavishly. . . . Its tale of a husband huntress obscured its evolutionary doctrine." The five-play cycle is the result of his desire "to make a second legend of Creative Evolution without distractions and embellishments," in which he will "abandon the legend of Don Juan with its erotic associations, and go back to the legend of the Garden of Eden."[1] *Saint Joan* is in its own way a legend-parable of Creative Evolution, less explicit than *Back to Methuselah* but clearly a play with cosmic implications, not merely demonstrating that women may be aggressors in war as well as in sex.

By choosing a story from the historical past, and then simplifying history, Shaw endows his fable of sainthood with symbolic significance and at the same time suggests that Joan's story is part of a continuum of human experience and development extending through the present into the future. Her legend is treated as though The Maid were one of Hegel's world-historical individuals who through their vitality and ambition and will push history to

1. *Back to Methuselah,* rev. ed. (New York: Oxford University Press, 1947), pp. lxxiii–lxxiv.

a new stage of development, a new synthesis.[2] For Shaw, of course, she is an agent of the Life Force. The opposition set against her, the obstacles to be overcome are literally and figuratively the forces of death, incarnate in the institutionalization of religious and political power: the Catholic Church and the feudal system. They represent the massive weight of the status quo, of stagnation, of resistance to change; and the play is about change: what it takes, and the price that must be paid, to make it happen. Joan is the agent of change; and while it is perhaps a cliché to say that the price of life is death, it is no empty paradox to affirm that in death there is life.

Shaw goes to great pains to weight the conflict evenly and, as in *Major Barbara,* to give both antitheses a fair showing. The representatives of the religious and political establishments of the time, Cauchon and Warwick, are characterized as intelligent and dedicated men, each convinced that the security and well-being of civilization rests on the solidity and stability of their respective institutions. Warwick is the less sympathetic, being concerned mainly with the continued supremacy of the barons, including himself, in the political hierarchy. He sees in the rising tide of nationalism only a new source of power for the king, by which, he says, "the king could break us across his knee one by one; and then what should we be but liveried courtiers in his halls?" Cauchon's fears, less immediately personal and parochial, arise from a vision of the social and moral chaos, the rending of the

2. Belfort Bax, in *The Ethics of Socialism,* discusses the operation of the dialectic in history of a somewhat later date: "With the Reformation the political power of the papacy was ended, and hence the two opposite checks to national centralization, the local [the feudal lord] and the cosmopolitan [the Catholic Church] were almost simultaneously abolished. On the ruins of feudalism and papal domination, then, arose the modern State-system of Europe." He goes on to observe that the new nationalism becomes the cornerstone of the capitalist system, with its individualistic ethic, but insists that the dialectic dynamics are in the process of replacing capitalism with "the socialist state as the synthesis." This is, of course, the Marxian party line; but Shaw may well have been introduced to "the uses of history" by Bax, who quite frankly treated history as the handmaiden to socialism. See Bax, *The Ethics of Socialism,* 3d ed. (London: Swan Sonnenschein, 1893), pp. 40 ff.

delicate fabric of human civilization that would attend "Protestant" inroads on the unquestioned authority of the Church: "What will the world be like when the Church's accumulated wisdom and knowledge and experience . . . are thrust into the kennel by every ignorant laborer or dairymaid whom the devil can puff up with the monstrous self-conceit of being directly inspired from heaven? It will be a world of blood, of fury, of devastation, of each man striving for his own hand: in the end a world wrecked back into barbarism" (II, 365). Later, Cauchon states Warwick's case in his own terms: "Divide [Christ's kingdom] into nations, and you dethrone Christ. Dethrone Christ, and who will stand between our throats and the sword? The world will perish in a welter of war."

In his superb defense of the Inquisition, preceding the trial, the Inquisitor points even more explicitly than had Cauchon to the central opposition between the need for freedom, for recognizing the validity of individual inspiration, for respecting the truth wherever it may be found, and the need for law, stability, and responsibility, a view of truth that sees it as winnowed from age to age and from level to level of ecclesiastical hierarchy. And the Inquisitor is a just and generous man: "Heresy at first seems innocent and even laudable; but it ends . . . always by vain and ignorant persons setting up their own judgment against the Church, and taking it upon themselves to be the interpreters of God's will. . . . They believe honestly and sincerely that their diabolical inspiration is divine. . . . Though the work I have to do may seem cruel to those who do not know how much more cruel it would be to leave it undone, I would go to the stake myself sooner than do it if I did not know its righteousness, its necessity, its essential mercy" (II, 392–393).

Of course, the bloody vision of the future conjured up by Warwick and Cauchon has to a great extent been fulfilled, and the accuracy of their prophecies is an essential part of Shaw's strategy in placing the events of the play at a sufficiently distant time that we can be aware of man's social and political history since. He is not concerned so much with Joan's conflict with the

English barons or with the Church as with the process in which they were all participants—a process that is still, and always has been, going on.

Joan is represented as being, in the context of her time, the first "nationalist" and the first "Protestant," questioning the authority and the permanence of the established institutional structures. In the conflict of the drama, they are engaged in a kind of dialectical struggle in which both antitheses are destroyed—and at the same time both, in different form, survive. What emerge—Protestant individualism and nationalist autonomy—are not to be seen as ultimate ideals. They incorporate not only the impulse toward freedom and self-determination represented by Joan, but also something of the social, political, and moral power and authority associated with the Catholic Church and the feudal system. With hindsight we know that the new freedom in its turn becomes institutionalized. Ironically, Joan might be called the saint of emergent capitalism, in which case some new saint will be required to move mankind to a still higher level.

That the Life Force manifests itself in many saints in many ages, who will destroy themselves by opposing society's established institutions with an energy that lifts both the saint and society to a new stage of evolution and being, is after all the substance of the play and most particularly of its epilogue. Ever since the early performances of *Saint Joan* the Epilogue has been objected to by the less perceptive critics as some kind of sentimental excrescence. On the contrary, in it lies the kernel of truth for which everything else is mere preparation, and which in a sudden epiphany opens out the play from the historical conflict of Joan and the Church to a drama of the Life Force and Creative Evolution.

Joan is a saint in the same way that all men could be saints, because they have God within them. Joan possesses the holy fire of imagination, the strength and loneliness of the true realist, the freedom of self-assurance, and a vitality that transcends death.

When the authenticity of her voices is challenged and they are dismissed as mere imagination, she acknowledges it: "Of course.

That is how the messages of God come to us." Imagination, then, is God's voice in man; and just as God is still aspiring to perfection, so the voices are not absolutely reliable. They have told her she shall not burn; but while they are wrong in fact they are right in spirit. When she discovers that the alternative to the fire is a life in prison, she knows that life and vitality mean much more than bare survival, and she willingly chooses the stake: "Light your fire: do you think I dread it as much as the life of a rat in a hole? My voices were right" (II, 407).

The assurance of her own rightness, her faith in her God-given imagination give Joan a particular kind of freedom, an intoxicating freedom from the petty, suspicious, self-serving counsels of her sometime friends. In the freedom of her clear-sighted vision lies her greatest strength and her fatal weakness. When King Charles complains that Joan "thinks she knows better than everyone else," she replies with sincere vehemence, "But I *do* know better than any of you seem to. And I am not proud: I never speak unless I know I am right" (II, 376). Mean-minded men cannot tolerate those with superior powers, and the very confidence that brings Joan victory alienates those for whom the victory was won.

In common with all Shavian figures who achieve anything approaching a heroic stature, Joan is a thoroughgoing realist from the very beginning. Her simple incisive way of seeing things cuts straight through cant and convention, hypocrisy and authority— but it does not make her popular with those who cling desperately to one another and to what everybody else believes for their security. The Archbishop of Rheims tells her: "You stand alone: absolutely alone, trusting to your own conceit, your own ignorance, your own headstrong presumption, your own impiety in hiding all these sins under the cloak of a trust in God." Her response shows Shaw at his finest:

Where would you all have been now if I had heeded that sort of truth? . . . Yes: I *am* alone on earth: I have always been alone. . . . Do not think you can frighten me by telling me that I am alone. France is alone; and God is alone; and what is my loneliness before the loneliness of my country and my God? I see now that the loneliness of God is His strength. . . . Well, my loneliness shall be my strength too: it is better to be alone with God. In His strength I will dare, and dare, and dare, until I die. [II, 382]

She will, she says, go out to the common people, and in spite of the jealousy and hate of the lords of the establishments of army, church, and monarchy, she will go through the fire to the hearts of the people "for ever and ever." Her imagination and realism and freedom give Joan a vitality that triumphs over the fire as it consumes her.

The Epilogue is a complex and often ironic tone poem on the motif of death and transfiguration. Set in some timeless dream world, not unlike that of "Don Juan in Hell," the episode brings together the major actors in Joan's drama purged of the passions and self-interest of the "real" world. The qualities that made her a saint survive the dissolution of her physical body, and each of her old antagonists or betrayers acknowledges his own inadequacy or incompleteness before the impulse embodied in Joan. The freedom she found in her faith in herself is justified by the Inquisitor: "The judges in the blindness and bondage of the law praise thee, because thou hast vindicated the vision and the freedom of the living soul" (II, 427). The validity of her private vision is acknowledged by Cauchon: "The girls in the field praise thee; for thou hast raised their eyes; and they see that there is nothing between them and heaven." The strength and loneliness she found in her sense of personal divinity Joan restates herself: "I shall owe nothing to any man: I owe everything to the spirit of God that was within me." In that personal divinity she finds her own victory over death: "My sword shall conquer yet: the sword that never struck a blow. Though men destroyed my body, yet in my soul I have seen God." In the power of imagination, however, lies the power to save the world. Cauchon sees the lesson in the example of the English chaplain, De Stogumber, who is redeemed by Joan's suffering, not by the more distant wounds of Jesus: "Must then a Christ perish in torment in every age to save those that have no imaginations?"

The Epilogue might appear to be an unqualified affirmation of the unconquerable and eternal spirit of man were it not for this suggestion that Christ is crucified again in Joan and in a hundred unsung saints who are destroyed in the moment of overcoming the opposition, transcending the world. In that transcendence they fulfill themselves and fulfill the will of the world, but at the same time something of themselves and part of the world dies. Christ *must* perish in every age—and be born in every age. It is an endless process of simultaneous dying and growing. It is a tragedy and a comedy, acted out over and over again with a repetition that is at once heartbreaking and reassuring. When Joan offers her old associates, who have justified and accepted the truth of all she represents, to return from the dead herself to the world of the living, she is shocked at their dismay: "What! Must I burn again? Are none of you ready to receive me?" Cauchon, sadly, speaks, if not for all mankind, for a major element of its nature: "The heretic is always better dead. And mortal eyes cannot distinguish the saint from the heretic." When Joan cries out in her agony, "O God that madest this beautiful earth, when will it be ready to receive Thy saints? How long, O Lord, how long?" the only possible answer is "never," at least as long as it *is* earth.

The mortal eyes that cannot distinguish saint from heretic are not only Cauchon's, but ours, and Shaw's. With 20/20 hindsight it is easier to spot the saints; but even with that advantage the Church rehabilitates Joan, as they had excommunicated her, largely for the wrong reasons, and for Shaw sanctity is wholly relative. Joan is a saint, not because she is a soldier of the Church, a worker of miracles, or an example of perfect virtue, but because her vitality and realistic vision and imagination caused her to participate as a moving force in man's social and political evolution. At a particular moment in history her will was that of the Life Force, the World's Will. Insofar as the movement to which she added her strength led the world, or at least the European part of it, down the road to Protestantism and nationalism, and beyond them to capitalism and colonialism, she has contributed to the "world of blood, of fury, of devastation" predicted by

Cauchon. Had Joan been a prophet as well as a realist she might well never have left the farm at Domremy; but she did, and the fact pushed the world on its stumbling, error-filled way. And if Joan is, among other things, a saint of capitalism, there must be other saints to pull or push resistant man to the next stage of his evolution. Bernard Shaw, for instance.

There is no doubt that Shaw saw more than a little of himself in his representation of Saint Joan. With tongue in cheek he referred to "Saint Bernard," and otherwise included his name in the rolls of the blessed. And he was only half-joking. He found in his own nature the same unlimited energy and will, the realistic vision, the somewhat cocky independence, the creative imagination; and he too had a cause. He was dismissed as a heretic, a fraud, a bumptious upstart, an idle paradoxer and jester; or worse, he was ignored. He saw the dominant values of his time antithetical to his own in every way. He saw himself, like Joan, locked in mortal combat with the vested interests and established institutions of his day, the State, the Church, and above all capitalist middle-class morality. In that struggle he could well be defeated—perhaps already had been; but his great source of hope was that out of the energy of the conflict a fire would be lit, a spirit would be moved, his will would live on—not as any individual victory, but as an advance for the Life Force.

Shaw's optimism, then, was characteristically rather tentative, and a little wistful. It was not personal optimism, but faith in a process. That the process should be fueled by opposition and consume its saints in the very effort by which they move it forward may be the source of regret, but in the longer view of reassurance. And the longer view is never dimmed, even though in the later plays there is an increasingly strong sensitivity to the short-term obstacles. While there is still an underlying conviction that for all the irregularity of its course, life is moving toward some ultimate fulfillment, more and more emphasis is put on the uncertainty, on the sense of difficulty and the inevitability of setbacks, on the fact that man himself, even inspired, realistic, clear-visioned man, can never be perfectly sure that he is on the right path—that he is not a heretic rather than a saint.

One of Shaw's last plays is very explicitly about an experiment of the Life Force that failed. *The Simpleton of the Unexpected Isles,* written in 1935, has been relegated by most critics to the scrap heap of Shaw's presumably senile efforts. It unquestionably lacks the strong dramatic movement of many of the earlier plays; but it is for all that an amusing and ingenious fantasy that carries on many of the motifs and concerns common to the later plays. Like *Misalliance,* it is concerned with questions of heredity and the paradoxes implicit in the eugenic-symbolic union of opposites; like *Heartbreak House,* it confronts humanity with a day of judgment; and like *Too True to be Good,* it dramatizes the efforts of seekers after salvation, pilgrims of the way of life.

For many years Shaw had been interested in the possibilities of improving the human species through some kind of eugenic control. In both the Don Juan episode and the "Revolutionist's Handbook" of *Man and Superman,* he speculates on ways of uniting the most desirable qualities of contrasting human types through breeding, whether directed by rational selection or by the instincts of the Life Force. In *Simpleton* the notion of an experiment in eugenics is combined with another of his interests, the multiple communal family. The six pioneers who have chosen to establish a colony on The Unexpected Isles, the priest and priestess of an unnamed Eastern sect and two English couples, have collectively become the parents of four children, the object of the experiment being "to try out the result of a biological blend of the flesh and spirit of the west with the flesh and spirit of the east" (VI, 570). Following a notion Shaw may have derived from some of the later writing of Belfort Bax, the results of this experiment evolve and put into practice "the idea that they were not to love one another, but that they were to *be* one another," with the result that they exist not as four separate individuals but one individual with four manifestations.

One might well suppose that this new stage of human evolu-

tion, like longevity in *Back to Methuselah,* represents a great
leap forward of the Life Force. "We are the way. . . . We are
the life. . . . I am the light. . . . I am the fire." So chant the
maidens of the mysterious foursome. But the brave new world of
promise they hold out is only an illusion, and the experiment is
a failure. The union of east and west, of flesh and mind has indeed produced a synthesis, but it is a synthesis of the worst of
both worlds. Pra, the priest, bewails that "the dream which united
Prola and Pra, . . . and then united us all six, has ended in a
single little household with four children, wonderful and beautiful, but sterile" (VI, 581). Although the quartet chants fine-
sounding phrases about love and beauty and joy in a maddening
epigrammatic counterpoint, they are little more than the emptiest
banalities of the idealists. Although the children are accomplished
and artistic, "they have not between the whole four of them a
scrap of moral conscience." They bore themselves and they bore
their parents. Pra, driven beyond his usual tolerance, tells them to
"stop screaming about nothing. . . . Use your minds"; and they
respond: "We have no minds." They are indolent and passive,
seeking in the will of others some point to their lives. They try to
elevate Prola to the position of queen and goddess, but she turns
on them: "Go and scrub the floors. Do anything that is dirty
and grubby and smelly enough to shew that you live in a real
world. . . . If I catch you grovelling to me, . . . I will beat
the slavishness out of your bones." But their only response is:
"Oh, what ecstasy to be beaten by Prola! . . . To suffer for
her! . . . How lovely is obedience! . . . Obedience is freedom
from the intolerable fatigue of thought" (VI, 593). When they
are gone, and their "real" names forgotten, all that is remembered
is that "their names were Love, Pride, Heroism, and Empire."

The children of hope turn out to be zombies of idealism: their
eyes blinded by visions of paradise, their force dissipated in
rhetoric, all action paralyzed by purposelessness. In the Day of
Judgment that provides the central action of the play they are
the first to disappear. As the angel tells the experimental family,
he and his colleagues have not come, as most people think, "to

dig up all the skeletons and put them through one of their shocking criminal trials," but "are executing a judgment. The lives which have no use, no meaning, no purpose, will fade out. You will have to justify your existence or perish" (VI, 598).

Amidst a barrage of satiric and sometimes farcical radio bulletins from the outside world reporting the progress of Judgment Day as it lays waste to the parliaments and palaces, to say nothing of the social elite, of the nations of the world, the six experimental parents wait anxiously to see if they too shall be judged useless and will vanish as though they had never been. Their prospects are doubtful, for all they have produced are their feckless, half-real foursome. One of the "mothers" acknowledges that they have produced only fools, and "there just shouldnt be any fools. They wernt born fools: we made fools of them." And Pra, the priest, tells the priestess: "The coming race will not be like them. Meanwhile we are face to face with the fact that we two have made a precious mess of our job of producing the coming race by a mixture of east and west. We are failures. We shall disappear" (VI, 610).

It is, however, their experiment that is a failure. They have failed—but they at least have tried. Iddy, the outsider who joins the experimental family as "husband" for the two daughters, says of love: "I love Vashti, I love Maya, I love Prola; and they all love me so wonderfully that their three loves are only one love. But it is my belief that some day we'll have to try something else" (VI, 585). Loving one another is too close to hating one another. And the experiment of the beautiful children in *being* one another ends in communal vapidity instead of communal effort. But the angel comments, as he has difficulty in becoming airborne: "An angel is far from being the perfect organism you imagine. There is always something better." In that faith Pra and the experimental family—or those of them that survive judgment—will continue to strive, and to hope, and to do the world's work as best they can. "We must stop making fools," says Pra. "When men no longer fear the judgment of God, they must learn to judge for themselves," says Prola. And another "parent" observes: "What we have learnt here today is that the day of judgment is not the end of the world but the beginning of real human responsibility."

Responsibility means working and not losing faith in life. "The fountain of life is within me," cries Prola; and although there is no security, and the changes are "never the changes we intend," "the future is to those who prefer surprise and wonder to security." Prola admits that she feels "like the leader of a cavalry charge whose horse has been shot through the head and dropped dead under him." But a dead horse is not necessarily the end of the battle: "There are still a million lives beyond all the Utopias and the Millenniums and the rest of the jigsaw puzzles: . . . Let men despair and become cynics and pessimists because in the Unexpected Isles all their little plans fail: women will never let go their hold on life. We are not here to fulfill prophecies and fit ourselves into puzzles, but to wrestle with life as it comes. And it never comes as we expect it to come." This should answer those critics who would find in *Back to Methuselah* Shaw's blueprint for the future of mankind, or at the other extreme who see the late plays as a testament to despair. The faith is as strong, and as tentative, as ever; and it is a faith in life rather than men, in the effort rather than in the results, in a process rather than in a utopian vision of The Good. The process is uncertain and experimental, a series of trials and errors, leading through relative falsehood to relative truth in a dialectic path that in human terms is unending. *The Simpleton* ends with a kind of dialectic exchange between Pra and Prola: "Every day must have its miracle, and no child be born like any child that ever was born before. And to witness this miracle of the children I will abide the uttermost evil and carry through it the seed of the uttermost good. . . . I must continue to strive for more knowledge and more power, though the new knowledge always contradicts the old, and the new power is the destruction of the fools who misuse it. . . . I need you and you need me. Life needs us both. . . . All hail, then, the life to come!"

11 *Every Ending Is a New Beginning*

The Simpleton of the Unexpected Isles, rather like the four-in-one offspring of the play, is a not wholly successful experiment in myth-making. Most of Shaw's later plays are experiments in both form and substance, and most have been considered in varying degrees unsuccessful. The plays and playlets he wrote in the last years—*Cymbeline Refinished, Farfetched Fables, Why She Would Not*—are generally set aside as the final feeble spasms of a once powerful mind, and there are those who wish that they had not been written. By then Shaw was in his nineties, and well aware of the narrowing range of his powers; but as long as any vital spark survived he was determined to devote it to the service of the one talent of which he was sure. In the Preface to *Buoyant Billions,* written when he was ninety-two, and his last sustained effort, he speculates as to why he cannot heed common sense and hold his tongue and his pen: "As long as I live I must write. If I stopped writing I should die" (*Plays,* I, 749). Writing plays was life to Shaw; and since, as he said elsewhere, "to do what was done last time . . . is virtually the law of death," he experimented, with rapidly failing energy, to the very end.

A long generation before Norman O. Brown, Shaw was preaching the religion of Life over Death. For him, as should be clear by now, the worship of life did not mean the worship of youth or of animal spirits, nor the thoughtless celebration of impulse, nor did it pursue novelty under the illusion that change is the same as vitality. Mindlessness was for Shaw a form of lifelessness, and change without growth was death-in-life. By the same token, turning one's back on the probability of personal extinction was a denial, not an affirmation, of the wholeness of life, and any viable theory of life had to be a theory of death as well.

Shaw always insisted that a religion, to achieve any kind of credibility in the present world, must have a solid basis in biology. And his own religion of Creative Evolution had a place for death as the mechanism by which the Life Force kept open space and food and resources for its own evolutionary experiments, for the eternal process of becoming—which *is* life. But for a religion of life to have any real hold it must also confront the fact of individual death, not as a universal biological necessity but as the most overwhelming and mind-shattering certainty of our personal existence.

Several broad possibilities have emerged from man's contemplation of the meaning of death, and Shaw at different times considered most of them. There is, for instance, the possibility that the old-fashioned preachers, with their eternities of bliss and their fire and brimstone, may have been right all along. Shaw rejected such notions, not because they are impossible, but because he could not accept the concept of a system in which good behavior is only a mercenary investment in a comfortable retirement home. More significantly, he saw that whatever the lures of paradise, it was really the fears of hell that mattered, and he found the world too full of fear already for it to provide an effective basis for a moral system. Even more sophisticated existential notions of a hereafter in which one is trapped eternally in one's mortal personality, with or without "other people," probably would have too much of the same "mind your p's and q's" element to have been of much interest to Shaw.

Other beliefs would make another existence, if any, wholly independent of behavior in this one, thereby justifying any self-indulgence, from the vulgarity of "eat, drink, and be merry" to the cultured hedonism in which the art of gracious living is life's highest achievement. There are those who find another existence of any sort inconceivable and who would seek immortality in monuments of stone, or charity, or in works of art, if they have means or ability, or in children or kindly memories if they have not.

In all these views, however, death is confronted with a personal orientation: Will I be happy then? Can I be happy now? Will the future think well of me? For Shaw such self-concern was essentially degrading. Like Montaigne, he thought a man should be at his best, should rise to death, not sink to it. Death should be faced with neither groveling nor a defiant sneer nor self-congratulation, but as a man proud of his humanity, with his last breath affirming that in spite of death being human is good—and that the only life, now and forever, is in humanity. Shaw would have had men come to death in no other way than this; but he also saw that in the present state of the world and its social organization suffering and degradation and fear are so common that the majority of mankind can not say that being human is good. That this should be so seemed to Shaw the greatest crime man could possibly commit. We hold our life as part of a common wealth; and denigration or lessening of life for any *one,* so that it is hateful to him, lessens the quality of life for all. John Donne notwithstanding, death does not lessen life; only we who are living do that.

But if death is the price of life, the warrant for our humanity, then it becomes in some sense coequal in magnitude or significance with life. Any serious writer must, if he deals with life, at least by implication deal with death, and to do otherwise is to run the risk of being trivial. When death is dealt with directly it is often called tragedy, but the association is not a necessary one. It is a common confusion to assume that tragedy inheres in death itself, rather than in what death has to tell us or remind us about life. And all art, even that focusing on death, is about life.

In tragedy, for instance, death is not "real," but as an artistic device it can be a forceful reminder of an essential quality of life that is desperately real: the irrevocability of time. In *Lear* the tragedy lies not in the death of the old king, for whom it is clearly represented as a release from suffering, but in the death of Cordelia, and the pain that brings Lear: the recognition of the harm he has done and cannot undo. Death is the final proof of the irreversibility of our acts and the inescapability of our responsibility—but it is not fundamental to tragedy. For Oedipus the tragedy is not death, and even the gouged eyes and the exile are only symbolic reminders of the blindness and the mistaken way, the angry blow at the crossroads, the proud marriage to the Queen of Thebes, the human frailty that becomes catastrophe by the inexorableness of time in our life. "Let no man be called happy until he has passed the day of his death."

Whatever death may be in "reality," in art it asks us to look more closely at life. Shaw does not, except possibly in *Saint Joan,* write tragedy; but death often intrudes into his comedies, usually with the effect of intensifying our awareness of life or of some quality essential to its fullest realization. In *Arms and the Man* Bluntschli's report of the death of his comrade-in-arms is a minor detail that underlines the distance between the violence, suffering, and urgency of his real war and the musical-comedy war of the Petkoffs and the Saranoffs, where no one would dream of hiding in a barn, let alone being burned to death in it.

Death is somewhat more immediate in *The Devil's Disciple.* Mrs. Dudgeon dies in Act Two, but it hardly moves us, for in her cankered bitterness and self-centeredness she is a life-hater, a representative of the death force, and her physical dissolution is nothing more than a fulfillment of her nature. Her son Dick does not die, but he is confronted by death as the consequence of one of the choices with which he is presented. He can accept death only when he has come to accept life, in recognizing both the integrity and importance of his individual humanity and his responsibility to a larger humanity. In much the same way, it is only when Blanco Posnet discovers the difference between the "great game" and the "rotten game," the game of life and the game of death, that he can choose the possibility of hanging to save the child's life. That the child subsequently dies in no way invalidates his decision, and it reminds us that death is real, is not bought off with good deeds, that playing the great game is an act of will and commitment to life and not a commercial transaction. Still later, in *Androcles and the Lion,* the manner in which the characters confront death is a measure of the quality of their dedication to life. Spintho, who is the only "Christian" terrified of death, is also the only one who dies; and it seems entirely appropriate, for he, like Mrs. Dudgeon, has all along been on the side of the death force. Lavinia, who has given herself fully to life, can give up her life in a martyr's death rather than give up her humanity by worshiping the Roman "God of Death."

In *Caesar and Cleopatra* death virtually appears on stage with the murders of Pothinus and Ftatateeta. Caesar, although a soldier, is another life-worshiper; and the death that lies just below the surface of the court life of Alexandria, behind the ideals of honor, justice, and patriotism, is part of a world of hate and blood and revenge through which he must make his way, and on which he will impose as best he can the way of life. And the fact that we know he will leave Egypt to be destroyed by the life-haters in Rome only enhances the sense of vitality, energy, and life that Caesar brings to the play.

The Doctor's Dilemma (1906) was written partly in response to William Archer's charge that Shaw was limited as a dramatist because he could not represent death effectively on the stage. The death of Louis Dubedat is not an artistic triumph, nor does it provide the emotional center of the play. That Shaw was less interested in the fact of Dubedat's death than in why he is allowed to die is suggested by the playwright's account of the origin of the play's central question. According to the story, he was present when a famous London physician, discoverer of a "cure" for tuberculosis, was confronted with the possibility of having more patients than he could treat. "We should have to consider," the doctor reportedly said, "which life is worth saving."[1] In the play as in life, death is certain, but who is to die is a matter not of chance but of choice. The imminence of death in the play and the possibility of choice make painfully urgent the question of

1. See Stanley Weintraub, *Shaw: An Autobiography 1898–1950* (New York: Weybright and Talley, 1970), p. 266, n. 9.

what qualities make one life more valuable, more worth saving, than another.

There are no deaths in either *Man and Superman* or *Major Barbara,* and yet the spirit of death looms large, and what might be called the Death Force constitutes one pole of the dialectic in each play. In the Don Juan episode the Devil is the quintessence of death: everything he stands for, idealism, complacency, fear of change, pursuit of happiness, is for Shaw another name for death. Juan, for whom creating new mind is a way of creating new life, must carry on the eternal war with death—presumably by being reborn in such frail human vessels as Jack Tanner. In *Major Barbara* Andrew Undershaft comes to represent both the power of death and the power over death. His religion is "Money and gunpowder. Freedom and power. Command of life and command of death." His high explosives and his aerial battleships can bring death indiscriminately to huge segments of mankind, or his power can be put to the service of life, to make a better life. It all depends, he says, which you want, and how far your courage will take you. Cusins understands that Barbara's ecstatic vision of "the raising of hell to heaven and of man to God" can be restated as "The way of life lies through the factory of death."

In *Heartbreak House* there are two literal deaths, of the two pirates, Mangan and Billie Dunn. But they too are life-haters, and no great loss. More significant is the brooding sense of impending death that dominates the end of the play. In several speeches by Hector and Captain Shotover, it is at least suggested that the angels of death, soaring overhead with grand Beethovian harmonies, are in fact agents of the Life Force, making use of death to clear the way for new experiments in life. For the mortals below, drifting is the way to death, steering is life. Through the proselytizing of Captain Shotover, Ellie Dunn seems to have become a worshiper of life, one who may in time learn navigation. But it is only a hope.

Back to Methuselah is a kind of evolutionary fulfillment of Donne's vision: "Death, thou shalt die." The power of death is defeated, and in Shaw's furthest fantasy life is victorious, life is everything. But, as Lilith points out, at this stage when all diversity is reconciled in unity, when there are no oppositions through which the dialectic can work, humanity ceases to be human, and life must seek out new worlds, and new deaths, to conquer.

With *Saint Joan* we are returned to the "real" world; and with the exception of the demise of Louis Dubedat, which hardly counts, the burning of Joan at the stake is the only death of a major character in Shaw's plays. But again, the play is about the triumph of life. In a literal historical sense, to be sure, the power of Warwick and Cauchon, of the status quo, of tradition, of human institutions, defeats Joan—as in the real world death always wins in the end. Yet the energy and vision and commitment of Joan's faith in life, gaining force from opposition, transcend death, and indeed because of the death her spirit and influence spread out to move others, and all mankind is moved a small way along the infinite evolution of life.

Shaw's comedy, being a form of worship of life, does not and could not ignore death. In a sense, of course, all comedy is a celebration of life. Life is protected by the unexpectedness and incongruities of comedy against the deadness of the stock response, or the unthinking, mechanical repetition of "what has always been done." It is protected by wit against dullness, by satire against stupidity, by irreverence against the complacency of the status quo. But comedy can affirm as well as defend; and although Shaw is best known for his biting wit, his irreverence, and his iconoclasm, behind every effort to shock, behind every question, lies an affirmation.

In virtually every one of Shaw's plays the movement of major characters is clearly defined from less life to more—more in the sense of broader, richer, more complete, more real, more aware that fulfillment lies outward rather than inward. Vivie Warren is isolated from both reality and life by the cocoon of protective fictions spun by her mother. And when she emerges, it is not to be a butterfly, but to live a fuller, more satisfying, less self-centered life. Raina and Sergius only live on the stage of Viennese light opera and have no more reality than actors playing a part, at least until Bluntschli jolts them out of their poses. In *Candida* both Morell and Marchbanks are playing out roles based on stereotyped images of themselves, until their interaction opens their eyes. In much the same way, both Dick Dudgeon and the Reverend Anthony Anderson in *The Devil's Disciple* are gradually losing their lives to fictions, of the reprobate and the pious parson respectively. Again there is a reciprocal enlightenment, in which each discovers himself in his opposite, and both are reborn into a new reality and a new life.

Captain Brassbound is trapped in a prison of unrealities called honor and justice, constructed by society. His obsession with revenge has sapped away all life and is making him into a mindless automaton—until Lady Cicely gives him his freedom, and with it new life. Jack Tanner, on the other hand, is by no means lifeless at the beginning of *Man and Superman,* and yet there is a certain sterility to his witty and cerebral iconoclasm. He appears to devote his energy to mocking life, or to running away from it; but he too has his eyes opened in the Mozartian dream, and thereafter embraces the Life Force, both as his fate and as unlimited potentiality.

In plays such as *Heartbreak House* and *Too True to be Good* the movement is more obvious at the same time that the reality achieved is less clearly defined. Ellie Dunn is freed at the cost of heartbreak from her world of romantic illusions, and after a brief escape into cynicism she recognizes as her natural captain and spiritual husband Captain Shotover, who has spent his life fighting against the death of drifting, dreams, and the lure of happiness. Finding her heart broken but her soul sound and strong, Ellie identifies herself with the Captain's determination to steer; but within the context of the play there is little opportunity for her to demonstrate the richer, more complete life we feel is open to her. At the end she, with some of the others, welcomes the catastrophe from the skies as a hope for a new order, a new dispensation in which their lives may find a new reality and a more satisfying fulfillment.

Joan is, of course, a realist, a lover of life, from the beginning of her play; and her only illusion is the failure to understand that the rest of the world does not march to the same drummer. Her isolation is at once her glory and her tragedy, and the greatest challenge to her faith in life is also proof of its temper: when she defies the power of the state and the church and the fire in affirming it. It may be carrying the spirit of paradox too far, but it is evident that Shaw intends us to conceive that Joan finds the ultimate reality of a rich, complete, rewarding life in her death.

In these and other plays Shaw is preaching the religion of the Life Force by glorifying life; and yet we can never get very far away from that central paradox of the *necessity* of death—the notion that there is no vitality without tension, that for life to be alive it must have opposition, contradiction, something to both wrestle with and triumph over and use, some "other" in which it can know itself.

Hegel, who appears to have provided, at least at one remove, a structural basis for a good many of Shaw's ideas about life and Creative Evolution, does not say much about death, because it does not in itself constitute a logical "category." Non-being, however, does; and as we have seen, being and non-being are, as categories, central to Hegel's thought. He does have a good deal to say about life, both as an abstraction and as a natural fact. Its essence, he says, lies in a dialectic relationship between unity and diversity. When Hegel speaks of evolution, it is more in a rational and metaphysical than a biological sense, but the concept itself is important: "In evolution, something that is undeveloped, undifferentiated, homogeneous, . . . and in this sense abstract, develops, differentiates, splits up, assumes many different, hence opposing or contradictory forms, until at last we have a . . . unity in diversity . . . a definite concrete reality in which the opposites are reconciled or united in the whole. . . . Without contradiction there would be no life, no movement, no growth, no development; everything would be dead existence, static externality."[2]

2. I turn once again for help to the summary of Hegel's thought in

Hegel defines life as a condition of diversity in unity, in which the dialectic tension between the two (diversity and unity) constitutes its life. To go back to our first illustration of the dialectic triad: becoming possesses both unity (it being a concept in its own right) and plurality (because it is a synthesis of, and hence subsumes, both non-being and being); and hence its "life" consists of the tension between the two. Remove one term, one pole of the opposition, and the system, he implies, collapses into lifelessness. Logically speaking, death is to be identified with non-being; it therefore follows that were the element or pole of death taken away from the life-giving triad that ends in "becoming" both the becoming and the life would cease to be.

Hegel does not come through as an enthusiast for life in the way that Shaw does, nor is Shaw's treatment of the relationship between life and death as theoretical and abstract as Hegel's. But death, as we have seen, does play a central role in Shaw's religion of life, as do opposition and contradiction, when it leads to a becoming, an evolution into something higher. Openness, alternatives, tentativeness are also crucial to his thinking—part of the same consistent view of life. For those who could not or would not take Shaw seriously, his pronouncements seemed the idle paradoxes of a summer's day. To those who took him seriously he sometimes seemed a social, political, and moral radical of the most dangerous sort. What he probably wanted more than anything else was to be thought of as a heretic, a heretic saint, like Joan, who might someday be seen to have risen above the mortal limitations of life and death, and through his heresy give man a religion, or at least a faith, that would enrich the quality of his life and move him ever so slightly on his evolutionary way toward becoming a god.

Frank Thilly, *History of Philosophy* (New York: Holt, 1914; rpt. 1945), p. 465; see also W. T. Stace, *The Philosophy of Hegel* (New York: Macmillan, 1924; rpt. New York: Dover, 1955), pp. 281–282.

Index

SHAW AND THE PLAY OF IDEAS

Designed by R. E. Rosenbaum.
Composed by York Composition Company, Inc.,
in 11 point Intertype Baskerville, 2 points leaded,
with display lines in Monotype Baskerville.
Printed letterpress from type by York Composition Company
on Warren's Number 66 text, 50 pound basis.
Bound by John H. Dekker & Sons, Inc.
in Columbia book cloth
and stamped in All Purpose foil.

Library of Congress Cataloging in Publication Data
(For library cataloging purposes only)

Whitman, Robert F
  Shaw and the play of ideas.

  Includes bibliographical references and index.
  1. Shaw, George Bernard, 1856–1950—Philosophy. 2. Shaw, George
Bernard, 1856–1950—Criticism and interpretation. I. Title.
PR5368.P5W5   822'.9'12   76–29866
ISBN 0-8014-1072-X